German Pop Culture

German Pop Culture

How "American" Is It?

Edited by Agnes C. Mueller

The University of Michigan Press   *Ann Arbor*

Copyright © by the University of Michigan 2004
All rights reserved
Published in the United States of America by
The University of Michigan Press
Manufactured in the United States of America
♾ Printed on acid-free paper

2007   2006   2005   2004   4   3   2   1

A CIP catalog record for this book is available from the British Library.

Library of Congress Cataloging-in-Publication Data

German pop culture : how "American" is it? / edited by Agnes C.
   Mueller.
       p.   cm. — (Social history, popular culture, and politics in
   Germany)
     Includes bibliographical references and index.
     ISBN 0-472-11384-4 (alk. paper)
       1. Germany—Civilization—American influences.   2. Popular
   culture—Germany—History—20th century.   3. Germany—Social life
   and customs—20th century.   I. Mueller, Agnes C., 1968–   II. Series.

DD239.G47   2004
306'.0943—dc22   2003025011

Preface

A lot has changed since this book was conceived. German-American relations have been transformed yet again, especially in light of the war against Iraq and all its surrounding issues. I will refrain from commenting on these most recent developments, but I would like to thank the numerous people and institutions who supported this project even before German-American relations once again became a topic for news headlines.

Before the essays collected here took their current form, they were presented and discussed extensively during a two-day German Studies Symposium held in April 2001 at the University of South Carolina. Several sponsors of the symposium have since made transitions also. I am grateful to Margit Resch, former chair of the former Department of Germanic, Slavic, and East Asian Languages, for being the first to provide funding and for encouraging a then very junior faculty member to plan and direct an international symposium. Joan Stewart, former dean of the College of Liberal Arts, supported the event generously and thoroughly impressed all participants with her witty and eloquent remarks at the opening dinner. Financial assistance from the university's Bicentennial Commission, its Comparative Literature Program (then directed by Allen Miller, who was also an active participant), and its Richard L. Walker Institute for International Studies helped to make the event possible. Beyond the University of South Carolina, the symposium received extremely generous support from the Max Kade Foundation in New York and from the DAAD (German American Exchange Service). Despite its own budgetary constraints, the Goethe Institute Atlanta also helped with some of the costs.

Of course, none of the above would have yielded any lasting results without the exemplary attention, patience, and cooperation of all the contributors to this book. I would like to thank everyone for responding so well to my occasionally overzealous timetable and, well, impatient emails. While academics are usually paid salaries, writers generally depend on receiving compensation for their writing. Therefore, special thanks to Thomas Meinecke and Matthias Politycki for donating their pieces.

I am thrilled that the University of Michigan Press took on this book and would like to thank Geoff Eley for his enthusiasm and support. It is a pleasure to work with him and with everyone at the press. The anonymous readers took exceptional care and their suggestions both for content as well as for the overall framing of the book were most useful; I thank them for their thorough engagement with the work.

Last but not least, I received various forms of support at home while working on this project. A College of Liberal Arts Scholarship Support award from the University of South Carolina in 2002 was in part used to complete work on the manuscript. Bill Edmiston, chair of the newly formed Department of Languages, Literatures, and Cultures, has been most supportive, as have my colleagues in the German Studies Program and my friends at the university. My husband, Nicholas Vazsonyi, not only sustains me daily as a friend and colleague, he also provided the model for the USC German Studies Symposium by organizing the first such event in 1999. And, speaking of changes, our daughter Leah, herself a German-American, has become my greatest source of inspiration.

Agnes C. Mueller

Contents

Introduction

Agnes C. Mueller

"German pop culture: how 'American' is it?" is a question that can never be answered. Accordingly, the essays presented in this volume do not aim to offer any clear-cut answers. Instead, the question represents a set of problems requiring different modes of investigation that interact, support, and build upon one another. As this volume will show, issues associated with Americanization and popular culture in Germany have been relevant throughout the twentieth century and today suggest renewed urgency, especially since the fall of the Berlin Wall. In the context of today's post–cold war, postcolonial, and perhaps even postnational global world, representations of hegemonic power structures are gaining in complexity, a complexity brought home with terrifying immediacy after September 11 and a complexity that demands urgent investigation with constantly reexamined sets of parameters.[1] Thus, the seemingly simplistic and naive question posed in the title of this book intends to provoke a thorough interrogation of current scholarship on German-American relations, of youth and popular culture in Germany, of consumer culture in the West, of "America" as an imaginary cultural entity, and of the multivalently coded expressions of those cultures.

Little did I know as a teenager working for McDonald's in Germany in the late 1980s that my experiences there would later become useful for the pursuit of such inquiries. As a high school student, my reasons for choosing to work at a much detested American fast-food chain[2] were mainly pragmatic and not culturally motivated, at least not consciously so. McDonald's hired students under the age of eighteen, and I could work flexible hours, including weekends and evenings.

As I started my work at McDonald's, the responses of people around me were rather uniform. There was some pity (*because every-*

one knew that McDonald's was the poster child of exploitive U.S. capitalism; after all, hadn't Günter Wallraff told us how bad it was?!), mixed with slight consternation at the idea of a dirty blue-collar job, and some questions on rumors they had heard (*did McDonald's really put appetite-stimulating chemicals into hamburger buns?*). But, as I continued to work, I actually liked it. What I liked was not so much the job itself but the somewhat mischievous notion of resistance against all the cultural and political objections raised by my peers concerning the supposed evilness of a company like McDonald's. My resistance to the resistance seemed validated by the sense of community I felt with the other employees, most of whom were Greek, Turkish, and Iranian but also included Hungarians, Arabs, and Pakistanis. In a curious twist, the partial ostracization I experienced from my peers provoked a sense of alterity I (a blue-eyed, almost blonde German) could share with my co-workers, from whom I learned about many distinct foreign cultures and their differences within and separately from the German context. As a result, I came to view McDonald's as an employer who, despite or perhaps because of its exploitive profit-driven company structure and low salaries, saved many foreign workers in Germany from unemployment since, unlike most German employers, it freely hired foreigners. Thus, against the as yet unspoken, highly problematic, but nevertheless lurking notion of a "Leitkultur," McDonald's became a polyvalently coded icon. Not unlike Levi Strauss and Coca-Cola in the 1960s, McDonald's, despite its role as a marker for American global economic imperialism, provided a mode of antiauthoritarian resistance, at least for me. But, beyond this, McDonald's—by opposing a dominant or traditional German culture—became a site, admittedly a highly exploitive one, that could function as a refuge for a host of Germany's displaced others. Consequently, the American company in Germany became a marker simultaneously for cultural diversity *and* for monocultural, homogenous, and homogenizing Americanness, for liberal employment politics *and* for an exploitive capitalist company structure. This complex power structure eliciting resistance and acceptance can also be subsumed under Antonio Gramsci's notion of hegemony, defined as a form of domination through consent on the part of the dominated.[3] The hegemonic economic success of McDonald's was all the more astounding given the timing of their big push into West Germany beginning in the early 1970s, shortly after the student protests against Vietnam and during the peak of anti-Americanism by German intellectuals.

But, it seems, even the intellectuals were not immune from succumbing to the beguiling ruse of marketing reason. Once I started my studies at the university, I decided to continue working at McDonald's even though I probably could have gotten a better employment situation elsewhere. The full extent of this decision and its cultural implications became obvious when the professor of my comparative and English literature seminar, an overtly career-minded woman in her mid-thirties, walked into the restaurant, spotted me behind the counter, and immediately scurried out, apparently hoping I hadn't seen her. The fact that going to McDonald's on her lunch break could trigger such embarrassment and guilt on her part started me to think about the cultural and political meaning of her reaction. Was she, as an academic working on Shakespeare's sonnets, intellectually opposed to "low" American culture, or was she more concerned with undermining a politically correct opposition to American capitalism and consumer culture? Either way, her reaction suggests a double standard associated with German intellectual responses to Americanism broadly conceived, a double standard that would merit further investigation.

This takes me back to the initial problem and my interrogation of the title. First, what is pop culture? I will not go into all that "culture" can mean; suffice it to underscore Raymond Williams's notion that it usually describes either, and more narrowly, a "cultivation of the mind" (in the arts or as intellectual work, including cultural criticism) or, more broadly, with John Clarke, the way "social relations of a group" are "structured, experienced, understood, and interpreted."[4] As opposed to the example of McDonald's, which would fall into the latter, broader category, most contributions in this book are more concerned with the former. In other words, while my illustration of McDonald's as a workplace belongs in the category of culture as lived practices, the essays in this volume are mostly concerned with culture as texts. Either way, Birmingham School notions of culture turn out to be hegemonic in effect, which for Dick Hebdige can be used to explain the formation of subcultures. According to Hebdige, the styles of subcultures do not simply resist or oppose hegemonic domination; rather, they hybridize new styles out of images and materials available to them in an effort to construct their own autonomous identity.[5] Given this reading, McDonald's as a workplace could indeed be considered a locus for the formation of a subculture—as a marker for an occupying power, it created a space for third-party resistance to the local dominant culture. Thus, new identities and communities were constructed out of the dominating hegemonic structures.

How, then, is "sub"culture related to popular culture or mass culture? Here, we might still wish to consider Adorno's notion of the "culture industry" and the resulting dichotomy between mass and high culture, or between low and high culture, which would implicitly suggest that popular culture belongs to low or mass culture. On the other hand, as the contributions to this volume also show, today's cultures are often hybrids of both high and low culture, rendering such a distinction impossible or even redundant. Instead of Adorno's, then, John Fiske's notion of pop or popular culture as an expression of power relations may prove more productive in that it allows for a dynamic model of constant struggle between domination and subordination, between power and various forms of resistance to it.[6] Along those lines, Fiske contends that "popular culture is deeply contradictory in societies where power is unequally distributed along axes of class, gender, and race."[7] Cultural commodities, he argues, have to meet contradictory needs, as the McDonald's example reveals. In this context, American popular culture does indeed seem to offer great opportunities for Germany's minorities to articulate ethnic and racial difference from German culture. In order for it to function, capitalism necessitates a hegemonic, massifying, centralizing, and commodifying economic structure. However, by their sheer existence, those same forces also pluralize meanings and pleasures of cultural commodities, compelling a struggle over the values of social or cultural experiences. In this sense, popular culture may at the same time be a response to the formation of subcultures, as it is an integral component of the hegemonic power's dominating culture. Pop culture, then, can also exemplify a further hybridization of subculture, by integrating the dominant culture into its struggle for a new identity. If we understand McDonald's as an icon of "German" pop culture, we find that it negotiates between hegemonic formations of American capitalism and culturally diverse representations of a multiethnic German subculture, while also acting as a contentious marker for public rejection and concealed acceptance.

How, then, does American culture become transformed or even deformed when introduced to Germany? From the perspective of a post–cold war, postunification Germany, the notion of "popular culture" can serve to investigate intersections of a newly evolving economic and ideological relationship between America and a now fully liberated Germany within a global setting. Just as pop culture—often via the formation of a subculture—negotiates between the dominant culture and its own autonomous identity, so are diverse modules of German pop culture today negotiating between domineering, hegemonic representations of U.S. culture and their own subversive adaptations thereof. Most contributions in this volume will address diverse aspects of aesthetic, artistic, and cultural representations within those intersections of popular culture and American culture, especially since World War II.

This transformation and hybridization of American culture in the German context often entails a distinct and deliberate deviation from traditional forms of German or European high culture, especially when we look at cultures as texts rather than as lived practices. The German reception of Andy Warhol's pop art may serve as an example of such a deviation, given its engagement with an aesthetics of the surface, thus openly seceding from high modernist European notions of the artwork as unique. Gerd Gemünden's recent study shows how Rolf Dieter Brinkmann adopted Warhol's aesthetics of the surface and his artistic techniques in order to create a new voice in West Germany's post-1968 literary scene.[8] By using Warhol's aesthetics for his poetics, Brinkmann also introduced the concept of postmodernism—albeit in an embryonic state—to a German audience. Fredric Jameson's concept of postmodernism similarly identifies a fascination with the surface as the artwork's main component.[9] Whether Warhol is represented "truthfully" or to what extent Brinkmann's poetics and writings can be described as Americanized, however, become less relevant in view of the cultural and political transformations taking place in the new, hybrid space between the realm of U.S. culture and the German-speaking audiences. The example of Warhol and Brinkmann is only one of many. Most others do not involve poetry or the fine arts but rather employ mass media, music, and especially cinema—artforms that helped to shape the aesthetic experience of the twentieth century.

In order to examine a wide scope of such transformations, it becomes necessary to look at different modes of cultural representation from a variety of disciplinary angles. While the project of cultural studies has gone a long way toward mediating between existing disciplinary boundaries, especially within the context of German studies, only a multiauthored volume can provide a truly interdisciplinary approach within an area that has so far been investigated mainly from the perspectives of "Germanistik" in the United States and "Amerikanistik" in Germany.[10] Much of this previous research has been devoted to German-American relations in the immediate wake of World War II. While still highly useful to historians, studies published before the 1990s usually follow the typical cold war paradigm of East versus West—communist-occupied German Democratic Republic

(GDR) versus capitalist U.S.-dominated Federal Republic of Germany (FRG).[11] Such contributions based on binary relationships have become outdated in German cultural studies to the extent that they cannot take into account the changes occasioned by German unification, changes significantly precipitated by how we (re)view pre-1990 German culture.

Apart from previous publications by the contributors to this volume, I would like to point to a few more recent studies especially on the nexus of Americanization. In his 1994 publication *Coca-Colonization and the Cold War,* the Austrian historian Reinhold Wagnleitner argues that much of the so-called Americanization of Europe should be understood as a more developed form of Europeanization in that capitalism and consumerism are products of the European Enlightenment. After this sweeping statement, Wagnleitner reiterates yet another binary, the familiar victim-oppressor dichotomy, which seems especially overdrawn since the undifferentiated claim of the victimization of Austria (and, by implication, West Germany) clashes with the author's own enthusiastic affirmation of U.S. pop culture in his introduction. Taking issue with such undifferentiated accounts, scholars of American studies residing in Germany (e.g., Berndt Ostendorf and Winfried Fluck) attempt more balanced views, but their contributions on the topic thus far have consisted mainly of individual articles published in Germany (and often in German). As Ostendorf observes in a 1999 article, instead of asking why American pop culture is so popular, even some of the most recent publications on the topic of the Americanization of Germany remain guided by a reductive dichotomy of good versus evil, dream versus nightmare, and love versus hate.[12]

On the other hand, the co-edited volume in 2000 by historians Wagnleitner and Elaine Tyler May on the foreign politics of American popular culture addresses some of the more current concerns. While the book productively engages a wide array of themes (from academia, cinema, and music to politics), only three of the nineteen essays (by Thomas Fuchs, Christoph Ribbat, and Michael Ermarth) deal with German-American relations, while all the others focus on different regions of the world.[13] In addition, valuable contributions by historians such as Kaspar Maase, Mary Nolan, and Volker Berghahn, as well as Uta Poiger and Heide Fehrenbach, represent efforts to arrive at a more differentiated understanding of German-American relations, setting the stage for the present volume.[14] Publications from the German Historical Institute's conference on Americanization in 1999 help to shed light on such key terms as "globalization" and, especially, "Americanization." Maase, Nolan, and Berghahn reject the notion of "Americanization" as a concept representing a one-way transfer in favor of a more dynamic model that allows for the description of more complex interactions between Germany and America. Most contributions to our present volume subscribe implicitly or explicitly to this more critical employment of the term, which also includes ongoing negotiations between Americanization and anti-Americanism. For the purposes of the essays collected here, Fehrenbach and Poiger's introduction to their volume provides an excellent account of the entanglement of Americanization with modernization. Their contention of American culture as a marker for "mutable, multidirectional, and often highly contested social and cultural processes involved in identity construction" (xvi) must serve as the backdrop to any future investigation of German-American relations, regardless of disciplinary or geographic specificity. For analytical purposes, we therefore need to concede that "Americanization" cannot be clearly defined, since, not unlike "globalization," it seeks to describe processes that involve constant negotiations and renegotiations among individuals, groups, and cultures.

Thus, a reexamination of the complex relationship between Americanization and pop culture in Germany from an interdisciplinary cultural studies perspective seems overdue, not only filling a lacuna but also taking the discussion out of some of its previous disciplinary boundaries while synthesizing ongoing discourses by presenting fresh assessments concerning the state of contemporary German film, literature, music, and national identity.

To this end, I found it useful to facilitate an exchange with the purpose of discussing those methodological and disciplinary questions both in theory and by focusing on specific examples. I therefore organized a German studies symposium at the University of South Carolina, to which experts from different fields (German studies, history, American studies, film/media studies, and women's studies, along with two German writers) residing in different countries (the United States, Canada, and Germany) were invited. The conversations at the symposium were centered around eight panels, each with two twenty-five-minute presentations with an additional forty minutes reserved for discussion. This format proved extremely productive in that it stimulated responses to individual presentations but also allowed for discussions reaching beyond the immediate subject of any one panel. One of the issues debated most intensely was the question of Americanization and its complex relationship with globalization, especially since participants attempted to take into account the previously mentioned recent discourses employing a more differentiated understanding of those terms. A majority of participants agreed that the term "Americanization" in its previous, traditional usage seemed too limited in that it neglected the inclusion of highly complex hybrid cultural representations, such as the emerging subculture of Turkish writers, singers, and filmmakers, and the complexities of late capitalist structures that are often precipitated by new modes of communication. While "globalization" seemed to be more closely associated with capitalism and its detriments in twentieth-century consumer culture, the term for some appeared too focused on issues of the global market economy, not taking into account the multitude of cultural utterances subverting that very concept (as Fiske suggests in his definition of pop culture). Several other symposium contributions, however, pointed directly to the fact that, as a result of the confrontation with globalizing impulses, a strengthening of local identity has taken place. Thus, "globalization" and "Americanization" are closely related concepts that merit careful consideration in each individual setting.

Some other more conceptual discrepancies can also be linked to questions of methodology. As Scott Denham, Irene Kacandes, and Jonathan Petropoulos illuminate in their *User's Guide to German Cultural Studies*,[15] such (productive) disagreements often surface where a truly interdisciplinary (as opposed to multidisciplinary) approach is sought. Along the same lines, despite the aim to be comprehensive, not all aspects of our question are examined to the same degree. Some readers may find the issue of the Americanization of GDR culture less evenly treated than other aspects. Although contributions by Uta Poiger and, to a lesser extent, Marc Silberman, Barbara Kosta, and Thomas Meinecke address the Americanization of GDR culture and juxtapose it with concurrent movements in the FRG, there is no contribution solely devoted to GDR culture. But this omission may illustrate a change in perception: More than ten years after unification, we no longer have to view the GDR as a separate entity requiring separate treatment but can instead choose to focus on the complex relationship among GDR culture, West German culture, the new Berlin Republic, and American culture. Furthermore, I think that the question of how American the GDR might have been during the cold war almost immediately raises the question of Sovietization, which would distract significantly from the focus of this collection.[16]

As the following brief overview of the essays in this book suggests, a cultural studies approach examining German issues from a variety of angles can prove most useful in sorting through some of the terminological and politically charged issues. The temporal focus of the collection is marked by two important transitions in the latter half of the twentieth century: the transition from Nazism to the cold war and, even more significantly, the transition from the cold war to the postsocialist, global-market, multicultural, unified Germany.

The noted German-based Americanist Winfried Fluck opens the discussion by combining a review of current (terminological and methodological) issues pertaining to the Americanization of Germany with a reassessment of Frankfurt School notions of the culture industry. As recent publications from both Germany and the United States indicate, the thesis of a culture industry and related charges of American cultural imperialism are outdated and, Fluck argues, should instead be replaced with models of self-empowerment through different modes of appropriation of popular culture—an argument developed further by, among others, Sabine von Dirke's investigation of the German hip-hop scene. While he does link Americanization with modernization, Fluck sees possibilities for (German) self-empowerment through a process of reappropriating American pop culture, given the broad variety of ethnicities found in the United States, which actually opens up a space for pluralities at a time of growing globalization.

Frank Trommler further pursues issues of Americanization and modernization by examining the communication revolution of the 1960s, specifically its relationship to high versus mass culture. Since the communication revolution has rendered "high" and "mass" culture indistinguishable, communication per se becomes culture, placing its transformative power in a category beyond Americanization. Trommler contends, however, that it is too early to determine whether and to what extent such transformations can indeed be termed "global."

Extending the focus back into the early twentieth century, historian Tom Saunders continues probing Americanization with an investigation of popular culture as conceived in Weimar and national socialist Germany. His provocative thesis, that Nazism contributed significantly more toward the Americanization of German popular culture than did the Weimar period, becomes especially productive when he turns his attention to cold war discourses of jazz and the concurrent fascination with the image of the "new woman," here meant to describe women's political and cultural emancipation represented by the "Bubikopf" of the 1920s.

Taking up the subject of the "new woman" during the cold war, Sara Lennox pursues the degree to which West German constructions of femininity during that era can appropriately be considered American. Her essay refutes earlier claims of a deliberate antifeminism embedded by the return of women to the domestic sphere. For Lennox, post–World War II German femininity can be regarded as Americanized, provided that one accepts the notion that women as consumers were important contributors to the U.S.-driven economy. As opposed to Saunders's piece, where political and cultural emancipation are at stake for the concept of a "new woman," the term is here employed to depict women in their newfound, self-conscious role as consumers.

Uta Poiger opens the second part of the volume, providing several specific examples of productive appropriations of American cultures by marginal identities. Her essay pursues the issue of jazz during the cold war period, with a special emphasis on the role of the GDR in the nexus of Americanization. Her point is that, during the 1950s, both East and West German jazz critics used "authenticity" as a qualitative marker to distinguish acceptable from unacceptable forms of jazz. The eventual and comprehensive East German rejection of jazz actually served to reinforce West German acceptance of Americanism and U.S. gender roles. Her suggestion that the West German acceptance of African-American jazz was used in part to overcome Nazi racism still seems to hold true for today's German hip-hop movements, as the following essay by Sabine von Dirke confirms. Despite some differences in methodology, the thematic intersections of the essays by Saunders, Lennox, and Poiger underscore the significant American impact on German culture from 1933 until the 1960s, especially in terms of film, gender, and music, connecting at least in this respect Nazi Germany with West Germany of the cold war period.

Continuing the broader topic of music and marginal identities, Sabine von Dirke delivers a fresh account of "old school" and "new school" hip-hop adaptations in Germany. She convincingly demonstrates why cultural imperialism and Americanization no longer work as analytical tools for investigating the German hip-hop scene. Instead, she sees processes of creolization/hybridization characterizing transatlantic transfers of pop music and at the same time challenging negative preconceptions of Americanization that, especially among German minorities, are more positively viewed, as my earlier example of McDonald's suggests.

Eckhard Schumacher turns his eye to another specific instance of American culture and its mediation to German audiences. German writer Rolf Dieter Brinkmann's deliberate "distortions," actually a desemantication and decontextualization, served as a model for the German reception of U.S. pop culture in the late 1960s and, as Schumacher argues, continue to do so. Brinkmann's strategies, including his aesthetics of the surface, are still evident in current German "fanzines" and pop magazines as well as in Germany's most recent pop music scene. Schumacher's essay thus illustrates the degree to which Germany's pop literature boom of the late 1990s is entangled with both earlier and concurrent affirmations and rejections of U.S. pop culture.

The third part of the book, a productive break from the academic discourse, is devoted to the voices of two contemporary German writers, Matthias Politycki and Thomas Meinecke, whose views on popular culture in general, and particularly on the Americanization of German culture, could not be more contradictory. Especially in light of the current debate on German "Popliteratur," it seems essential to include the voices of those "on the ground." Politycki's polemic against the Americanization of German culture and especially of the German language, caused by America's dominance as a global player, calls for reinventing a European aesthetics, in the case of language even by insisting on German traditions. Despite Politycki's aim that his arguments not be subsumed under any politically motivated anti-Americanism, his thesis may be read as a problematic turn toward an all too familiar, Nazi-tainted conservatism. His views seem especially controversial considering that American popular culture also serves as a site of empowerment and resistance for those marginalized in German society, as some of the contributions to the present volume contend. On the other hand, Politycki's advocacy of a renewed attention to German language and culture could also be interpreted as an affirmative and vital element in the conceptualization of the new Berlin Republic within a newly conceived Europe, an element represented in several of this volume's essays (e.g., Koepnick, von Dirke, Gemünden, and Kosta). Even though Politycki seems to regard Americanization as disabling rather than empowering in its potential to create new "hybrids" (in that he rejects foreign influence not dissimilar to the *Sprachgesellschaften* of the seventeenth century), his polemic clearly signals the desire for a renewal of German (national?) identity.

Although, along with Politycki, he fiercely rejects the notion of traditional forms of linear narration and plot construction, Thomas Meinecke presents a totally opposite viewpoint. Meinecke uses his postwall experience as a writer by embracing both Americanisms in language as well as America's daily cultural intrusion into German music and literature. He acknowledges that his very existence as a writer is deeply indebted to a culture that is neither purely German nor completely American but rather a hybrid he calls "pop," emergent from Warhol's techniques of reference and abstraction or pop/techno music's subjectivity. Meinecke's pop manifesto (which is decidedly not a manifesto) deconstructs both the traditional author figure as well as the subject, a deconstruction he sees as a political necessity given today's discourses. Pop, for Meinecke, is neither a concept nor a program but rather a self-referential moment in the deconstructive process. In regarding the deconstruction and hybridity as opportunities for the development and empowerment of the self, Meinecke's take on Americanization and popular culture is in line with the findings represented in the scholarly essays of this volume.

It is especially interesting that two writers of the same generation (both were born in 1955) come to such widely divergent conclusions on Americanization and popular culture. Despite their differences, however, both writers emphasize an urgent desire to revisit or come to terms with a postwall Germany that seems desperate to break free from the U.S. dominance of the 1960s and earlier, while at the same time negotiating the predominance of U.S. icons in everyday language and culture.

Accordingly, the last part of the book is concerned with the formation and establishment of the more recent discourse of the 1990s. Not surprisingly, perhaps, the medium of cinematic representation—with its combination of visual, acoustic, and linguistic forms and its essential contemporaneity in its response to current innovation in media technologies—seems to yield the most productive insights. Along those lines, the film historian Marc Silberman examines both the infrastructural shifts in the film industry and the discursive conceptualizations and significations of national cinema(s) per se accompanying those shifts. He also sets out some of the parameters that have given rise to the complaints and hype surrounding developments of popular film and television genres in Germany during the last decade of the twentieth century.

Barbara Kosta's essay on the popular success *Run Lola Run* investigates more recent German filmmaking and its shift from the entrenched forms of New German Cinema toward renewed appropriations of Hollywood themes and aesthetics. Actually, recent German films present a hybrid of elements from both New German Cinema and Hollywood filmmaking traditions while simultaneously and playfully undermining these same modes. Perhaps more importantly, Kosta shows how cinematic projections of the image of yet another concept of "new woman" and representations of romance and (German) history have helped to shape the identity of the new Germany.

Gerd Gemünden's essay "Hollywood in Altona" looks at other examples of current German filmmaking, this time within the minorities discourse. Again, if we keep in mind my comments on the effect of McDonald's on minorities in Germany, it comes as no surprise that the new German minority film auteurs such as Fatih Akin and Fatima El-Tayeb and Angelina Maccarone incorporate Hollywood images and language instead of availing themselves of the politically more subversive aesthetics of New German Cinema. It is not without a certain sense of irony that Americanization and its path to popular culture seem to offer greater opportunity for Germany's minorities to articulate ethnic and racial difference (from their German hosts) than do the ideologically more subversive and nominally liberal modalities of New German Cinema with its Brechtian claim of transformative potential. While Gemünden's essay emphasizes the negative aspects of such (Americanized) globalization, it also points to a transcendence of the traditional nation-state for the cultural expression of minorities in today's Germany, similarly demonstrated in von Dirke's essay on hip-hop culture.

Lutz Koepnick's essay brings to a close both the book's part on current film as a discursive path to the 1990s and the volume as a whole. Koepnick argues the existence of a new genre of the German heritage film in which characteristics of its British highbrow model are replaced by a turn toward popular and mass culture. As such, these films become integral to the recent Berlin Republic's aim to reinscribe and renew twentieth-century German history and German national identity. The emergence of the new genre illustrates that globalization produces new desires for localization, thereby challenging traditional models of American filmmaking. This thesis provokes Koepnick to ask whether categories of Americanization/Hollywoodization or even the concept of a national cinema are still useful when describing the more recent reinvention and redefinition of German film. Koepnick's essay rounds out the last part of the book by taking issue with the arguments put forth previously by Kosta, Gemünden, and von Dirke, urging us all to revise and reconsider current interpretative tools. At the same time, Koepnick's findings for the German heritage film point the way to other postnational German cultural representations of the postwall era.

In addition to documenting new understandings of Americanization, the contributions in this volume tackle the delicate nexus of U.S. popular culture as a tool for the subversion of a dominant German culture or the subversion of U.S. culture in Germany. With the end of the cold war, revisiting the complex ways in which American culture may be used and understood abroad poses a new set of challenges. As the essays here demonstrate, America and its cultures—both its culture of global capitalism and its popular culture—frequently serve as tools for other nations and communities to come to terms with their own political and cultural problems. In the case of Germany, those issues range from creating Nazi Germany in the 1930s, to coping with the Nazi past during the 1960s, to (re)establishing a "new" German identity in the postwall era, to locating minority cultures within the dominant German discourse. Therefore, in the present context, terms such as "Americanization" or even "globalization" need to be employed with caution. Instead, we might wish to consider that, in today's world, cultures are more clearly defined along the lines of dominant versus subversive spaces. In this respect, to borrow a line from one of the contributors to this volume, the answer to the impossible question of how "American" is Germany would be "very" as well as "not at all."

NOTES

1. An example of the more recent turn in German-American relations after September 11 is the debate on America's "justified" war, documented in *Der Spiegel,* which also invites German intellectuals to respond. Peter Schneider, "Die falsche Gewissheit," *Der Spiegel* 35 (2002): 168–70.

2. The numerous reasons for many Germans' rejection of McDonald's are, to some extent, similar to those outlined in George Ritzer's *The McDonaldization of Society,* rev. ed. (Thousand Oaks, CA: Pine Forge Press, 1996). Although Ritzer uses the example of McDonald's to analyze today's society at large, many Germans find those same problems (overrationalization and dehumanization, health concerns, environmental concerns) embodied by McDonald's. Here is not the place to critique Ritzer's highly simplified approach; suffice it to say that the success of his book as a teaching tool proves that he delivers a useful account of many Americans' perception regarding the downside of the fast-food industry. From the German perspective, however, the issue becomes more complex, given their perception of the company as a symbol for American economic imperialism.

3. Antonio Gramsci, *Selections from the Prison Notebooks,* ed. and trans. Quintin Hoare and Geoffrey Nowell Smith (New York: International, 1971). While Gramsci's concept of hegemony is more concerned with the working class's failure as a revolutionary subject in Western industrial societies and its subsequent integration into existing orders, the concept can also serve to illustrate the acceptance of U.S. domination in West Germany, in this case by "displaced others."

4. Raymond Williams, *Sociology of Culture* (New York: Schocken, 1981), 11, and John Clarke et al., "Subcultures, Cultures, and Class: A Theoretical Overview," in *Resistance through Rituals: Youth Subcultures in Post-War Britain,*

ed. Stuart Hall and Tony Jefferson (London: Hutchinson, 1976), 9–74 (quotes from 10–11).

5. Dick Hebdige, *Subculture: The Meaning of Style* (London: Methuen, 1979).

6. John Fiske, *Understanding Popular Culture* (Boston: Hyman, 1989), 19.

7. Fiske, *Understanding Popular Culture,* 4.

8. Gerd Gemünden, *Framed Visions: Popular Culture, Americanization, and the Contemporary German and Austrian Imagination* (Ann Arbor: University of Michigan Press, 1998), 43–65.

9. Fredric Jameson, *Postmodernism, or the Cultural Logic of Late Capitalism* (Durham, NC: Duke University Press, 1991), 9.

10. For an example of "Germanistik" in the United States, see Frank Trommler and Joseph McVeigh, eds., *America and the Germans: An Assessment of a Three-Hundred-Year History: Vol. I, Immigration, Language, Ethnicity; Vol. II, The Relationship in the Twentieth Century* (Philadelphia: University of Pennsylvania Press, 1985), and for a recent example of Amerikanistik, see Berndt Ostendorf, "The Final Banal Idiocy of the Reversed Baseball Cap: Transatlantische Widersprüche in der Amerikanisierungsdebatte," *Amerikastudien/American Studies* 44, no. 1 (1999): 25–48, or Winfried Fluck (this time published in a German studies venue), "The 'Americanization' of History in New Historicism," *Monatshefte* 84, no. 2 (1994): 220–28.

11. Trommler and McVeigh, *America and the Germans,* vol. 2.

12. See Ostendorf, "The Final Banal Idiocy"; Alf Lüdke, Inge Maßolek, and Adelheid von Saldern, eds., *Amerikanisierung: Traum und Alptraum im Deutschland des 20. Jahrhunderts* (Stuttgart: Franz Steiner, 1996); and Richard Pells, *Not Like Us: How Europeans Have Loved, Hated, and Transformed American Culture since World War II* (New York: Basic Books, 1997).

13. Reinhold Wagnleitner and Elaine Tyler May, eds., *"Here, There, and Everywhere": The Foreign Politics of American Popular Culture* (Hanover and London: University Press of New England, 2000). In this present context, Christoph Ribbat's contribution on hip-hop in Germany is especially elucidating; see "'Ja, ja, deine Mudder!' American Studies und deutsche Populärkultur," in *Kulturwissenschaftliche Perspektiven in der Nordamerika-Forschung,* ed. Friedrich Jaege (Tübingen: Stauffenburg, 2001), 145–60.

14. See those works in the bibliography, and in particular: Heide Fehrenbach and Uta G. Poiger, eds., *Transactions, Transgressions, Transformations: American Culture in Western Europe and Japan* (New York, Oxford: Berghahn, 2000), and Raimund Lammersdorf, ed., *GHI Conference Papers on the Web: The American Impact on Western Europe: Americanization and Westernization in Transatlantic Perspective,* <http://www.ghi-dc.org/conpotweb/westernpapers/index.html>.

15. Scott Denham, Irene Kacandes, and Jonathan Petropoulos, eds., *A User's Guide to German Cultural Studies* (Ann Arbor: University of Michigan Press 1997).

16. For the earlier postwar period, this question has been researched thoroughly in Konrad Jarausch and Hannes Siegrist, eds., *Amerikanisierung und Sowjetisierung in Deutschland 1945–70* (New York: Campus, 1997), and looking at the time beyond 1970—indeed a most deserving project—would require separate treatment.

Part I

Approaches to Americanization, Globalization, and Hybrid German Identities

The Americanization of German Culture? The Strange, Paradoxical Ways of Modernity

Winfried Fluck

How "American" is German popular culture? How serious is the threat of Americanization? Until recently, the answer seemed to be quite clear. Following in the footsteps of Max Horkheimer and Theodor Adorno's chapter on the culture industry in their book *Dialectic of Enlightenment,* several generations of German cultural critics have harshly criticized the growing influence of American mass culture in Germany. This development, they argue, will lead to increased cultural homogenization and the dominance of an escapist entertainment culture that erases the true task of culture, namely, to function as a counterforce to the alienating forces of modernity.[1] With the student movement of the 1960s this critique gained an additional political dimension. Americanization was now seen as the epitome of cultural imperialism, because the growing role American mass culture played in Germany was attributed not to the attraction of the product itself but to the worldwide market dominance of American companies that pushed competitors and artistically more ambitious alternatives out of the market.[2]

This was the time in which the television series *Dallas* gained central importance in German cultural criticism because its worldwide dissemination seemed to confirm the enormous power that the leading content providers for television entertainment, at the time the three major American networks, could wield. The German Research Foundation (Deutsche Forschungsgemeinschaft) provided considerable financial support for a research project on the harmful impact of *Dallas* on German society that claimed that it was now high time to put the criticism of Americanization on a systematic, scientifically rigorous basis in order to convince German society that the menace was real and the danger of the Americanization of German society imminent.[3] Ironically, however, this attempt to objectify cultural criticism was the beginning of the end of the Americanization thesis in its simple, literal-minded form. For as various studies of the impact of *Dallas*—for example, by Ian Ang; by Elihu Katz and Tamar Liebes in Israel; and by Ellen Seiter and colleagues in their project sponsored by the German Research Foundation[4]—all demonstrated with surprising unanimity, the cultural imperialism thesis was based on a surprisingly naive theory of effect and completely disregarded the possibility that different audiences can make different uses of one and the same program.[5] With these results, studies of the impact of *Dallas* and other television programs confirmed a basic insight of reception aesthetics: in order to give a fictional text meaning, the reader or spectator has to draw on his or her own associations, emotions, and bodily sensations as an analogue and in the process creates a new object.[6]

This transfer process lies at the center of our encounters with fictional material. It explains the interest we have in fictions, for otherwise it would make little sense that we expose ourselves again and again to stories that we know very well are invented. But although reception aesthetics in its classical form restricts its description of the transfer process that takes place in the act of reception to high literature, one may very well argue that it is also at work in popular culture[7] and, contrary to arguments by Wolfgang Iser and others, in film and other forms of visual representation.[8] For the reception of American popular culture in Germany, this means that material that in one context may have no other function than that of mere escapism can have quite different functions in other contexts, as Kaspar Maase has demonstrated in his study *BRAVO Amerika.*[9] In contrast to the then standard view of the topic, Maase shows the extent to which American popular culture played a liberating function for Germany's postwar generation by undermining key elements of the authoritarian personality structure, for example, by replacing the still lingering ideal of the military man with rock ' n' roll heroes like Elvis Presley, by glorifying youthful rebellion through film stars like James Dean or Marlon Brando, and by opening up new spaces for self-fashioning and self-expression without a loss in respectability through the playful exhibitionism of female actors like Marilyn Monroe.[10] The result of Maase's study and others since can be summarized by arguing that, in the context of postwar Germany, American popular culture played an important—and, I think, largely positive—role in the Westernization of German society.

Maase's study poses a significant departure from Horkheimer and Adorno's position, especially in its view of modernity. Classical Weberian theories of modernity saw modernity as characterized by a steady increase of bureaucratization, rationalization and standardization and placed their hopes on culture as a counterrealm. The major thrust of *Dialectic of Enlightenment* consists of the claim that instrumental reason and its relentless drive for rationalization have by now also affected and deformed the realm of culture.[11] Although there remains a remnant of ambivalence, Maase's description has an altogether different thrust and deserves to be quoted at length:

> One of the results of the influx of attitudes that can be found in American popular and everyday culture into German society was that young people in the Federal Republic of Germany developed civil habits (habitus). "Civil" here refers to three aspects. The first reference is to commercial attitudes that were still labeled "materialistic" at the time. The idols of pop culture knew how to take advantage of the market. They made no bones about the fact that they wanted to make money instead of preaching any type of message. This undermined a long-cherished German tradition of appealing to idealistic principles for the justification of one's own behavior and, consequently, of thinking in either-or, friend-foe dichotomies. This change of attitude paved the way for a more flexible approach to dealing with conflicts of interest and an increased willingness to compromise. The second reference is to a growing informality in social interaction that, in turn, diminished the symbolical distance between groups that were traditionally in unequal positions of power: women and men, young and old. It is therefore not far-fetched to claim that this growing informality contributed to the democratization of German society. Finally, the new civil habit also affected traditional gender concepts: it strengthened a new view of masculinity in which the ideal of military discipline was replaced by a more relaxed conception that can even accommodate feminine aspects.[12]

The recognition that cultural material is never simply absorbed as a model of behavior but is reappropriated in different contexts for different needs and purposes is, I think, the bottom-line consensus at which the Americanization debate has arrived.[13] In his excellent discussion of theories of cultural imperialism, John Tomlinson summarizes the debate: "The general message of empirical studies—informal ones like Ang's and more large-scale formal projects like Katz's and Liebes's—is that audiences are more active and critical, their responses more complex and reflective, and their cultural values more resistant to manipulation and 'invasion' than many critical media theorists have assumed."[14] The cultural imperialism thesis has thus been replaced by models of negotiation, hybridization, and creolization,[15] and if one returns with that perspective to our starting question—How "American" is German popular culture?—then the somewhat unexpected answer must be that it is actually far less so than the question seems to imply. German popular culture today is a very mixed bag. While Hollywood dominates the German film market, by a staggering 80 percent, the role of American series on television has decreased considerably (in view of the *Dallas* hysteria, one might even say dramatically). There are comparatively few American series to be seen, most of them are relegated to the late hours, and few capture any attention. Moreover, driven by the insatiable need for programs that six major and several minor television networks have, German production companies of television series have not succumbed to American market power but have blossomed lately and are actively pursuing foreign markets themselves, especially in Middle and Eastern Europe.

In music, Turkish-German rap groups have become the German epitome of the idea of cultural hybridization.[16] There are several successful versions of German rock music, and there is an influential appropriation of Detroit techno music (patterned, in turn, to a large extent on the experimental electronic music of the German group Kraftwerk) that has made Berlin a center of techno music, made famous by, among other things, the annual Love Parade. Finally, two examples highlight the possibility of successful self-assertion against the seemingly overwhelming market power of American multinational companies: (1) the German video clip channel Viva, which puts heavy emphasis on German popular music and uses German for all of its announcements, has passed MTV as the leading video channel in Germany and has forced MTV to offer nationally and regionally varied versions of its program—a reorientation that has in the meantime become an international policy of the company; (2) to counter the plans of Viacom-owned Nickelodeon to establish a children's channel program financed by advertising only, the two major German public television networks have created a children's channel of their own that has not only successfully held its ground against American competition but driven profit-conscious Nickelodeon out of the German market.

How "American" is German popular culture then? In the cultural imperialism thesis, German popular culture seems to be in danger of being swallowed up wholesale, while in the reappropriation and hybridization paradigm, the issue seems to dwindle down to selective use.[17] Does this mean that we can close the book on the issue? It all depends on what we actually mean by "American." If "American" refers to national ownership, then Americanization, perhaps with the exception of the film industry, does appear to be no longer a pressing issue.[18] But if "American" is meant to refer to a certain type of culture, developed and made popular in the United States, then the issue becomes more complicated. For it may be true that, at least as far as market shares in the television and music industry are concerned, the influence of American companies has not become overpowering. But the programs produced even by those German companies that have successfully managed to assert themselves against the American competition—the new production companies for television series, the television station Viva, or even the Turkish-German rap groups—continue to pattern their products after American models. A Frankfurt School–inspired cultural critic might argue, therefore, that German society no longer needs to import American mass culture because it is now "advanced" enough to have an American-style culture industry of its own.

However, what is the explanatory power of such a view of American popular culture with its association of a standardized form of escapism? Is American popular culture just mass-produced trash?[19] If not, what explains its stunning worldwide resonance? It is here that the Americanist can perhaps be of help, for one cannot study American society without coming to terms with the crucial role that popular cultural forms play in American culture.[20]

The significance of the phenomenon of popular culture for cultural history lies in its response to the problems of cultural access and accessibility (in the sense of cultural literacy). Traditionally, access to cultural life in Western societies depended on social standing, economic means (books before the nineteenth century were expensive), and a fairly high degree of cultural literacy. Basically, the term "popular culture" refers to cultural forms that undermine or abolish these conditions of access. In this sense, American society was especially effective for a number of reasons, among them the lack of strong national cultural centers that could shape cultural development on the basis of aesthetic or educational criteria of an elite.[21] Within this dehierarchized, socially, regionally, and ethnically diversified context, two factors made American popular culture unique, gave it a head start internationally, and explain its amazing worldwide popularity. Both factors are tied to the multiethnic composition of American society. First, American popular culture profited from a variety of multiethnic influences. This is most obvious in the realm of popular music, where the result was a hybrid mix of European and African traditions that was highly original and clearly something no other country had to offer at the time. Second, because of the multiethnic composition of its audiences, American popular culture encountered a market that resembles today's global market in its diversity and multilinguistic nature, so that a need emerged early on to find a common language that would be able to overcome the heterogeneity of the audiences.[22]

The response of American popular culture to this challenge—and, by implication, to the issues of access and accessibility—was reduction. The novel, which is the first example of modern popular culture in the Western world, is already a reduction of the epic; the dime novel, in turn, is a reduction of the novel in terms of narrative and characterization. Each of these reductions increases cultural accessibility, and because this accessibility means increased sales and cheaper production, social access is also increased. However, in order to read a dime novel, one still has to be able to read English. In terms of accessibility, writing, no matter how reduced it is in its requirements for cultural literacy, has obvious limits. Images and music, on the other hand, have obvious advantages. And while even the image still requires a certain literacy in the sense of being able to master a visual code, music can reduce such potential barriers of accessibility even further. Thus, film, television, and, above all, popular music have been the driving forces in the Americanization of modern culture.

Traditionally, it is exactly this phenomenon of reduction that has been the target of cultural critics, because it is seen as the result of a race for the bottom line in taste. But when silent movie directors such as D. W. Griffith and Erich von Stroheim tried to develop a filmic language that would be superior to theatrical melodrama in terms of accessibility and effect, they did not do this in search of the lowest common denominator in taste. They pursued their goals because they realized that the reduction in communication made possible by the image opened up entirely new possibilities of expression. The reduction I am talking about here is, in other words, primarily a result of a transformation of cultural expression by technological developments such as printing, film, electrified music, and so on—developments that facilitate accessibility but, at the same time, also create new possibilities of expression and aesthetic experience.[23]

In my opinion, there is an unmistakable direction in which this development has gone, redefining, in the process, criteria of cultural literacy. Cultural access and accessibility are constantly widened for the individual. At the same time, the individual's wishes for imaginary self-empowerment have been served more and more effectively—up to a point, for example, where the representation of violence has been taken almost completely out of moral or social contexts and is now presented largely for its own sake, that is, for the thrill it gives Hollywood's main target group: young (or not so young) males. This is an important point, because it captures the major paradox produced by the development I have sketched: contrary to the conventional wisdom of a standardized mass production, American popular culture has been driven by a promise of providing ever more effective ways for imaginary self-empowerment and self-fashioning.[24] In this sense, it has contributed to an accelerating process of individualization in society.

This individualization provides a third reason for the worldwide success of American popular culture: its deeply ingrained strand of antiauthoritarianism, ranging from stances of mere informality to absorbing stories of youthful rebellion and embracing provocative, shrill, even deliberately vulgar and trashy forms of expression that take pleasure in violating socially established norms of taste. Fittingly, Maase characterizes these heightened forms of self-expression as "sensuous-expressive, shrill, unrepentant and overpowering in their rhetorical means; socially they are close to the taste and behavior of the lower classes and marginalized cultures."[25] American popular culture is antiauthoritarian not only in its withdrawal from moral and social contexts but also, and even more so, in its willful disregard of established hierarchies of culture. However, as many cultural critics have pointed out, individualization is a double-edged sword: it is both liberating and potentially antisocial. It increases the social and cultural space of the individual but often at the cost of undermining social values and the possibility of social cooperation.

If popular culture is driven by increasing possibilities for imaginary self-empowerment and cultural self-fashioning, then Americanization, understood as growing, worldwide dissemination of a certain type of culture, means that a process that, for a number of reasons, is most advanced in the United States is taking hold in other parts of the world as well. This process is usually driven by the demands of a younger generation that is in flight from a tradition it considers restrictive.[26] What many cultural critics—including Americans who are embarrassed to have American society associated primarily with consumer culture and fast-food icons—often do not understand is that even the most conventional and most maligned symbols of American consumer culture, such as Coca-Cola or McDonald's, bear a connotation of informality that can be experienced as liberating by young people in most parts of the world.[27] Americanization in this sense is an effect of modernization—not in the sense of sociological and economic modernization theory but in the sense of modernity's promise of self-development.[28] The problem, however, is that Americanization is an unforeseen, almost embarrassing result of modernity's promise for self-development, for in place of self-cultivation and increasing self-awareness we get unrepentant forms of imaginary self-empowerment and self-fashioning. What we have to realize and acknowledge in dealing with American popular culture is that, contrary to its image as a mindless, standardized mass product, it is not the deplorable counterpoint to this modern culture of self-development but rather an unexpected manifestation and consequence of it.

The United States is a society dominated by business interests, and it would be naive indeed to forget that business tries its best to take commercial advantage of the individual's seemingly insatiable hunger for imaginary self-empowerment. But although these commercial interests should be acknowledged, they do not get to the core of problem. Clearly, the same hunger manifests itself in societies that are quite different in political and economic structure. Nevertheless, each of these societies has to come to a decision about what institutional structures it wants to maintain for cultural production and expression. Or, to come back to our starting question, Germany may not be as American in terms of cultural homogenization and market monopolies as many critics fear, but it is certainly far advanced in patterning itself after models coming from the United States. In view of my explanation of the emergence and function of American popular culture, this development must be seen as an inevitable consequence of the Westernization of German society (which, one may claim, has saved German society from itself). One may look at American culture ambivalently, but one cannot have only half of it. The Americanization of modern culture comes along with other aspects of modernity.

Maase's *BRAVO Amerika* must by now be one of the most quoted books on the topic of Americanization in Germany—deservedly so, I think, because Maase was the first to tell differently a story that had been watered down to a mere formula. Mary Nolan, on the other hand, in a comment on the concepts of Americanization and Westernization, rightly insists that we need to extend the analysis of Americanization to the contemporary period. The extent to which the 1950s still dominate debates about the Americanization in Germany is striking indeed.[29] One obvious reason is that the period marks the beginning of full-scale Americanization.[30] But another reason may be that, as part of the cold war period, the 1950s still hold the promise of a dramatic narrative along classical generic lines: There is the drama of victory and defeat, there is the cold war, and there is the question of how to treat the defeated. There are victors who have political interests, and there are those who do not realize that entertainment can be politics too. Critics do not quite agree on the result of this plot constellation, but the narrative provides a welcome opportunity to tell the story again and to tell it differently each time: either as a tale of victimization by American cold war policies; as an upbeat story of Westernization, that is, liberation from the authoritarianism of German society; or as a story of subcultural resignification of culturally dominant forms and hence of successful resistance to cultural hegemony.

These narratives, in turn, are useful because they still provide a basis for large-scale generalizations. Whether the issue is discussed explicitly or not, each of these narratives of Americanization illustrates an underlying view of American society and its relation to the rest of the world. Hence, interpreters draw different conclusions from their descriptions of Americanization in the 1950s, documented in exemplary fashion in the papers from the conference "The American Impact on Western Europe."[31] They see Americanization as a means of cultural dehierarchization (Maase's grass roots Americanism);[32] as an instance of—not entirely successful—hegemonial policies;[33] as—overdue—Westernization;[34] or, more recently, as a kind of pseudo-democratization that masks the fact that the American liberal system is fundamentally constituted by racism and sexism and does not hesitate to export this legacy in a seemingly democratic or liberal form.[35] In each case, a different view of American politics and society determines what course the narrative of Americanization will take. Strangely, however, these underlying views have not yet become a topic of debate. Could it be that there is a persistent interest in the continued focus on the 1950s because certain generalizations about America are still possible?

In effect, however, the narrative of Americanization has by now become considerably more muddled. This holds true for both of the main features of the conventional narrative of Americanization: the question of national ownership and the question of whether American popular culture is really a debased form of mass culture. In a time when corporations such as Sony, Murdoch, Vivendi, and Bertelsmann own large pieces of the American entertainment pie, Americanization can no longer be assessed primarily in terms of national ownership. At the same time, American popular culture has become part of a dehierarchized postmodern field of hybrid cultural forms in which "high" and "low" are no longer helpful markers of aesthetic distinction and in which models of imposition or unilateral cultural transfer have to be replaced by myriad constellations of negotiation, appropriation, and transformation. Can we rest easy then and regard the challenge of Americanization as an inevitable result of modernity and its growing plurality of cultural and life-style choices? Or are there new issues that should move to the fore of the Americanization debate? If we no longer want to remain on the relatively superficial and, in itself, often contradictory level of the cultural imperialism paradigm without, on the other hand, discarding the question of cultural politics altogether, then we have to include two aspects into our discussion that can help to bring the discussion up to current states of complexity. One of these aspects is the problem of the organization of culture, the other a differentiation about what we are actually talking about when we use the term "Americanization" and refer to the United States in the process.

Let me begin with the latter aspect. One of the main difficulties in discussions of Americanization is that, as a rule, two different Americas are conflated in the debate. One is the territory we call the United States, which has a distinctive economic and social structure; the other is an imaginary, deterritorialized space that is filled with a selection of objects of choice, evoking strong fascination or disgust. This America is an America of the mind, whose protean, chameleon-like shape constantly changes according to different collective and individual needs. When we pick out cultural features such as jazz or rap music, to name just two out of a sheer endless reservoir of interesting cultural forms, we create our own deterritorialized, imaginary America of the mind. Consequently, "Americanization" can have at least two meanings that should be kept apart. Americanization through an imaginary America of jazz, rock 'n' roll, or rap promises reinvigoration, if not regeneration, of one's own culture without, on the other hand, having to import those social conditions that played a significant role in creating these cultural forms. Those happy apologists for American popular culture who celebrate only its vitality and antiauthoritarian thrust are, in fact, oblivious to those economic and social contexts. They want rock 'n' roll, not a widely unregulated free enterprise system or urban slums.

The question that the Americanization debate has to face is how the two Americas are related. In the beginning, in the period of the mass culture debate and cultural imperialism paradigm, the implication was that American popular culture would be the bait to make the world ready for American capitalism. The infatuation with an imaginary America would pave the way for the transformation of German society on the American model. The reappropriation and hybridization model of reception that has taken the place of the cultural imperialism paradigm claims that this is an unwarranted causal connection. Fascination with an imaginary America does not necessarily lead to fascination with the American economic and social system. It may, in effect, have no other consequences than leading to a better cultural mix at home and hence to a different, less suffocating form of modernity. On the other hand, where concerns about Americanization have not abated, the basic fear still is that the imaginary America of popular culture may function as a kind of Trojan horse, that it may be the entry gate for establishing American conditions in German society. There is indeed one aspect of cultural life for which this may be true—which brings me to a second important point of differentiation in the Americanization debate.

"Americanization" is a term that refers to the relations between nations. It evokes questions of national self-definition and, by implication, self-determination. When the term is used critically, it suggests that one's culture is no longer one's own but decisively influenced, perhaps even controlled, by someone else. The term draws its polemical force from the fear that one may be in danger of losing control over one's own culture.[36] However, in the age of globalization, such thinking seems to have become increasingly obsolete. For one thing, it clings to an outdated notion of national self-control or even nationhood, in this case of a Germanness that is in danger of being diluted or polluted. Moreover, it appears hopelessly outdated at a time when national ownership of media or other cultural resources can no longer be neatly distinguished. (There is concern in the United States, for example, about the dominance of American quality publishers by German companies.) In view of the fact that national boundaries can and should no longer be neatly maintained, my argument so far has been to take the melodrama out of the Americanization debate by identifying the emer-

gence and worldwide triumph of American popular culture as the
enactment of a cultural logic of modernity, although an unexpected,
largely unacknowledged, and perhaps not altogether welcome part.

In a certain sense, modernization cannot be avoided. As Tomlinson
puts it in his critique of the cultural imperialism paradigm, we are condemned to modernity.[37] The increasing demands for individual freedom and self-realization that are part of modernity's promise of self-
development cannot be ignored or suppressed by prohibitions, unless
one lives in a fundamentalist culture. However, there are more and less
radical manifestations of this phenomenon, and in this respect historical and social developments can be influenced and shaped. There are,
after all, multiple modernities, each with its own specific sources and
configurations of the basic process of modernization. For reasons
given in this essay, we may not even want to fight against the Americanization of German culture. And since German popular culture is,
despite the current increasing number of instances of successful self-
assertion against the dominance of American companies, after all patterned after American models, it would be especially absurd to argue
for non-American purity in this case. The questions that remain are
how much we want of this type of culture and whether the increasing
Americanization of German culture should also lead to an American-
style organization of culture.

If we look at the issue of Americanization from this point of view,
the major challenge of Americanization consists neither of the question
of national ownership, which has become muddled in an age of economic globalization, nor of the question of content, since, as we have
seen, one and the same cultural text or object can have entirely different functions in different contexts of use. The major issue at stake in
the relationship of, and comparison between, American and German
culture today is the question of how, or on what principles, culture
should be organized and financed. In the United States, the organizing
principle is mainly commercial. Except for the National Endowment
for the Arts, the state does not consider itself responsible for culture, so
therefore cultural production has to find financial support somewhere
else. Spending taxpayers' money on opera, musical performances, theater productions, or public television—that is, cultural forms that cannot fully support themselves financially—is rejected. In consequence, a
rich culture of philanthropy and sponsorship has developed in the
United States.

In Germany, on the other hand, there still exists a public consensus
that such cultural forms should be supported by direct or indirect

forms of taxation, although there is an unmistakable tendency to take a page from the American book and to encourage the active search for sponsorship. Therefore, the real issue in the challenge of Americanization today is, I believe, no longer whether we get the wrong kind of culture but rather whether we are drifting toward an American model of organizing and financing culture. It is one thing to welcome the various forms of American popular culture as additions to cultural variety but quite another to organize a whole culture primarily on commercial principles. Or, to put it differently, it is one thing to welcome somebody as a guest in the house but another to make sure the guest does not take over the whole house!

NOTES

1. The term "modernity" is used here in the broad sense of Neuzeit, that is, the beginning of the modern period around 1600. It is set in motion, at different times in different places, by the drive of the individual to escape the seemingly god-given social and cultural hierarchies of feudal and aristocratic societies. One consequence is a growing differentiation of social and cultural spheres and, as a result, an increasing pluralization of values and life-styles. The process by which secular values of Western societies such as the doctrine of individual rights, religious freedom, liberal democracy, or civil society become the inspiration for value change is called Westernization; the process by which specific elements are adapted from American society and culture is called Americanization. Culturally, Germany was part of modernity long before the twentieth century, but it was only after 1945 that values of the Western liberal tradition gained a growing influence, strongly aided by the process of Americanization. For an interesting, though eventually inconclusive, debate on whether Westernization or Americanization is the most fitting term to describe Germany's postwar development, see the papers from the 1999 conference "The American Impact on Western Europe: Americanization and Westernization in Transatlantic Perspective" (Raimund Lammersdorf, ed., *GHI Conference Papers on the Web: The American Impact on Western Europe: Americanization and Westernization in Transatlantic Perspective,* <http://www.ghi-dc.org/con potweb/westernpapers/index.html>). In contrast to the conference participants, I do not think that the issue is one of an "either-or" choice, since the terms "modernity," "modernization," "Westernization," and "Americanization" describe different aspects of cultural developments in Western societies and have a different explanatory range. The link between modernity and Americanization is also emphasized in Mary Nolan's *Visions of Modernity: American Business and the Modernization of Germany* (New York: Oxford University Press, 1994) and in the introduction to *Transactions, Transgressions, Transformations: American Culture in Western Europe and Japan,* ed. Heide Fehrenbach and Uta G. Poiger (New York: Berghahn Books, 2000) (see especially the section "American Culture,

Nation-States, Modernity," xviii–xxiv). However, in both cases the term "modernity" is restricted to the twentieth century.

2. One of the most recent and most emphatic of these cultural critiques of Americanization is Benjamin Barber's *Jihad vs. McWorld: How Globalism and Tribalism Are Reshaping the World* (New York: Ballantine, 1995). For earlier versions of the cultural imperialism thesis, see, for example, Herbert Schiller, *Mass Communications and American Empire*, 2d ed. (Boulder: Westview, 1992), and Ariel Dorfman and Armand Mattelart, *How to Read Donald Duck: Imperialist Ideology in the Disney Comic* (New York: International General, 1996).

3. In its more pointed versions, the cultural imperialism thesis always carried the implication of an act of colonization, as expressed, for example, in words like "Coca-colonization" or the "McDonaldization" of the world. Occasionally, the claim was extended to that of a colonization of the mind. German filmmaker Wim Wenders even claimed that Hollywood had successfully colonized the European subconscious.

4. See Ian Ang, *Watching Dallas* (London: Methuen, 1985); Elihu Katz and Tamar Liebes, "Mutual Aid in the Decoding of *Dallas:* Preliminary Notes from a Cross-Cultural Study," in *Television in Transition,* ed. Philip Drummond and Richard Paterson (London: BFI, 1986), 187–98; Ellen Seiter, Hans Borchers, Gabriele Kreutzner, and Eva-Maria Warth, eds., *Remote Control: Television, Audiences, and Cultural Power* (London: Routledge, 1989); and Hans Borchers, Gabriele Kreutzner, and Eva-Maria Warth, eds., *Never-Ending Stories: American Soap Operas and the Cultural Production of Meaning* (Trier: Wissenschaftlicher Verlag, 1994). A particularly telling example of the very different ways in which one and the same program is seen in different national and cultural contexts is provided by the American television series *Holocaust,* which found quite different receptions in Germany and the United States, despite the fact that in both contexts the basic attitude toward the program was predominantly positive. Cf. Bruce A. Murray, "NBC's Docudrama, *Holocaust,* and Concepts of National Socialism in the United States and the Federal Republic of Germany," in *The Americanization of the Global Village: Essays in Comparative Popular Culture,* ed. Roger Rollin (Bowling Green: Bowling Green State University Popular Press, 1989), 87–106.

5. Even for sympathetic commentators, the cultural imperialism thesis has some serious shortcomings. John Thompson, for example, draws attention to Katz's and Liebes's study of the very different ways in which the American television series *Dallas* was viewed by various ethnic groups in Israel and arrives at the following conclusion: "Studies such as this have shown convincingly that the reception and appropriation of media products are complex social processes in which individuals—interacting with others as well as with the characters portrayed in the programs they receive—actively make sense of messages, adopt various attitudes towards them and use them in differing ways in the course of their day-to-day lives. It is simply not possible to infer the varied features of reception processes from the characteristics of media messages considered by themselves, or from the commercial constraints operating on the producers of TV programs. . . . This line of criticism presses to the heart of the cultural imperialism thesis. It shows that this thesis is unsatisfactory not only because it is outdated and empirically doubtful,

but also because it is based on a conception of cultural phenomena which is fundamentally flawed. It fails to take account of the fact that the reception and appropriation of cultural phenomena are fundamentally hermeneutical processes in which individuals draw on the material and symbolic resources available to them, as well as on the interpretative assistance offered by those with whom they interact in their day-to-day lives, in order to make sense of the messages they receive and to find some way of relating to them." *The Media and Modernity: A Social Theory of the Media* (Palo Alto: Stanford University Press, 1995), 172.

6. In popular culture studies, it has been John Fiske, above all, who has stressed the considerable freedom of appropriation on the side of the recipient. See, for example, his essays "Popular Culture," in *Critical Terms for Literary Study,* ed. Frank Lentricchia and Thomas McLaughlin (Chicago: University of Chicago Press, 1995), 321–35, and "Moments of Television: Neither the Text nor the Audience," in *Remote Control,* ed. Seiter et al., 56–78, as well as his book *Power Plays, Power Works* (London: Verso, 1993). A helpful summary of research on spectator activity in watching television is provided by David Morley in "Television: Not So Much a Visual Medium, More a Visible Object," in *Visual Culture,* ed. Chris Jenks (London: Routledge, 1995), 170–89.

7. Terminology is already telling in this debate. With the advent of a more differentiated and potentially positive view, the term "mass culture" was usually replaced by "popular culture," which has become the standard term by now. I will therefore stick to the term "popular culture."

8. For a discussion of this issue, see Wolfgang Iser, *The Act of Reading: A Theory of Aesthetic Response* (Baltimore: Johns Hopkins University Press, 1978), 137–38, and my counterargument in "Aesthetic Experience of the Image," in *Iconographies of Power: The Politics and Poetics of Visual Representation,* ed. Ulla Haselstein, Berndt Ostendorf, and Hans Peter Schneck (Heidelberg: Carl Winter, 2003), 11–41.

9. Kaspar Maase, *BRAVO Amerika* (Hamburg: Junius, 1992). *BRAVO* was the name of the most popular German teenage magazine in the 1950s; it was the main interpreter of American films and popular music for many of the German baby-boomer generation and therefore also had a strong influence on the perception of American society and culture in that generation.

10. Cf. Heide Fehrenbach's characterization of the impact of the rebel-hero on American popular culture: "Through casual clothes and youthful self-assurance, Brando and other American male stars represented a romantic, rebellious macho—a brand of antiheroic individuality and self-expression attractive for its generational- and class-specific packaging. Set against the cultural stereotype of the socially formal, physically stiff, 'soldierly' German male of the Nazi period and the softer, more humble postwar version projected in *Heimatfilme,* it spoke to them of adventure and sexual expression, freedom from restriction and want." *Cinema in Democratizing Germany: Reconstructing National Identity after Hitler* (Chapel Hill: University of North Carolina Press, 1995), 167. An analysis of German reactions to Elvis Presley is provided in Uta G. Poiger's *Jazz, Rock, and Rebels: Cold War Politics and American Culture in a Divided Germany* (Berkeley: University of California Press, 2000), chap. 5.

11. Adorno's essay on jazz, "Perennial Fashion—Jazz," in his *Prisms* (London: Spearman, 1967), 119–32, provides one of the most interesting documents of the encounter between the European philosophical tradition and American popular culture.

12. Maase, *BRAVO Amerika*, 14–15; my translation.

13. For studies of Americanization not only in Germany but in the larger European context, see, for example, Rob Kroes, Robert W. Rydell, and Doeko Bosscher, eds. *Cultural Transmissions and Receptions: American Mass Culture in Europe* (Amsterdam: VU University Press, 1993); Rob Kroes, *If You've Seen One, You've Seen the Mall: Europeans and American Mass Culture* (Urbana: University of Illinois Press, 1996); Richard Kuisel, *Seducing the French: The Dilemma of Americanization* (Berkeley: University of California Press, 1993); George McKay, ed., *Yankee Go Home (& Take Me with You): Americanization and Popular Culture* (Sheffield: Academic Press, 1997); Reinhold Wagnleitner, *Coca-Colonisation und Kalter Krieg: Die Kulturmission der USA in Österreich nach dem Zweiten Weltkrieg* (Vienna: VG, 1991); Ralph Willett, *The Americanization of Germany, 1945–1949* (London: Routledge, 1989).

14. John Tomlinson, *Cultural Imperialism: A Critical Introduction* (Baltimore: Johns Hopkins University Press, 1991), 49–50. For a more recent assessment of the Americanization debate from a similar perspective, see Ronald Inglehart and Wayne E. Baker, "Modernization's Challenge to Traditional Values: Who's Afraid of Ronald McDonald," *Futurist* 35 (2001): 16–21. The authors argue: "The impression that we are moving toward a uniform 'McWorld' is partly an illusion. The seemingly identical McDonald's restaurants that have spread throughout the world actually have different social meanings and fulfill different social functions in different cultural zones" (18). "Economic development tends to push societies in a common direction, but rather than converging they seem to move along paths shaped by their cultural heritages. Therefore we doubt that the forces of modernization will produce a homogenized world culture in the foreseeable future" (20).

15. Cf., for example, Joana Breidenbach and Ina Zukrigl, *Tanz der Kulturen: Kulturelle Identität in einer globalisierten Welt* (Hamburg: Rowohlt, 2000), and Ulf Hannerz, *Cultural Complexity* (New York: Columbia University Press, 1992). In his essay "Networks of Americanization," Hannerz has found a helpful formulation for applying this "tool-kit" view of culture to the question of Americanization: "As an alternative to the phrase 'the American influence on Sweden,' we could speak of 'American culture as a resource for Swedes,' and then find that it consists of a great many parts, of different appeal to different people." In *Networks of Americanization: Aspects of the American Influence in Sweden*, ed. Rolf Lunden (Uppsala: Almquist and Wiksell, 1992), 15.

16. One should also add that there exists a fairly lively subgenre of Turkish-German film productions that deal with issues of cultural contact between German society and its large Turkish minority, initially often in melodramatic fashion but more recently also with ironic distance. The essay collection by Ruth Mayer and Mark Terkessidis, *Globalkolorit: Multikulturalismus und Populärkultur* (St. Andrä-

Wördern: Hannibal, 1998), contains a number of interesting discussions of the state of Turkish-German popular culture.

17. In this view, one may say, "American" becomes something like a brand name for cultural material that specializes in certain generic features and thrills. In "Is Hollywood America? The Trans-Nationalization of the American Film Industry," Frederick Wasser gives an interesting example of this kind of "staged Americanism": "In my conversations with American film executives, it was obvious that they perceive the world wide market as desiring a certain image of America to be featured in the movies. Each executive may have different and changing notions of the desired image—one season it may be hedonist consumers on the open road with fast cars—the next season it may be the American ethic of an individual hero struggling against all corrupt collectives. The point is not whether international viewers are actually seduced by such images but that film producers set for themselves the task of portraying an 'America' that is a dreamscape for 'universal' desires rather than a historic reality." *Critical Studies in Mass Communication* 12 (1995): 423–37, here 435.

18. The German film industry, which was clinically dead in the 1970s (the period, interestingly, of the greatest international success of German auteur filmmakers such as Wenders, Herzog, and Fassbinder), recovered somewhat in the 1990s and has established a steady output, but its market share remains regrettably low.

19. In his study of American cultural policies after World War II, Volker Berghahn provides a useful reminder that this aversion against American popular culture was a widespread attitude not just of European elites but also of elites in the United States, to whom the worldwide identification of American culture with American popular culture was (and often still is) a source of embarrassment: "In the eyes of many European intellectuals on the right and the left, but also among the educated middle classes, the United States did not really have a culture at all. It seemed more like the end of civilization. What was coming out of America had no sense of quality. It was judged to be vulgar mass culture of the worst kind that could not possibly be compared with the high-cultural achievements of the Europeans." "Philanthropy and Diplomacy in the 'American Century,'" in *The Ambiguous Legacy: U.S. Foreign Relations in the 'American Century,'* ed. Michael Hogan (New York: Cambridge University Press, 1999), 396; see also Berghahn's comprehensive study *America and the Intellectual Cold Wars in Europe: Shepard Stone between Philanthropy, Academy, and Diplomacy* (Princeton: Princeton University Press, 2001). As Berghahn argues, American cultural policies after World War II set out to prove, in Germany mainly through the institution of the Amerikahäuser, that the United States did indeed have remarkable cultural achievements on their own. Today, in view of the worldwide triumph of popular culture, American cultural policies seem to have developed new priorities. Except for the occasional support of ethnic writers in order to bolster the image of a multicultural America, there is no longer any American effort to "sell" American high culture abroad. Instead, the main line at present is to work against international criticism of Americanization. The battleground of the future, however, will be

somewhere else. It is announced by the title of Tyler Cowen's recent book *In Praise of Commercial Culture* (Cambridge: Harvard University Press, 1998). Cowen argues, "I seek to redress the current intellectual and popular balance and to encourage a more favorable attitude towards the commercialization of culture that we associate with modernity" (1).

20. I have addressed this issue in other contexts and publications, to which I have to refer those readers who may be dissatisfied or not convinced by the current condensed version of an originally much more detailed historical account. In view of the available space, I have to summarize an extended argument in the shortest possible fashion here. Cf. my essays "Emergence or Collapse of Cultural Hierarchy? American Popular Culture Seen from Abroad," in *Popular Culture in the United States*, ed. Peter Freese and Michael Porsche (Essen: Die Blaue Eule, 1994), 49–74; "'Amerikanisierung' der Kultur. Zur Geschichte der amerikanischen Populärkultur," in *Die Amerikanisierung des Medienalltags*, ed. Harald Wenzel (Frankfurt/Main: Campus, 1998), 13–52; and "Amerikanisierung und Modernisierung," *Transit* 17 (1999): 55–71.

21. In his study *Highbrow/Lowbrow: The Emergence of Cultural Hierarchy in America* (Cambridge: Harvard University Press, 1988), Lawrence Levine has traced the emergence of the idea of highbrow culture in America. However, it is significant that his narrative stops before the arrival of American modernism with its dehierarchized, often vernacular, and racially hybrid forms. In the way it is described by Levine, highbrow control over American culture is a phenomenon of the Victorian period.

22. One of the answers at the time of increased immigration around 1900 was the development of a nonverbal culture of performance that draws its attraction from the presentation of spectacular skills, appearances, or acts "for their own sake," that is, without implying any deeper meaning. Important aspects of this development around the turn of the century are described by John Kasson, *Amusing the Million: Coney Island at the Turn of the Century* (New York: Hill and Wang, 1978); Lewis Erenberg, *Steppin' Out: New York Nightlife and the Transformation of American Culture, 1890–1930* (Chicago: University of Chicago Press, 1981); Robert Snyder, *The Voice of the City: Vaudeville and Popular Culture in New York* (New York: Oxford University Press, 1989); David Nasaw, *Going Out: The Rise and Fall of Public Amusements* (Cambridge: Harvard University Press, 1993); William Leach, *Land of Desire: Merchants, Power, and the Rise of a New American Culture* (New York: Pantheon, 1993); Kathy Peiss, *Cheap Amusements: Working Women and Leisure in Turn-of-the-Century New York* (Philadelphia: Temple University Press, 1986); Lauren Rabinowitz, *For the Love of Pleasure: Women, Movies, and Culture in Turn-of-the-Century Chicago* (New Brunswick, NJ: Rutgers University Press, 1998); Miriam Hansen, *Babel and Babylon: Spectatorship in American Silent Film* (Cambridge: Harvard University Press, 1991), and various essays in the book *Cinema and the Invention of Modern Life*, ed. Leo Charney and Vanessa Schwartz (Berkeley: University of California Press, 1995). In order to describe the special contribution of the silent film to the new culture of performance and exhibition, Tom Gunning has introduced the useful term "cinema of attractions." The concept draws attention to the fact that, in their initial stage, silent movies gave

priority to the extraordinary spectacle or the spectacular technological effect over narrative continuity and plausibility. "The Cinema of Attractions: Early Film, Its Spectator, and the Avant-Garde," in *Early Cinema: Space-Frame-Narrative,* ed. Thomas Elsaesser (London: BFI, 1990), 56–62.

23. This holds true even for the dime novel, which gained influence in American culture after new printing techniques made it possible to sell a novel for a dime and thus to open up a market for young adolescent readers who for a number of reasons, would not touch the longer and more expensive type of historical novel that dominated the market up to then. The dominant dime novel genre, the Western novel, was, in fact, only a reduction of the type of historical novel made popular by James Fenimore Cooper.

24. The term "self-empowerment" is employed here in a much larger sense than meaning an identification with a better version of oneself. Because of the processes of reduction to easily accessible visual and aural forms and the textual fragmentation of cultural objects into short segments, single images, or musical moods, the individual encounters ever more improved conditions for satisfying imaginary longings, emotional needs, and bodily impulses. A superb illustration is provided by Gerhard Bliersbach in *So Grün War die Heide: Der Deutsche Nachkriegsfilm in neuer Sicht* (Weinheim: Beltz, 1985): "Ich liebte am amerikanischen Kino die Reifungsprozesse im Zeitraffer-Tempo mit glücklichem Ausgang; es hatte die Geschwindigkeit meiner Tagträume. Wie kein anderes Kino hat Hollywood die Strapazen der Reifung, die Ängste und Konflikte, die Phantasien und Wünsche auf die Leinwand gebracht" (23). [What I loved about American film was to be able to mature to a fast-paced tempo and a happy-ending; it had the speed of my daydreams. Like no other cinema, Hollywood captured the strains of adolescence—the anxieties and conflicts, the fantasies and desires (trans. Heide Fehrenbach)].

25. Maase, *BRAVO Amerika,* 28; my translation.

26. The habitual criticism of the destruction of native cultural traditions through American culture never considers the possibility that, as a form of cultural self-definition, these traditions may be very limited and may be experienced even as suffocating by the individual, because, in reflecting a strict social hierarchy, they only provide one possible role and source of self-esteem. Usually, the demise of these preindividualistic traditions is bemoaned by those Western individuals on the outside who would like to escape the leveling effects of democracy by having a whole array of cultural choices spread out before their eyes. On this point, see the acute observation by Tomlinson: "The critique of homogenization may turn out to be a peculiarly Western-centered concern if what is argued is that cultures must retain their separate identities simply to make the world a more diverse and interesting place." *Cultural Imperialism,* 135.

27. The crucial role youth has played in the worldwide reception of American popular culture is emphasized by David Ellwood in "Anti-Americanism in Western Europe: A Comparative Perspective," in *Occasional Paper No. 3, European Studies Seminar Series* (Bologna: Johns Hopkins University Bologna Center, 1999), 25–33. Ellwood provides a quote by Alexander Cockburn that gives a nutshell summary of the attraction that the informality of American popular culture had in an English context: "American culture was liberating, whether in the form

of blues, jazz, rock or prose. Here was escape from airless provincialism, BBC good taste and the mandates of the class system" (28). See also Volker Berghahn in his introduction to the German Historical Institute conference "The American Impact on Western Europe": "On the German side the 'Americanizers,' it seems, were very much young people who responded positively, indeed enthusiastically, to what arrived from across the Atlantic. The resistance to these imports came from an older generation who rejected rock and jazz, James Dean and Coca-Cola as products of an *Unkultur.*" "Conceptualizing the American Impact on Germany: West German Society and the Problem of Americanization," 7.

28. For brilliant analyses of cultural modernity as a culture of restless individualism, driven by a promise of self-development, see Marshall Berman, *All That Is Solid Melts into Air: The Experience of Modernism* (London: Verso, 1983), and Tomlinson, *Cultural Imperialism,* chap. 5.

29. A study of the influence of American culture in the 1960s is provided by Gerd Gemünden, *Framed Visions: Popular Culture, Americanization, and the Contemporary German and Austrian Imagination* (Ann Arbor: University of Michigan Press, 1998), but Gemünden focuses on responses to American culture in German-speaking literature and film, that is, on cultural production and not on consumption.

30. The other often discussed period is the 1920s, but, as Nolan points out in her essay "America in the German Imagination," Americanization, although a matter of concern, was not yet a social reality: "But the American model of modernity—prosperous, functional, materialistic, and bereft of tradition, domestic comfort, and *Kultur*—did not become the German reality in the 1920s. Americanization was contained both by Germans' poverty and limited consumption and by German capital's reluctance to embark on a full Fordist restructuring of the economy. . . . After 1945 . . . Germans no longer invented America from afar or on the basis of limited firsthand experience; America came to Germany." In *Transactions, Transgressions, Transformations,* ed. Fehrenbach and Poiger, 17–18. In contrast to earlier periods, anti-Americanism "coexisted with a pervasive Americanization of German life" (21). As Gemünden puts it: "What is new here is that an entire generation—roughly those born after 1938—was brought up with American popular culture from its members' earliest childhood on." *Framed Visions,* 23.

31. <http://www.ghi-dc.org/conpotweb/westernpapers/index.html>.

32. Kaspar Maase, "'Americanization', 'Americanness', and 'Americanisms': Time for a Change in Perspective?"

33. Volker Berghahn, "Conceptualizing the American Impact on Germany: West German Society and the Problem of Americanization."

34. Anselm Doering-Manteuffel, "Transatlantic Exchange and Interaction—The Concept of Westernization."

35. Mary Nolan, "Americanization or Westernization?": "As many historians and political theorists have argued, liberal values were raced and gendered, and liberal universalism and tolerance masked the exclusion of women, non-Whites and colonial subjects from full participation in projects of democratization, modernization, and Westernization" (8). What is introduced as anti-elitist culture is, it seems, an excuse for the perpetuation of a sexist and racist culture.

36. For the crucial role of invasion metaphors in discussions of Americanization, see my essay "*Close Encounters of the Third Kind:* American Popular Culture and European Intellectuals." *Annals of Scholarship* 12 (1998): 235–51.

37. "Cultures are 'condemned' to modernity not simply by the 'structural' process of economic development, but by the human process of self-development." Tomlinson, *Cultural Imperialism,* 141.

Mixing High and Popular Culture: The Impact of the Communication Revolution

Frank Trommler

Thanks to electronic technologies of reproduction, the trade in images, stereotypes, fictions, myths, and fantasy has become a more significant economic factor than ever before. Cultural criticism of the superficial stimuli of television and entertainment electronics has tended to make the discourse about popular culture into a stocktaking of image production and semiotic strategies. The following observations try to go beyond this stocktaking and focus on the specific expansion of the international, especially American, communication industry across the Atlantic since the 1960s. It seems that the cultural implications of this expansion—often called a revolution—have rarely received the appropriate attention since most of its factors are tied to the realm of political economy rather than to the debates in the humanities. While the mixing of high and popular culture has been an ongoing process, it has visibly accelerated under the impact of the communication revolution—to the point where the boundaries between them lose their distinction and the overlap with communication fosters new notions of culture.

Culture as an Agent of Social and Political Change

First, let me sketch out some general remarks about the political and social importance of culture—including both high and popular culture from rock and pop music to movies, television, and literature—in the transformations of Europe in the era of the cold war.[1] Crucial is, of course, the distinction between high and popular culture, in which the latter was increasingly associated with the American entertainment industry, although music and movie production for the masses had been a thriving European industry for a long time. In contrast, high culture was understood to represent the major achievements in literature, drama, classical music, and the arts with which the European nations had self-consciously built much of their identity over the centuries. In the first decades after World War II the rebuilding of Europe meant that politics rather than culture received primacy. Dependency of doctrines about art in each system—the contrast between (Western) modernism and (Eastern) socialist realism—seemed to offer proof for this. In the 1960s, however, not only did concepts of "art" and "culture" change, but the ways in which these concepts referred to politics also shifted. A new generation of artists, intellectuals, and cultural managers found ways to free themselves from the primacy of politics and demonstrated the transformative power of culture on society. This was a culture embodied by a new generation of youth, which broke free from hierarchies and the restraints of representation. Culture liberated itself from its aesthetically internalized labels, which in the case of modernism were supposed to prove the freedom of the Western individual, and, in the case of socialist realism, the superiority of a communist social order. But culture held itself within the parameters of international confrontation, which became explosive with the Vietnam War: national elites tended to understand culture (mostly in terms of high culture) as an alternative order to politics, an expression of human values set against the deadly manipulation of political hierarchies and monopolies.

This liberation also meant a liberation from a fixation on the dichotomy between high and mass culture that had predominated in the 1950s, a process that took on a special dynamic in the United States. The battles around civil rights and the Vietnam War in American society made extensive use of cultural expression, especially marshaling rock and pop music in the service of oppositional culture. Rejecting the difference between high culture and the market-oriented culture of light entertainment that was traditionally seen as lesser and lower, the student movement in America, with its growing counterculture, developed a cultural consciousness. It saw itself as an active way of life organized through a great variety of forms of aesthetic and emotional involvement. This became a worldwide model for opposition to established life-styles and power relations. It provided inspiration for new tactics in the struggle for minority rights and the equality of women.

In the 1970s many factors contributed to giving culture a key role in the debates over democratization of societies that had become fossilized through decades of war and the cold war. In the United States these factors were strongly linked to the rejection of the political order and the whole military and industrial establishment during the Vietnam conflict. Interest in culture was more intense in the quarters of those pursuing oppositional life-styles, particularly the younger generation, which had begun seeking contact with Europe through film, travel, cuisine, and enthusiasm for art. In West Germany the reform policies of the coalition of Social Democrats and Liberals elected in 1969 provided significant impetus in democratizing culture. Here the interest in culture was more strongly channeled through initiatives on the state and community level and through new social groups. Despite talk of an "extended concept of culture" and the (slow) acceptance of intertwining its "high" and "popular" forms, culture in the European context retained more of its traditional representational function. While the young generation in Europe absorbed and extended American counterculture with much aplomb, one should not forget that it was due to the traditional notion of its high status that culture was able to become a liberating force on both sides of the Iron Curtain.

The American Impact on the Communication Revolution

At the end of the 1970s the increasing dominance of the American media and communications industry became an important topic of contention in European and developing countries. The common denominator of international reactions, which were voiced above all in UNESCO, was resistance to American mass culture. On this basis—playing on well-established cultural anxieties vis-à-vis an invading giant—the omnipresence of American media lost its bonus as part of the fortification of the West in the cold war confrontations. Although the Vietnam War, sometimes called the "television war," revealed the overextension of the United States as a global power, it did not diminish the American media industry's dominance of the world market. On the contrary, it resulted in an even more outspoken determination of American political and business elites to use every possible means to ensure America's media presence.[2] The aim was to guarantee the "free flow of information" through an internationally ratified information agreement that would allow the American communications and media industry access to all national domestic markets.[3] American businesses dominated more than 80 percent of distribution and production in the world communications market, as Zbigniew Brzezinski ascertained in his influential book *Between Two Ages: America's Role in the Technetronic Era*.[4] This fact led to heated debates within UNESCO, with the third world countries and some European countries such as France becoming particularly agitated. In 1974 Finnish president Urho Kekkonen summed up the mood of the time: "Might it not be the case that the prophets who preach the unimpeded flow of information are not at all interested in equality between nations, but are simply on the side of power and wealth?"[5]

While the American debate on multiculturalism, which promotes greater sensitivity toward other cultures, was relegated to the sphere of education, the U.S. government made use of cold war rhetoric to enforce the opening up of the media markets of other nations for the American communications industry. They claimed that the state or the media in these countries were practicing a form of antidemocratic control. The great significance of these critiques of cultural or communications policy in the United States was revealed by the reaction of the American government in 1984 to UNESCO's refusal to comply with American demands. The United States promptly left the most important international cultural agency.

The French government organized an international effort against American cultural imperialism[6] in France mainly over the question of economic control over film and television. Under President Mitterand this effort culminated in France's attempt to take a lead in Europe in the defense of national traditions of media culture and high culture. The central concept used was that of France's "cultural identity." While Minister for Culture Jack Lang linked this concept to the idea of "cultural democracy" at an international conference at the Sorbonne in 1983, Mitterand emphasized the economic dimension of promoting culture: "Investing in culture means investing in the economy. It frees the future and thus contributes to giving back to life its whole meaning."[7] International cultural policy should "prevent market mechanisms and the economic power struggle from imposing stereotyped, culturally meaningless products on individuals of other nations," he argued.[8] The participants agreed to complement the notion of cultural identity with that of cultural democracy, aware of the fact that cultural self-expression has great potential for economic gains or can, at times, compensate for insufficient economic gains. Yet, the core of the conflict over cultural identity with America was without doubt economic. By 1989 the states of the European Community alone were paying more than $1 billion in licensing fees to American television companies. In the same year the American film industry had an export surplus of $2.5 billion, second only to the aviation and space industry.[9]

Unlike France, the Federal Republic of Germany did not play a prominent or official role in this conflict. The cultural sovereignty of its *Länder,* or regional states, meant that a unified policy on such matters only came together in exceptional circumstances.[10] Scholarly debates were still influenced by Theodor Adorno and Max Horkheimer's concept of the "culture industry," but they rarely had access to the real workings of this industry, in which records, books, films, radio, television, the press, photography, reproduction of art and advertising, audiovisual products, and services were all competing with one another and were determined by international trends. The realization was slow in coming; it was no longer possible to view this problem in terms of the contrast between high and mass culture and thus to reduce the cultural presence of America to its dominance of the mass market. Those who worked in the industry knew that true access to the international communications market could only be gained by renouncing cultural sovereignty.

The 1980s became the crucial decade for a twofold readjustment of the redefined and broadened concept of culture, which, in the 1960s, had been extricated from the dichotomies of high and mass cultures. Both readjustments originated in the United States and were routinely attributed to this origin, often with open resentment of the intellectual elites against the constant influx of mass and popular culture. The first was, under the strong dominance of American music, movie, and media culture, the wide acceptance of the commercial conditions of cultural production, including those of high culture and art. The obligation to provide support for arts and culture, which European state institutions and cities had traditionally assumed and broadly extended in the 1970s and early 1980s, was increasingly questioned and put under financial scrutiny. By the 1990s, the established system of arts sponsorship—in Germany about 90 percent from public sources and 10 percent from private sources—was beginning to unravel. In the United States, where about 10 percent of outlays for arts and culture come from public sources and 90 percent from private sources, the few national agencies of public arts sponsorship such as the National Endowment for the Arts were almost shut down by the Republican Congress. Only heavy emphasis on the social usefulness of culture, which also informed the public commitment in European legislative bodies, saved public sponsorship on the national level. Demonstrating the economic benefits of arts and culture—both high and popular—for a city or region emerged as the most effective counterargument.

The other readjustment of the broadened concept of culture occurred under even stronger influence of the United States in the area of communication, where technological advances, especially the digital revolution, transformed the notions of time and space on a global scale. Communications technology reconstituted the relationship among economic, political, and cultural actors, absorbing functions and practices that traditionally had been considered to belong to the cultural realm. In his analysis of this process, Belgian communications scholar Armand Mattelart illuminates that both technological and nontechnological factors contributed to the readjustments of the 1980s that resulted in the realization that communication, long associated only with its technologies, would have to be considered part of culture:

> Communication is also *culture*. Placing thought about communications under the sign of culture, however, was not a major concern of the theories and strategies of international communications in the course of their history, because of their technicist and economist drifts. It was only recently, in the 1980s, that the recentering on culture acquired its legitimacy, as centralized models of the management of culture in the welfare states entered into a crisis and as the world market became a space of transnational regulation of the relations between nations and peoples.[11]

It is not surprising that Europeans were more resistant to recognizing communication as culture. The conservatives and Marxists, though separated by different social goals, found themselves to be companions in the offensive against American dominance in mass culture and communication. Traditionally part of conservative vocabulary, denigration of mass culture as an expression of low taste met with the attack against the commercialization of culture in the interest of American media conglomerates, which the Left had reformulated in the ideological battles of the 1960s. One of the most influential responses on the American side was already formulated in 1970 in *Between Two Ages,* in which Brzezinski projected the crucial role of the United States in disseminating the technetronic revolution. It would lead, Brzezinski conceded, to a "new imperialism" that, however, would soon be challenged and replaced, as the new communication practices would enable other nations to compete and catch up. He described America's impact as disseminator of the technetronic revolution in this contradiction:

> it both promotes and undermines American interests as defined by American policymakers; it helps to advance the cause of cooperation on a larger scale even as it disrupts existing social or economic fabrics; it both lays the groundwork for well-being and stability and enhances the forces working for instability and revolution.[12]

Brzezinski's projection of enormous advancements of global economic and social policies on the basis of the communication revolution and his insistence that the role of the United States as disseminator would not go unchallenged has held its ground for many years. His listing of stabilizing and destabilizing factors can be applied to the age of the Internet, as can the response on the Left that also "the new communication technologies are, in fact, the product and a defining feature of global capitalism that greatly enhances social inequality."[13] What has become more concrete with the Internet is the potential of overriding "the antidemocratic implication of the media marketplace." Whether more democratic media and a more democratic political culture will ensue, however, is open to debate.[14]

Both adjustments of the extended concept of culture were anchored and monitored, as mentioned, in the realm of political economy, not in traditional humanities or liberal arts discussion. As a consequence it left academic and educational communities that engaged in cultural studies as a new heuristic and theoretical device in a precarious position of entrenchment. It is no coincidence that the adversarial promotion of culture as a manifestation of diversity took shape in the 1980s, most prominently and polemically in the academic world, which found it a convenient vehicle for renewing the tradition of cultural pluralism as part of the democratic ideal. The contest between cultural conformity, intensified by the growth of mass culture and communication, and cultural diversity, enhanced by the academic yearning for distinction and *différence,* absorbed a great deal of critical energy. Eventually it became the terrain in which multiculturalism shifted the frame of reference away from the Eurocentric basis of American education toward the concept of culture as a vehicle of personal, ethnic, or racial identity.[15] The so-called cultural wars of the 1980s that were fought over the definition of American identity either from the traditional consensus position or from the multicultural fabric of the country made this terrain part of the confrontations, as it reflected America's close ties to the cultures of

Europe. These ties, weakened by the end of the cold war, were seriously threatened both by technoculturalism and multiculturalism.[16]

It has been called a great irony that "America's belated attention to its multicultural makeup . . . occurred just when the electronic media and technology are perfecting our ability to obliterate diversity."[17] Upon closer look, the connection is less ironic than causal. The fact that multiculturalism became the focal point of the American democratic agenda should not obliterate this dialectic. Europeans did not overlook the connection, although they found the American model of multiculturalism appealing especially at a time when ethnic clashes in the Balkans triggered the worst atrocities since World War II. With the debate about globalization, the arguments about obliterating cultural diversity have again turned against the United States although globalization has been increasingly conceptualized under the decentering omnipresence of the Internet, not only under the principles of corporate expansionism.

Among the many irritations that surface in the transatlantic quarrels about directing globalization, one question clearly reflects the recent shifts in the conceptualization of culture: whether Europe still participates in defining universalism as culture's mission, of which it was the guardian for centuries, or whether it has shifted to enforcing culture in its resistance potential against economic globalization. Slavoj Žižek has formulated it for the case of France, always the most alert critic of American hegemony:

> The paradox is that the proper roles seem to be reversed: France, in its republican universalism, is more and more perceived as a *particular* phenomenon threatened by the process of globalization, while the United States, with its multitude of groups demanding recognition of their particular, specific identities, more and more emerges as the universal model.[18]

And yet France is only part of the emerging Europe. What is threatened by globalization is not the particularity of a region or culture but "universality itself, in its eminently political dimension."[19] As Europe increasingly tries to unite nationalities and not just ethnic cultures, the search for an universalism beyond the economic and technological agenda becomes crucial. The ability to integrate socially determined goals into international politics will determine the success, as will the ability to reshape the concept of culture and to activate its prospective and anticipatory qualities.

Communication as Culture

With the end of the cold war and the integration of Europe, the discourse on the European-American relationship in the area of communication has been transformed. The arguments of political and economic dependencies have lost their urgency as the predominance of politics in the public sphere has diminished and as economic globalization is drawing attention away from national models. Most obvious is the emergence of a new media order in Europe, which is supposed to promote integration and cohesion, while Japanese, British, Australian, and German companies have taken over parts of the American publication and media industries.

One can argue that the transformations of the nature of both the broadcast media and the public sphere that occurred in the 1990s have been even more fundamental to culture than those of the 1980s. As long as the cold war endorsed the political and moral weight of culture vis-à-vis the military and political stalemate, the traditional association with the status of high culture provided public interest and representational functions even for the most commercial ventures in film, television, and other visual media. Yet the erosion of the differences between high and popular culture, already far advanced in the 1980s, intensified in the 1990s, when the antiuniversalistic aesthetic currents that had been elevated under the sign of postmodernism converged in an all-encompassing commercial universalism. If every item of everyday life becomes part of the ever-expanding aestheticism of our consumerist existence, art and culture lose whatever distinction they bestow on their audience. Their prominence in producing identity is being successfully challenged by other constituents of contemporary life, especially those that help us function as subjects in the aesthetic consumerism and absorbing communication experience of today. Consumption itself has transformed from mere use—the "realization" of the product—to communication, and the consuming-communicating subject itself is becoming "creative." "The fact that immaterial labor simultaneously produces subjectivity and economic value shows how the capitalist mode of production has penetrated our life and torn down established distinctions between economy, power, culture, and knowledge."[20]

Under these auspices communication has indeed become culture, providing identity through a kind of consumerist creativity that even Joseph Beuys, the propagator of the aesthetization of everyday life, might not have recognized as such in the 1970s. At the same time the devalorization of reality has been intensified by the media and the Internet. The disorientation of the public has resulted in inhibiting its access to political consciousness. The "very ideal of public opinion" is being undermined, "the belief that public knowledge can, and should, inform and shape political life."[21] Recognizing the "force of the image that now prevails," Ignacio Ramonet assesses the culturalist dilemma: "the objective is not to make us understand a situation, but to make us take part in an event." This occurs, he adds, at an enormous social cost: "Becoming informed is tiring, but this is the price of democracy."[22] While functioning more as a catalyst of identity than ever, communication as a mode of existence dissipates its long-standing public mission of facilitating informed understanding of the political process. (Often quoted as a powerful example is the talk show as the conduit to political information and electoral behavior.)

Europeans have been more forthcoming with the warning that this means a decline of civic and political culture.[23] The American doctrine of the free flow of information through commercial channels has clearly contributed to dislodging the European public service broadcasting, but it remains to be seen whether the new European media order can check the privatization and commercialization of all public communication, thus preventing public information from fully turning into a mere vehicle for advertising.

All in all, it should have become obvious that the communication revolution, which drew its dynamic from American business interests, has impacted greatly not only the transformation of concept and practice of culture in the late twentieth century, leading from a mixing of high and popular culture to a merging of many of their functions in society, but also the nature and function of communication itself. While it is still too early to ascertain the full consequences of the fact that communication *is* culture by generating identity in a new matrix of consumption and production—which projects itself on both national and international markets and politics—it is not too early to show that the transformations have gained momentum that places them beyond the traditional notions of "America" and "Americanization." Whether they are truly global remains to be seen.

NOTES

1. For a comprehensive overview, see Frank Trommler, "Neuer Start und alte Vorurteile. Die Kulturbeziehungen im Zeichen des Kalten Krieges 1945–1968," in

Die USA und Deutschland im Zeitalter des Kalten Krieges: Ein Handbuch, ed. Detlev Junker (Stuttgart/Munich: Deutsche Verlags-Anstalt, 2001), 1:567–91; and "Kultur als translatlantisches Spannungsfeld 1968–1990," in *Die USA und Deutschland im Zeitalter,* 2:395–419.

2. Anthony Smith, *The Geopolitics of Information: How Western Culture Dominates the World* (New York: Oxford University Press, 1980), 58.

3. Emily S. Rosenberg, "Cultural Interactions," in *Encyclopedia of the United States in the Twentieth Century,* ed. Stanley I. Kutler et al. (New York: Charles Scribner's Sons, 1996), 2:710.

4. Zbigniew Brzezinski, *Between Two Ages: America's Role in the Technetronic Era* (New York: Penguin, 1976).

5. Cited in Jörg Becker et al., eds., *Informationstechnologie und internationale Politik* (Bonn: Friedrich-Ebert-Stiftung, 1983), 13.

6. John Tomlinson, *Cultural Imperialism: A Critical Introduction* (Baltimore: Johns Hopkins University Press, 1991).

7. Cited in Chantal Cinquin, "President Mitterand Also Watches Dallas: American Mass Media and French National Policy," in *The Americanization of the Global Village,* ed. Roger Rollin (Bowling Green: Bowling Green State University Popular Press, 1989), 21.

8. Ibid., 19.

9. Marie-Luise Hauch-Fleck, "Die Rollen werden neu verteilt: Europäische Produzenten wehren sich gegen die Vormachtstellung der Amerikaner," *Die Zeit* (overseas ed.), May 25, 1990, 10.

10. Klaus von Bismarck et al., *Industrialisierung des Bewußtseins: Eine kritische Auseinandersetzung mit den "neuen" Medien* (Munich/Zurich: Piper, 1985), esp. 189–90.

11. Armand Mattelart, *Mapping World Communication: War, Progress, Culture* (Minneapolis/London: University of Minnesota Press, 1994), xv.

12. Zbigniew Brzezinski, *Between Two Ages,* 34.

13. Robert W. McChesney, "The Internet and United States Communication Policy-Making in Historical and Critical Perspective," *Journal of Communication* 46 (1996): 99.

14. Ibid.

15. David A. Hollinger, *Postethnic America: Beyond Multiculturalism* (New York: Basic Books, 1995), 100.

16. Stephen Langley, "Multiculturalism versus Technoculturalism: Its Challenge to American Theatre and the Functions of Arts Management," in *The American Stage: Social and Economic Issues from the Colonial Period to the Present,* ed. Ron Engle and Tice L. Miller (Cambridge: Cambridge University Press, 1993), 278–89.

17. Ibid., 279.

18. Slavoj Žižek, "A Leftist's Plea for Eurocentrism,'" *Critical Inquiry* 24 (1998): 1007.

19. Ibid., 1008.

20. Stephan Schmidt-Wulffen, "Die Kunst von heute braucht kein Haus:

Warum das Museum seine gesellschaftliche Funktion verloren hat," *Die Zeit* 13 (March 25, 1999): 55.

21. Kevin Robins, "The Politics of Silence: The Meaning of Community and the Uses of Media in the New Europe," *New Formations* 21 (1994): 99.

22. Ignacio Ramonet, "L'Ère du Soupçon," *Le Monde Diplomatique* (May 1991): 12, 99.

23. Jay G. Blumler, "Political Communication Systems All Change: A Response to Kees Brants," *European Journal of Communication* 14 (1999): 245–46.

How American Was It? Popular Culture from Weimar to Hitler

Thomas J. Saunders

The categories with which scholars have understood and analyzed Americanization have largely been inherited from the interwar period. Two broad lines of inquiry emerged. The first sought to identify and quantify the increase in European exposure to the American way of life as evidenced by the combination of travel to the United States and, more essentially, the marketing and appropriation of elements of American popular culture in Europe. The second endeavored to conceptualize the parallels and contrasts between European and American culture and to assess the impact of the latter on the former. Both approaches have been differentiated and reformulated over recent decades through analytical categories of modernization, Westernization, and globalization. Some commentators have discarded the notion of "Americanization" as too general, unilateral, and mechanical for analyzing the nature of cultural interchange.[1] Yet if, as interwar observers already recognized, the line between Americanization and modernization can blur, one can still question how American German popular culture was between the wars.

The burgeoning literature on the Americanization of Germany since World War II cannot escape the intense debates of the 1920s.[2] Those debates have long been taken as an indication that in the period before 1945 Germany was the European country most exposed to American influence. Among recent formulations of this phenomenon, Janet Lungstrum calls the Germany of the 1920s Europe's most Americanized counterpart; Sabine Hake locates in this era "the rise of Americanism as the main paradigm of mass culture."[3] A host of familiar images fuels these perceptions—jazz in Berlin nightlife, the prevalence of American movies, preoccupation with American achievements, visits by Josephine Baker and Charlie Chaplin, the popularity of the

Bubikopf, and the emergence of the so-called new woman. Whether one refers to clothing and hairstyles, music and dance, or media and advertising, America figures as the primary foreign element in Germany's development. American fashions are credited with setting trends in work and leisure and with enhancing the popularity of sports and physical fitness.[4]

The broad consensus that identifies the 1920s as the high-water mark of Americanization before 1945 presents America's cultural presence as a smorgasbord of modernity and technological progress appropriated by Germans according to inclination and need.[5] America specifically functioned as a point of departure for intellectuals and artists intrigued by the alternative it offered to domestic traditions they found worn out and stultifying. America therefore served as a promising or baleful signpost to Germany's future, a *Sonderweg* promising redemption for those disenchanted with Germany's own path or a threatening deviation from the German norm. Beeke Sell Tower's claim for Weimar artists applies very broadly: "In imagining America . . . artists took a spirited part in Weimar Germany's discourse on modernity and on America as either admirable model or specter of Spenglerian decline."[6]

The literature on Americanization in Weimar has generally focused on the ideas of those intellectuals who looked to America with curiosity or enthusiasm for answers to German problems. Without ignoring the undeniably strong currents of anti-American sentiment in Weimar, historians have paid these less attention.[7] From Mary Nolan's examination of alternatives offered by the American model in the economy and society to David Bathrick's exploration of the infatuation among the avant-garde with boxing, America figures as the incarnation of values judged modern if not always admirable.[8] Liberal and left-wing observers predominate. It is these same intellectuals who are tacitly referenced in Nancy Nenno's claim that "Berlin conducted a love affair with things American, attempting to model itself as Europe's most modern city."[9]

The rather more limited literature on Americanization in the Third Reich shifts perspective, emphasizing the resurgence of anti-Americanism and at best the ambivalence of Nazi observers toward America. Historians generally highlight the growing official hostility toward America and the marginalization of popular culture imported from the United States. As an exercise in national renewal and assault on what was labeled Jewish modernism and cosmopolitanism, national socialism foregrounded many of the negative stereotypes of America held by conservative nationalists who were on the defensive in the 1920s. Denunciation of America as racially mixed and degenerate, restrictions on jazz music, and the gradual elimination of American motion pictures from German theaters all suggest a rejection of American popular culture.[10]

However, closer examination shows inconsistencies in perceptions and in the appropriation of America. Not only did elements of American popular culture continue to circulate widely in Germany—there was no sudden break in 1933—but respect for the American achievement in creating a broadly popular culture remained, even when coupled with derision toward the specific nature of that culture. This is consistent with the broader recognition that the Third Reich, despite its integral nationalism, cannot be neatly pigeonholed as reactionary. Rather, as Jeffrey Herf has suggested, it represented a form of "reactionary modernism" and in this regard at least may be classified with the broader phenomenon of interwar fascism.[11] For evaluating Americanization in the Third Reich one must certainly be attentive to the tension between the modern and antimodern in Nazism, but one must also not become preoccupied with it. Similarly, one should assume neither continuity nor break between Weimar and Nazi Germany in respect to American popular culture as a market force and reference point.

My own work on American cinema in Weimar has hitherto tended to adopt the conventional pattern, highlighting the ideas of those who grappled seriously, though by no means uncritically, with the American model. It shares the premise of Weimar's remarkable indebtedness to American culture, even as it leaves open the question about the relationship between Weimar's experience and developments after 1933.[12] But having agreed with those asserting the breadth of American inroads in the 1920s (which tends to prejudge the case for discontinuity after 1933), I would like to revisit both that premise and the relevance of American popular culture for Nazi Germany. Without denying the extent to which America functioned as a reference point for Weimar intellectuals and, in a different way, for Nazi ideologues, I would like particularly to challenge the picture sometimes drawn of the ubiquity of American popular culture in Germany after World War I.

There is little doubt that the United States played a noteworthy role as a point of departure for German debates about social, economic, and cultural development. There is also ample evidence that America functioned as a model for a life-style understood to be more modern and democratic. It has not, however, been demonstrated that interwar

German popular culture became particularly American. There is a notable tension between assumptions about America's omnipresence in the 1920s and the contemporary, often academic debate about how extensively Germany borrowed from America. The literature on Weimar's encounter with America primarily engages absence, not presence. Such phenomena as the popularity of the German translation of Henry Ford's autobiography confirm this: not automobiles or marketing schemes crossed the Atlantic but a set of images and ideas. Indeed, one could argue that the debate over America raged precisely because of its (still) relative remoteness from everyday German life. Granting a major exception to this rule, the case of cinema, one can pose the following counterfactual question: Without American popular culture, how different would German popular culture have been before 1945?

To pose the question this way is to recognize, as did some contemporaries, that America represented a specific version of modernity already apparent in Germany. Yet conceding this point, and the transnational potential of modern popular culture, in interwar Germany neither radio, popular fiction, nor sporting events were American in a literal sense.[13] The unprecedented awareness of American counterparts actually underscores the domestic provenance of popular culture. Germans were not obliged to digest American popular culture regularly. Many, however, felt an obligation to have an opinion about it. The great debates of this era, not least of which was the one over the "new woman," revolved primarily around images of America rather than American popular culture in Germany. Thus the question regarding how American German popular culture was before 1945 differs substantially from the question of what Germans thought or wrote about America in this period.[14]

For illustrative purposes, jazz in Weimar offers a useful case study. Historians, myself included, well aware that Berlin was not Germany, have nonetheless followed certain contemporaries mesmerized by currents in the capital in adopting jazz as a buzzword for American inroads into German music, dance, and fashion. Only recently has anyone probed the surface of this image. In the words of J. Bradford Robinson:

So domineering is our picture of bare-kneed flappers dancing the shimmy with tuxedoed lounge lizards in post-war Berlin, a city caught in a frenzy of sexual excess and political thuggery, that few have bothered to ask those mundane questions so obvious to social historians: Who actually consumed this music, and in what amounts? Where did Germany's jazz originate? How was it imported, learnt, and disseminated?

Robinson goes on to argue that the Jazz Age was a myth propagated by the Weimar media: "The music, dance forms, and cultural epiphenomena that bore this label captured the imagination of German journalists and intelligentsia to such an extent as to elevate jazz, a music entirely foreign to German traditions and ethos, to the level of what was called by one of its champions a *Zeitfrage.*"[15] The music itself touched only a small group of the urban middle-class. Moreover, what passed as jazz in Germany had little to do with its American variant. Most Germans "had little inkling of the nature of this music and still less desire to consume it." Robinson demonstrates that what passed for jazz in Weimar was "commercial syncopated dance music," mostly homegrown to an imagined notion of jazz.[16] Jazz became code for any music from America or music perceived to be in the American style. In short, jazz was a heavily overdetermined site of debate about America's meaning for Weimar, more specter than actuality.[17]

The limitations Robinson notes with regard to the marketing of jazz in Germany—mass culture as a whole still in its infancy, a weak currency until the mid-1920s, and at best embryonic means for dissemination of music to a mass audience—have wider implications.[18] If jazz was fundamentally the property of urban middle-class cognoscenti and the subject of artists and literary intellectuals ruminating about the nature of their age rather than part of the mainstream of popular culture, then we have confused cause and effect. Not only, as Cornelius Partsch has observed, did jazz in Germany, as in America, remain outside the cultural mainstream, but jazz also never became broadly popular.[19] Its falsely implied ubiquity, on the basis of very limited exposure to the original American music or bands, can be taken as evidence of just how German, and impervious to America, popular culture remained. Here, as elsewhere, the longing among certain intellectuals for cultural renewal valorized an otherwise marginal cultural phenomenon.[20]

A parallel, though inverse case can be developed for the Third Reich, where the official denigration of American music and dance politicized popular culture. Jazz enthusiasts and "deviant" youth whose musical preferences included jazz had those preferences "elevated" to the level of choices for or against the ethos of national socialism. American music offered not only the lure of the foreign and the taint of the unclean but also an index of conformity and political loyalty. Even though Goebbels never totally excluded American dance music from radio, since he respected the extent to which it had found popularity in Germany, swing youth, who found in American music a symbol of independence, were persecuted as rebels.[21]

TO CONFRONT THE questions of the social historian posed by Robinson helps correct problematic generalizations but hardly exhausts the meaning of "American" for German popular culture. That jazz was a parallel rather than a borrowed form is no witness by itself against America's importance for German culture after 1918. Popular culture is about images and icons as well as products and consumption. The fact that German jazz was a bastardization of the real item and thus un-American scarcely nullifies the German equation of jazz with modern (American) dance music. Rightly or wrongly, jazz stood in for the blend of primitive and modern elements in the American cultural matrix, with the saxophone as its unmistakable icon. This argument can be widened to other cultural phenomena, where the icon substituted for America. Even boxing could become a site of discourse on American modernity. "If sport, along with jazz, dancing revues, Josephine Baker, or the pragmatic Henry Ford came to symbolize American toughness and the up-to-date, then the figure of the boxer served as its corporeal representation par excellence."[22]

If the distinction between the imagined or iconographic America and American cultural imports is understood, a reference such as Tower's to the "enormous success of America-style mass culture" belongs clearly to the former category.[23] Neither American music, American literature, nor American sports overwhelmed German counterparts. Nor did the "new woman," however much she reflected gender anxieties in Germany, represent Germany's conquest by the American girl. Rather, it was the image of America, simultaneously identified as modern, that she enshrined.

In only one area of popular culture was America as much literally as iconographically present (although the distinction becomes somewhat ironic in a medium devoted to images). Hollywood movies represented a direct rather than mediated contribution to German culture, while generating, like jazz, a set of icons and values (including that of the "new woman") with resonance well beyond the screen. After an extended hiatus caused by the war, German theaters began to show American movies regularly again in 1921. By mid-decade they were releasing hundreds of Hollywood pictures annually, a pattern checked only partially by the introduction of talkies. Well into the early years of the Third Reich American movies were familiar in German theater programs. While these imports were retitled and later dubbed, and often re-edited for German release, they were widely circulated and were not, as often is the case of jazz, weak facsimiles of the original.[24]

American movies did not single-handedly pose the challenge of a medium commanding images; they did help frame it, however. Members of Parliament were not concerned about American film imports when in 1919–20 they debated and then reinstituted censorship for movies alone after general abolition of censorship in the revolution of 1918. They were giving expression to widespread sentiments, especially among the educated bourgeoisie, that cinema adulterated culture. Movies were commonly dismissed as hopeless kitsch, but their broad popularity, perceived persuasiveness, and aggressive advertising, especially aimed at young people, made them appear threatening.

The physical and commercial ubiquity of Hollywood leaves open, of course, complex questions about the appropriation and meaning of American films for German audiences. Several general observations are in order. First, despite its newly won international dominance, Hollywood was not yet synonymous with motion picture entertainment. German production expanded dramatically during and immediately following the war and sustained itself, amid turbulent economic circumstances, right through the interwar period. American and domestic movies appeared side by side in roughly equal proportions through the second half of the 1920s. Second, although not all American genres found broad popularity in Germany, most of them became familiar. Depending upon the sources one consults, the American imports can be judged either as alien and generally unpopular or as welcome variety and essential stimulants to a national production that otherwise would have become insular and pedestrian.[25] Westerns, slapstick, and select blockbusters certainly found German audiences. Third, American movies were a strong enough presence on the German market and in the visual imaginations of German producers and directors—prominently Erich Pommer and Fritz Lang—that it is scarcely possible to understand German cinema in this period apart from its steady dialogue, both friendly and hostile, with Hollywood. Finally, American movies not only disseminated images of the American way of life (moral and material) but also brought with them advertising techniques and marketing values. Hollywood therefore played a crucial role in the contest to dominate the realm of images and icons and, with these, distraction and consumerism. It was precisely this contest that riveted Nazi attention on the motion picture and has sustained the view that the Third Reich aimed to reduce Hollywood's presence.

THAT AMERICAN MOVIES were domesticated in Germany in the 1920s means that, whether appreciated or condemned, they participated, more than any other American cultural import, in the formation of Germany's modern media culture. The motion picture was the leading medium of an age inundated with images en route to becoming icons. This is not to suggest that the rise of film marginalized aural or literate culture. On the contrary, cinema became *the* medium of the twentieth century precisely because it synthesized the literate, the visual, and the aural. Its mechanisms operated in everything from the consumption of sporting events to fashion shows. Already in the 1920s it was observed that the essence of American movies was advertising—not primarily or necessarily for products but for poses, values, and visual pleasure. Here the spectator and consumer merged, a development critical for understanding modern popular culture in general. It is also critical for grasping Nazi culture in particular.

While popular culture traverses national borders, the icons of the twentieth century, whether corporate, political, or from the realm of entertainment, were often identified with nations. America was the twentieth century's most fertile producer of images and icons. Nazi Germany was a somewhat distant second. To assess the meaning of American popular culture for interwar Germany therefore requires consideration of the extent to which American images and icons became household items in Germany. Reference has already been made to Chaplin, the *Bubikopf* and the "new woman." Regardless of their popularity, each gained considerable resonance as symbols of America's cultural weight. Like Hollywood, national socialism sought to capture the popular realm with its images and icons. Both Hitler and Goebbels recognized a fundamental principle of advertising and applied it to politics in the time of struggle: better to be resented than ignored. Not to figure in the thicket of images and slogans that dominated the public realm meant to surrender without a fight. And the Nazis, of course, saw themselves engaged in a struggle for culture, one whose leitmotif was purification—that is, the removal or stripping away of the debasements of modernism and adulterations from abroad that denationalized and thus falsified authentic German culture.[26] Nazism had multiple cultural enemies, from expressionism and primitivism to cosmopolitanism. However, it also posited the creation of a truly popular culture, suited to the modern age.

What then of America and popular culture in the Third Reich? Thematically, Hitler's Germany was about the restoration of a national, racially pure culture against an international or cosmopolitan culture, which scarcely endeared it to the American model. Structurally, it was about mechanisms of oversight and control. The Reichskulturkammer, with its seven departments, provided a framework for oversight of all areas of cultural life. Motion pictures and radio, the two media apart from the press that enjoyed the broadest resonance, were particularly important for setting the tone of popular culture in the Third Reich. In terms of content, each laid claim to national orientation and was to serve the regime. Yet the operative principle of each, especially cinema, was entertainment. Goebbels famously objected to pedantry even in propaganda—to be obvious and boring was the cardinal sin.[27] Although American movies were increasingly marginalized as a source of film entertainment and then disappeared during the war, I would argue that Hollywood was internalized. The politics of image, whether in the political arena or in motion pictures, came to characterize public life.

From this perspective the marginalization of the "authentic" images of America, such as Hollywood movies, mattered less than it might appear. In the early Hitler years, American movies continued to feature in German theaters. Thanks in part to the introduction of talking pictures in the late 1920s the American share of the domestic market had shrunk significantly even before the Nazis took office. Growing chauvinism in trade circles during the Depression did not translate into demands for a ban on the import of American films. Film experts and audiences welcomed American specialties, such as Disney's animation or star vehicles for performers such as Greta Garbo or Joan Crawford. Had Hitler not been bent on a war in which America was certain to become an antagonist, and thus the object of attack for German propaganda, American movies would not have been banned altogether as they were from 1940. Whatever economic and diplomatic considerations came into play, American movies otherwise complemented more than threatened Nazi culture.

It is no accident that Hitler and Goebbels admired Hollywood's achievements. For them culture and politics merged in the ambition to enthrall and rally followers and to provide the pleasure of distraction—which Hitler himself indulged through hours of movie watching. Both men were, of course, obsessive stage managers, Hitler to the point of dissolving the distinction between stage and reality. Compared to the political leaders of Weimar they could well have been Hollywood directors à la Cecil B. de Mille. Preoccupation with mise-en-scène, lighting, and creating moods became the very stuff of politics. Whereas Weimar governments thought primarily in terms of controlling and taxing cinema, and had at best vague hopes that it might serve republican purposes, Nazism harnessed it not only for direct propaganda effect but also for distraction, creating communal daydreams to mask the mundane and increasingly regimented experience of everyday life.[28]

The achievements of Nazi cinema in creating pleasurable distraction, and the remarkable increase in cinema going, belonged to a broader trend. For decades social historians have debated national socialism's role in forging a modern mass society through dissolution of historically entrenched distinctions of region, class, and political loyalty.[29] Parallel with this debate has been the study of Hitler's ideas and priorities and elements of Nazi socioeconomic policy that credit Nazism with a modern social vision.[30] On balance historians have related the emergence of a modern consumer society after 1945 more to the destructive impact of war and its aftermath than to Nazi *Gleichschaltung*—the *Volksgemeinschaft* has not received a very congratulatory press. Similarly, while accepting that there were elements of a modern social vision in Nazism, historians have not been prepared to consider these as the driving force behind developments in the Third Reich, which followed racial obsession to war and destruction.[31]

There is no need to reinvent or "relativize" Nazism to see its popular culture as a badly distorted yet recognizable variant of the American model. Indeed, it was a caricature of the caricature of American popular culture that circulated in Germany in the 1920s: at once homogeneous, conformist, youthful, and energetic, easily swayed and easily distracted rather than reflective or critical.[32] It would at once reward conformity and performance and offer amusement and distraction. In affirming, however self-servingly, the elements of modern consumer societies, the Third Reich inadvertently aligned itself with American popular culture.[33]

Structural parallels between mass culture in Germany and the United States still yield no simple formulas. We can certainly not draw a line of influence from new world to old and assert the Americanization of the Third Reich. Unlike the period after 1945, there was clearly no vacuum into which American popular culture or consumer products could readily flow after 1933. The same applies before 1933, when exposure to American culture was intense enough to cause the skeptical to reference and denounce the proverbial German openness to things foreign—and by extension disregard for its own heritage. With partial exception for the case of cinema, popular culture in Germany was not literally American, even leaving aside important questions of how foreign culture was appropriated. The inroads after 1933 of a product such as Coca-Cola, wonderfully symbolized by the image of Hermann Goering taking a swig from a bottle of Coke at Düsseldorf's counterpart to the World's Fair in Paris in 1937, point both forward (beyond 1945) and beyond Nazism.[34] The power of this image is surely the incongruity it suggests as much as the assimilation it implies, even as it testifies to the transferability of popular culture, at once transnational and beyond ideological sanction.

To describe the culture of Hitler's Germany with the label of "reactionary modernism" therefore exposes some but not all of its peculiarities. The backward-looking connotations of "reactionary," whether applied to politics or culture, pose particular problems. For national socialism the past, apart from indeterminate racial antecedents, held little appeal, for even the racial community they trumpeted had never existed. The reactionary element in Nazism should therefore be seen primarily as a generalization of its ambition to isolate insiders from outsiders, thus its integral nationalism and xenophobia. The tension is not that between backward- and forward-looking elements but that between participation in modern Western culture and preservation of national distinctiveness. Nowhere was this tension more evident than in confrontation with American popular culture, above all the motion picture. Although German culture was not defined by America, it could not be identified without reference to or reaction against America.[35]

Baldly put, Nazism set itself the task of creating for the twentieth century, in which American popular culture was internationally dominant, a national popular culture that was both historically rooted and modern. Nazism was therefore less reactionary than atavistic, appealing through hopelessly muddled racial metaphors to sentiments of tribal identity and exclusiveness in the attempt to birth a distinctive culture. It did this despite some recognition that tribal exclusiveness was an impossibility, that popular culture was hybrid and showed limited interest in national borders. The proof of this is found both in the export of German movies across Europe in the Hitler era and in the resonance of Nazi icons and symbols after 1945.[36]

If one reads Nazi popular culture as fundamentally modern in aspiration, while entertaining atavistic impulses, it is surprising neither that American cultural products were marginalized nor that they found popular appeal. Understanding popular culture in the age of the mass media as the marriage of image or icon, entertainment, and advertising, Hitler's movement firmly grasped the need to reorient German culture. Early in his political career Hitler borrowed from critics of Germany's propaganda efforts in World War I the notion that Germany had lost the international war of images to Britain and the United States. The attempt of his regime to reverse that alleged defeat, long before war was declared on the United States in 1941, necessarily paid tribute to the enemy. American popular culture may have played a declining role in the later years of the Third Reich, but Nazism ultimately made it *gesellschaftsfähig*.

NOTES

1. Cf. the papers presented to the German Historical Institute's conference in March 1999: *GHI Conference Papers on the Web: The American Impact on Western Europe: Americanization and Westernization in Transatlantic Perspective*, ed. Raimund Lammersdorf, <http://www.ghi-dc.org/conpotweb/westernpapers/index.html>. See especially the papers by Volker Berghahn, Kaspar Maase, and Anselm Doering-Manteuffel.

2. There is a brief recent summary in Anselm Doering-Manteuffel, "Dimensionen von Amerikanisierung in der deutschen Gesellschaft," in *Archiv für Sozialgeschichte* 35 (1995), 1–34. On images inherited from before 1914, see Alexander Schmidt, *Reisen in die Moderne: Der Amerika-Diskurs des deutschen Bürgertums vor dem Ersten Weltkrieg im europäischen Vergleich* (Berlin: Akademie, 1997). For samples of the contemporary debate in English, see Anton Kaes, *Weimar Republic Sourcebook* (Berkeley: University of California Press, 1994), 393–411. Further references to Weimar's encounter with America are in Thomas J. Saunders, *Hollywood in Berlin* (Berkeley: University of California Press, 1994).

3. Janet Lungstrum, "The Display Window: Designs and Desires of Weimar Consumerism," *New German Critique* 76 (winter 1999): 123; Sabine Hake, "In the Mirror of Fashion," in *Women in the Metropolis: Gender and Modernity in Weimar Culture*, ed. Katharina von Ankum (Berkeley: University of California Press, 1997), 193.

4. Hans Ulrich Gumbrecht, *In 1926* (Cambridge: Harvard University Press, 1997), 17, cites the characteristic generalization of *Berliner Tageblatt* (July 25, 1926): "Being cosmopolitan means being Americanized. It also means being influenced by sports and health concerns."

5. Detlev Peukert, *The Weimar Republic*, trans. R. Deveson (New York: Hill and Wang, 1992), 178–90.

6. Beeke Sell Tower, "'Ultramodern and Ultraprimitive': Shifting Meanings in the Imagery of Americanism in the Art of Weimar Germany," in *Dancing on the Volcano: Essays on the Culture of the Weimar Republic*, ed. Thomas Kniesche and Stephen Brockmann (Columbia, SC: Camden House, 1994), 85. On Josephine

Baker, cf. Nancy Nenno, "Femininity, the Primitive, and Modern Urban Space: Josephine Baker in Berlin," in *Women in the Metropolis: Gender and Modernity in Weimar Culture,* ed. Katharina von Ankum (Berkeley: University of California Press, 1997), 146: "As an icon of jazz, her Charleston echoed the sounds of the city. As an American, she represented ultra-up-to-dateness."

7. For a recent summary of anti-American sentiments, see Adelheid von Saldern, "Überfremdungsängste: Gegen die Amerikanisierung der deutschen Kultur in den zwanziger Jahren," in *Amerikanisierung: Traum und Alptraum im Deutschland des 20. Jahrhunderts,* ed. Alf Lüdtke, Inge Maßolek, and Adelheid von Saldern (Stuttgart: Steiner, 1997), 213–44.

8. Mary Nolan, *Visions of Modernity: American Business and the Modernization of Germany* (New York: Oxford University Press, 1994); David Bathrick, "Max Schmeling on the Canvas: Boxing as an Icon of Weimar Culture," *New German Critique* 51 (fall 1990): 113–36.

9. Nenno, "Femininity, the Primitive, and Modern Urban Space," 146.

10. The most comprehensive recent assessment of this issue, with further references, is Phillip Gassert, *Amerika im dritten Reich: Ideologie, Propaganda, und Volksmeinung, 1933–1945* (Stuttgart: Franz Steiner, 1997).

11. Jeffrey Herf, *Reactionary Modernism* (Cambridge and New York: Cambridge University Press, 1984).

12. Saunders, *Hollywood in Berlin,* 3: "In the postwar decade Europe experienced a massive invasion of American culture. . . . Jazz bands, sports heroes, troupes of dancing girls, movie stars and tycoons were its personal representatives. American literature, fashions, mores, and aspirations were its commercial counterparts."

13. Cf. Karl Christian Führer, "A Medium of Modernity? Broadcasting in Weimar Germany, 1923–33," *Journal of Modern History* 69 (1997): 722–53; Frank Becker, *Amerikanismus in Weimar: Sportsymbole und politische Kultur, 1918–1933* (Wiesbaden: Deutscher Universitäts-Verlag, 1993).

14. Cf. Eve Rosenhaft, "Lesewut, Kinosucht, Radiotismus: Zur (geschlechter-) politischen Relevanz neuer Massenmedien in den 1920er Jahren," in *Amerikanisierung,* ed. Lüdtke, Maßolek, and von Saldern, 119–43.

15. J. Bradford Robinson, "Jazz Reception in Weimar Germany: In Search of a Shimmy Figure," in *Music and Performance during the Weimar Republic,* ed. Bryan Gilliam (Cambridge: Cambridge University Press, 1994), 107.

16. Ibid., 113. Cf. the introduction to Michael Kater, *Different Drummers: Jazz in the Culture of Nazi Germany* (Oxford: Oxford University Press, 1992), 3–10, where the picture of a jazz-inspired culture is seriously qualified by the analysis of its dissemination in Germany.

17. This is apparent in Tower, "Ultramodern and Ultraprimitive," 93.

18. Robinson, "Jazz Reception," 116.

19. Cornelius Partsch, "Hannibal ante Portas: Jazz in Weimar," in *Dancing on the Volcano: Essays on the Culture of the Weimar Republic,* ed. Thomas Kniesche and Stephen Brockmann (Columbia, SC: Camden House, 1994), 105. Partsch implies that Berlin's jazz scene largely catered to foreign visitors.

20. Cf. Kater, *Different Drummers,* 17, where the passionate interest of left-wing intellectuals implies popular sympathies.

21. Cf. Kater, *Different Drummers;* Detlev Peukert, *Inside Nazi Germany,* trans. R. Deveson (London: Penguin, 1987), 154–69.

22. David Bathrick, "Max Schmeling on the Canvas," 118.

23. Tower, "Ultramodern and Ultraprimitive," 94.

24. Details on the trends described here and in the following paragraph are in Saunders, *Hollywood in Berlin.* Cf. Markus Spieker, *Hollywood unteim Hakenkrenz: Der amerikanische Spielfilm im Dritten Reich* (Trier: Wissenschaftlicher Verlag, 1999).

25. Cf. Saunders, *Hollywood in Berlin,* 149–61; Joseph Garncarz, "Hollywood in Germany: The Role of American Films in Germany," in *Hollywood in Europe: Experiences of a Cultural Hegemony,* ed. David Ellwood and Rob Kroes (Amsterdam: VU University Press, 1994), 94–135.

26. The essays in Glenn Cuomo, ed., *National Socialist Cultural Policy* (New York: St. Martin's, 1995), offer a useful survey of the issues.

27. For Goebbel's role in cinema, see Felix Moeller, *Der Filmminister: Goebbels und der Film im Dritten Reich* (Berlin: Henschel, 1998).

28. See Eric Rentschler, *The Ministry of Illusion* (Cambridge: Harvard University Press, 1996); Linda Schulte-Sasse, *Entertaining the Third Reich* (Durham, NC: Duke University Press, 1996).

29. The pioneering work is David Schoenbaum, *Hitler's Social Revolution* (Garden City, NY: Doubleday, 1966).

30. Cf. Rainer Zitelmann, *Hitler: Selbstverständnis eines Revolutionärs* (Stuttgart: Klett/Cotta, 1987); Ronald Smelser, *Robert Ley: Hitler's Labour Front Leader* (Oxford and New York: Berg, 1988).

31. For a brief discussion, see the latest (fourth) edition of Ian Kershaw, *The Nazi Dictatorship* (London: Arnold, 2000), 243ff.

32. These stereotypes are nicely represented in Fritz Giese's *Girlkultur: Vergleiche zwischen amerikanischem und europäischen Rhythmus und Lebensgefühl* (Munich: Delphin-Verlag, 1925).

33. On this theme cf. Thomas J. Saunders, "A 'New Man': Fascism, Cinema, and Image Creation," *International Journal of Politics, Culture, and Society* 12 (1998): 227–46.

34. I am grateful to Jeff Schutts for allowing me to consult portions of his dissertation on Coca-Cola in Germany.

35. The distinction drawn by Goebbels between form and content in an American film reflects this reality more than it confirms the ambivalence of "reactionary modernism." See Gassert, *Amerika im dritten Reich,* 65. This distinction was recycled endlessly by film critics in the 1920s as a way of distinguishing between the sensibilities of American and German movie audiences.

36. Anton Kaes, *From Hitler to Heimat* (Cambridge: Harvard University Press, 1989).

Constructing Femininity in the Early Cold War Era

Sara Lennox

In 1963 Betty Friedan's *The Feminine Mystique,* examining the unnamed malaise that seemed to have befallen American housewives, posed the question about women after 1945 that has haunted feminism ever since: "Why did women go home again?"[1] Friedan seems to be able to document a sudden shift, around 1949, in American women's understanding of their own possibilities; after a half-century of agitation for women's increased opportunities in the public arena, women in the United States were now content to confine their activities only to the domestic sphere. In Germany, national socialism had, of course, constricted women's ability to participate in domains defined as male, though it also encouraged women to take part in Nazi-sponsored activities outside of the home; under the desperate conditions of the immediate postwar era, however, *Trümmerfrauen* in West Germany took charge of most areas of daily life until—or so the story goes— their men came back and they meekly resumed their old submissive domestic roles again. (As many feminist and other scholars attentive to class issues have pointed out, such narratives ignore the fact that many working-class women in the United States and the Federal Republic of Germany [FRG] were compelled to continue working outside the home after 1945, though the kinds of jobs available to them may have shifted—but this is not the point that my essay pursues.) From the earliest days of the women's movement in the FRG, feminists there, like their American sisters, puzzled over the question of their mothers' betrayal: Why did West German women also return to the home?

Though it is not my project here, it would be very easy to describe how "American" West German feminism is; from the earliest translated *Raubdrucke* of the U.S. women's liberation movement to Suhrkamp's feminist series entitled—in English—"Gender Studies,"

Anglo-American feminist theory and, to some degree, practice have been responsible for determining the emphases and analyses of feminism in West Germany. With a little help from Engels, Bebel, and Simone de Beauvoir, this has also been the case with respect to the terms feminists used to understand their—and our—mothers' confinement to the domestic arena. At least since the beginning of the industrial era—and not, of course, just in feminist texts—men's realm has been considered to be the public, the modern, and the historical, while the domestic world to which women were restricted was the private, traditional, timeless, and unchanging. But, oddly, though U.S. and West German feminists have employed similar categories to describe women's condition post-1945 and prefeminism, the particular explanations for *why* women went home again have remained resolutely national. Thus West German women's retreat into domesticity, for instance, has been viewed as a response to the turmoil of the 1945–47 period in Germany—though women's redomestication in the late 1940s seems to have assumed very similar forms in all the Western industrialized countries.

In this essay I want to investigate two issues. First, I want to suggest that our feminist understanding of our mothers' "return to the home" as a retreat from public politics to a timeless realm of traditional domesticity is at best an oversimplification, if not outright wrong. I want instead to regard women's experiences in the postwar period not as extrinsic to, but as fundamentally connected to, the general history of their time. Second, I want to investigate the degree to which it is possible to adduce supranational explanations for changes in women's situation in the late 1940s and, more specifically, how the new definitions of femininity in West Germany in the postwar era might be connected to or influenced by larger imperatives of the U.S. occupation of Germany and the early cold war. That is, I want to explore how American the construction of West German femininity in the early cold war era might be.

A number of recent studies begin to help us understand these issues. In his book *More: The Politics of Economic Growth in Postwar America,* the economic historian Robert M. Collins explores how and why U.S. policymakers became centrally and single-mindedly committed to the pursuit of a policy of expansive economic growth in the period after 1945. In the immediate postwar era, Collins observes, "the growth regime expressed in the arena of political economy the ascendant values of modern consumer culture," and those values, he argues, "would so thoroughly color American life for the remainder of the twentieth century that most Americans assumed that the consumer culture *was* America and vice versa."[2] Collins concurs with the German historian Charles Maier's assessment that this "politics of productivity" was also the "American organizing idea for the postwar economic world," a policy that, among other things, explicitly aimed at convincing European working-class parties and workers themselves that economic growth could and should supplant class politics.[3] Collins thus emphasizes that the policy of economic growth based on "consumption, more consumption" so energetically and determinedly pursued by the U.S. government was not a substitute for political ideology but rather was its embodiment and expression.[4] In *An All-Consuming Century,* the American historian Gary Cross advances an argument about economics and ideology that elaborates upon Collins's. Cross maintains that the victorious ideology of the twentieth century in the United States and increasingly across the globe is that of American consumerism: "the belief that goods give meaning to individuals and their role in society"; "a choice, never consciously made, to define self and community through the ownership of goods."[5] To be sure, he argues, consumerism is so centrally intertwined with all other aspects of U.S. society "that it is difficult for Americans to consider any serious alternatives or modifications to it" (5), and they accept as natural the trade-off between the effort they invest at the workplace and the freedom they have to purchase consumer items with the money they earn. Cross traces the steps in the triumph of consumerism through the century with a particular emphasis on how Americans' "exuberant spending on cars, houses and appliances" after 1945 "confirmed a form of domestic consumption that today we associate with the 1950s, but that in fact had roots in the longings of the 1930s" (67). As numerous manufacturers emphasized in the wartime advertisements that Cross cites, this culture of ever-expanding domestic consumption was the content defining the American Way of Life. This was, one advertiser proclaimed, what World War II was all about: "For years we have fought for a higher standard of living, and now we are fighting to protect it against those who are jealous of our national accomplishments" (84). Collins and Cross suggest that a politics of both productivity and consumerism, promoted by powerful government forces *and* widely supported by the populace, characterized both the postwar period in the United States and the policies the United States attempted to encourage elsewhere.

How do women figure in this picture of postwar prosperity? They are not mentioned in Collins's study and play only a minor role in

Cross's. Again, several suggestive studies point us in promising directions. In a review of Cross's book, Lawrence Glickman stresses more strongly than Cross himself "that the consumerism of the postwar years was not hedonistic but 'domesticated,' focused on the suburban home and the nuclear family."[6] He faults Cross for failing to investigate the role of women since, "[a]s men and women's organizations recognized early on, women have performed the vast majority of the unpaid labor of consumer society: the shopping, budgeting and refashioning of older items" (36). In *Homeward Bound: American Families in the Cold War Era*, Elaine Tyler May also emphasizes, beyond the tasks connected to consumption itself, the range of social and psychological needs met by the domestic unit vis-à-vis a new postwar order that seemed full of possibilities but also replete with dangers and insecurities ranging from nuclear war and communism to workplace alienation and juvenile delinquency. "The legendary family of the 1950s," May tells us, "complete with appliances, station wagons, backyard barbecues, and tricycles scattered on the sidewalks, represented something new. It was not, as common wisdom tells us, the last gasp of 'traditional' family life with roots deep in the past. Rather, it was the first whole-hearted effort to create a home that would fulfill virtually all its members' personal needs through an energized and expressive personal life."[7] From such observations, we might tentatively conclude that the accusations earlier feminists directed at their mothers' generation were falsely formulated. Postwar women neither "returned" to the traditional home, nor did they retreat from the public arena into a timeless domestic world oblivious to the course of general history; rather, women after 1945, in their specifically female way as wives, mothers, and household managers in a newly configured domestic unit, took on a role of central importance to postwar economic expansion, progress, and the triumph of the American Way.

Two studies addressing the situation of postwar women outside the United States also suggest that the analytical framework earlier feminist scholars used to understand postwar women elsewhere may also have misrepresented their intentions and experiences. In an examination of women in Australia after 1945, Lesley Johnson challenges Friedan's narrative of women's subjection in *The Feminine Mystique*. In Johnson's view, Friedan's book "told the story of women's emancipation in the form of the classical account of the emergence of the modern subject."[8] Friedan decries women's entrapment in the traditional, private, and secure realm of the suburban home and calls upon them to dare to embrace the freedom to define themselves in the more risky public arena of work and political life. But Johnson's own research on Australian women shows, in contrast, that housewives after 1945 explicitly understood themselves as participating in the creation of the new postwar world. Thus, Johnson argues:

> In certain contexts in the 1940s and 1950s, home represented for women the site of their agency. Defined as the suburban house with its modern appliances, planned spaces, garden, and comfortable domestic existence, it constituted the sphere of everyday life which they were actively involved in making. . . . Their capacities and responsibilities in this sphere gave women a stake, as they saw it, in the life of the nation and in building modern life in Australia.[9]

If women's embrace of domestic consumerism in the post-1945 period is indeed a transnational phenomenon taking place in many countries with market economies, Johnson's study of women in Australia raises provocative questions about women's purported "return to the home" that may also be relevant for women in the United States and West Germany.

More specific to the German situation, Erica Carter's *How German Is She?* (a book whose very title, of course, suggests an application broader than that of the FRG) views West German women after 1945 not as the hapless, victimized objects of an expanding consumerism but "as the hegemonic model of a new consuming citizen."[10] As such, they, like their contemporaries in Australia, made a contribution to national recovery via both the physical and cultural labor they invested in consumption and in their role as cultural agents producing meaning and value. Indeed, Minister of Economic Affairs Ludwig Erhard had emphasized in 1953 that women's role as guardians of consumption, spending the money men earned, was crucial to the *Wirtschaftswunder.* The *Wille zum Verbrauch* Erhard so often touted "was the engine that drove uninterrupted output, economic rationalization, efficiency, and gains in productivity; as 'economics ministers' of their families, women controlled the throttle."[11] West German market analysts also remarked on "the new status of women as chief purchasers in the family unit," calculating that women were responsible for disposing of 70 to 80 percent of family income.[12] Carter observes as well that women's capacity for thrift and rational household management was a crucial factor in "the accumulation of capital savings for major family purchases—kitchen gadgets, media technology, fittings, and furniture" (55) and thus from the early 1950s onward was an essential element in the development of the German consumer economy. Like Johnson in Australia, Carter concludes that the housewife's role in consumption functions as a *"public* contribution to national reconstruction" and, though it cemented a hierarchical gender division of labor, also "offered women a route to public agency" (71).

How did it happen that, around the world, postwar women in industrialized societies based on market economies embraced *this* construction of femininity rather than some other? As May has emphasized, even a society organized around consumption could have chosen a different course:

> The Great Depression of the 1930s brought about widespread challenges to traditional gender roles that could have led to a restructured home. The war intensified these challenges and pointed the way toward radical alterations in the institutions of work and family life. Wartime brought thousands of women into the paid labor force when men left to enter the armed forces. After the war, expanding job and educational opportunities, as well as the increasing availability of birth control might well have led young people to delay marriage or not marry at all, and to have fewer children if they did marry.[13]

But in the 1950s the "housewife marriage" seemed the form of domestic organization best suited to support what Cross has termed Americans' "unacknowledged decision to build a consumer culture around personal products" (250), and American women both actively chose and were vigorously encouraged to embrace the model of female domesticity that seemed best to anchor that familial structure. Vice President Nixon made precisely that point in his famous 1959 "kitchen debate" with Khrushchev. Strolling with Khrushchev through the model home displayed at the American exhibition in Moscow, Nixon insisted vehemently that consumer choice was the form in which Americans experienced democracy and freedom and that the suburban home, where housewives presided over consumption, comprised the essence of the American Way of Life. "To us," Nixon maintained, "diversity, the right to choose . . . is the most important thing. . . . We have many different manufacturers and many different kinds of washing machines so that housewives have a choice. . . . Would it not be better to compete in the relative merits of washing machines than in the strength of rockets?"[14] In his formal speech opening the exhibition, Nixon emphasized the 44 million families in the United States who owned 56 million cars, 50 million television sets, and 143 million radios, three-quarters of whom also owned their own home. Like U.S. housewives, I want to argue, women in industrialized countries around the world who wished to claim such consumer wonders for themselves also actively embraced the ideal of female domesticity as the most effective way to assure that they, their families, and their nations would also be able to claim their share of the American Way.

And, indeed, as a wide range of commentators have shown, this project was not even a new idea but rather an expansion and intensification of an old one: the connection of femininity, consumer goods, modernity, and the American Way of Life can be traced back at least to the 1920s, if not before. Emily Rosenberg has documented government, corporate, and individual efforts to facilitate American economic expansion by "spreading the American dream" that stretch back to at least the 1890s.[15] Mary Nolan has shown that, by the Weimar period, "America" was generally taken to represent "the physical appropriation [of nature], social transformation, and economic development, built on new technologies, ways of organizing production, and approaches to management and marketing."[16] Despite the rhetorical anti-Americanism of the Nazis, Hans Dieter Schäfer has demonstrated, access to American consumer items and culture was widespread during the Nazi era, and Rainer Zitelmann argues convincingly that Hitler's conception of America deeply influenced his thinking about consumption practices under national socialism.[17] There is no reason not to assume that the tension Victoria de Grazia discerns among Italian women between fascist and commercial cultural models in Mussolini's Italy was not also at play in Hitler's Germany.[18] In the German imagination, "America" had also enabled a dangerous empowerment of consuming women, both in the form of the "new woman" enthralled with mass consumption and the competent middle-class woman who held a job and "managed a modern home, replete with appliances and canned goods."[19] Tellingly, Nolan observes, in the postwar period "[w]omen, long considered susceptible to the dangerous allures of Americanism, were expected to negotiate its adoption" (19). On the other hand, in conceptualizing postwar women as conscious agents deliberately engaged in the process of rebuilding their nation, it is also possible to understand their actions as manifesting a continuity rather than a rupture with national socialism, which also mobilized women's domestic efforts for the common good. For, as Michael Wildt argues, the transformation of West Germany into a consuming nation during the course of the 1950s demanded a particular engagement from women: "Consumers, or more specifically, housewives, had to acquire all sorts of new habits. They had to navigate through a complex, unstable, and confusing new world of commodities; learn the new language of advertisers; and decipher the various semiotic codes underlying the presentation of goods."[20] But, as Wildt also emphasizes, it was the transformation of West Germany into the affluent society of the *Wirtschaftswunder* that helped to induce its citizens to embrace new political ideals: "The perspective of more welfare, economic growth, and a gradual but steady rise in the standard of living created not only consumers but also democrats" (315).[21]

In the past decade, a number of historians of gender in West Germany have produced pathbreaking studies exploring questions of postwar domesticity and women's agency. Together with Carter's examination of the constitution of West German women as subjects of consumption, Robert Moeller's *Protecting Motherhood* argues for the centrality of conservative gender politics and policies to the course the FRG charted in the 1950s. In *What Difference Does a Husband Make?* Elizabeth Heineman expands on Moeller's observations to demonstrate that marital status (particularly whether they could be defined as "women standing alone") profoundly affected women's possibilities in postwar West Germany (and was of remarkably little relevance in East Germany), while her essay "The Hour of the Women" shows how after 1945 the purported activities of women—conceived variously as industrious *Trümmerfrauen*, promiscuous *Amiliebchen*, or benighted rape victims—were deployed as metaphors that helped to shape emerging West German identity.[22] These studies, however, examine West German women's lives in the 1950s solely within a national context. More recently, Uta Poiger and Maria Höhn have begun the work of exploring the U.S. impact on the post-1945 period: Poiger's *Jazz, Rock, and Rebels* explores American culture's effect on postwar East and West German culture, including gender relations among rebellious youth, and Höhn's *GIs and Fräuleins* pursues the consequences of "fraternization" for debates over gender policy in the 1950s, but their investigations focus mostly on informal and unofficial contacts between Americans and West Germans.[23] Here, though, I want to maintain that, particularly in the late 1940s and 1950s, the FRG can be understood only very imperfectly if U.S. pressures to conform to American policies are not taken into account—and those pressures also affected women. As the cold war took shape, U.S. wartime propaganda organizations were given new life, and the United States Information Agency (USIA) and the CIA were given the task of managing the government's so-called information programs or of subsidizing organizations that were already pursuing activities in the national interest. Though those organizations hatched any number of conspiracies in the early postwar period, it is not necessary to attribute the construction of a new model of West German femininity to a deliberate conspiracy. Instead, other deliberate, though somewhat more indirect, forms of pressure influenced the choices that West German women would make. As, in the aftermath of the war, the U.S. government aggressively took upon itself the task of creating what Rosenberg has termed "a more integrated, liberalized, and regulated world system, one which could presumably offer prosperity to those who cooperated and punishment to any who remained outside and who tried to create a restricted sphere of interest,"[24] West German women en passant, so to speak, were also induced to embrace a construction of femininity then conceived as most apt to produce the model of prosperity the Americans promoted.

Certainly, as Höhn emphasizes, the presence of huge, healthy, and overfed GIs in postwar Germany left a strong impression on many young West German women, whom they would immediately relate to the pleasures of consumption, as GIs distributed chocolate, chewing gum, nylons, and other delicacies to the fräulein of their choice and often to her entire family. Reinhold Wagnleitner, who as a young Austrian boy profited from GI beneficence, recalls: "It was not long before those *Fräuleins* and many other European women began to look like their American sisters, wearing more colorful dresses than European women had worn before, using American makeup, and pressing their figures into American-modeled brassieres which formed huge conic breasts that made even the real ones appear artificial." And, Wagnleitner continues, throughout Europe the United States was represented by Europeans themselves as a consumer paradise for women:

> Not only conservative publications but also socialist and trade union journals insisted that the *average* woman in the United States could afford beautiful dresses, wear makeup all the time, take a bath every day, run a functional household with washing machines and vacuum cleaners, and rule over a modern kitchen with gas or elective stoves, mixers, refrigerators, and even dishwashers; work was minimal because American women used canned or frozen food they had bought in supermarkets in great quantities and brought home to their suburban houses in their cars.[25]

Such tales suggest that the European construction of America was itself in part responsible for women's choice of a way of life that seemed to promise what America had to offer.

But the United States of the early cold war era was not prepared to leave the task of informing a recovering Europe about the American Way of Life to lively European fantasies alone. An aspect of the Marshall Plan's European Recovery Program (ERP) much neglected by scholarship is its propaganda dimension. The German edition of the *Reader's Digest,* which began publishing in 1949, and the *International Herald Tribune* enjoyed Marshall Plan subsidies,[26] but the Economic Cooperation Administration (ECA), which managed the ERP, also seized upon a much wider, and wilder, variety of mechanisms to encourage acceptance of the principles that the Marshall Plan promoted, including newspapers, pamphlets, postcards, postage stamps, stickers, exhibitions at industrial fairs, competitions, radio programming, movies, and puppet shows. Traveling exhibitions were carried by auto caravan, ships, and trains. A fifteen-car "Train of Good Will and Peace" carrying products produced by more than 350 West German manufacturers toured West Germany in 1950 and 1951 and was visited by more than 1.3 million Germans in its stops at fifty cities and towns. The "Train of Europe," which left Munich in 1951 and ended up in Vienna in 1953, used four of its seven cars as exhibition areas, while a fifth car was used as an auditorium for films and puppet shows. All ERP-sponsored activities (including the construction of the Limburg Dam in Austria, which assured that the Austrian housewife "no longer needs to worry of a breakdown in the supply of electricity") were lavishly documented by photographs that were then distributed widely.[27] Early on, the occupying military government had arranged for U.S. documentary films dealing with topics ranging from malaria to the New Deal's Tennessee Valley Authority to be shown in a range of venues from movie theaters to schools, town halls, and the outdoors, by 1951 reaching, it was claimed, about 2 million people a month. The documentary films were also frequently shown together with U.S. feature films and a newsreel, "Welt im Film," whose viewing was compulsory through 1949.[28] After the onset of the ERP, U.S.-focused documentaries were supplemented by over two hundred films that documented the achievements of the Marshall Plan.[29] "Prosperity Makes You Free" was the slogan posted on the Marshall Plan trains; the Marshall Plan message was "You Too Can Be Like Us." Paul Hoffman, administrator of the ECA, recalled in his memoirs, "They learned that this is the land of full shelves and bulging shops, made possible by high productivity and good wages, and that its prosperity may be emulated elsewhere by those who will work towards it."[30] It was a lesson that was not lost on West German women.

In a memo to the U.S. military administration in Germany, Billy Wilder, on his way to Berlin to direct *A Foreign Affair,* argued that U.S. efforts to promote reeducation via the use of documentaries was doomed to failure and that feature films à la Hollywood would perform such propaganda tasks much more effectively.[31] During the war, the director of the U.S. Office of War Information had expressed a similar opinion: "The easiest way to inject a propaganda idea into most people's mind is to let it go in through the medium of an entertainment picture when they do not realize that they are being propagandized,"[32] while Gerald Mayer, head of the International Division of the Motion Picture Association, connected Hollywood film directly to the promotion of the consumption of American products:

> The modern American motion picture, almost beyond any possible comparison with other items of export, combines considerations of economic, cultural and political significance. . . . No one has ever attempted to calculate—and it would probably be an impossible task—the indirect effect of American motion pictures on the sale of American products, not only on display, as it were, but in actual demonstrated use. Scenes laid in American kitchens, for example, have probably done as much to acquaint the people of foreign lands with American electric refrigerators, electric washing machines, eggbeaters, window screens, and so on, as any other medium. . . . There has never been a more effective salesman for American products in foreign countries than the American motion picture.[33]

Writing in the fall 1950 issue of *Public Opinion Quarterly,* Walter Wanger, head of Walter Wanger Pictures, Inc., proclaimed that the film industry represented a "Marshall Plan of ideas."[34] Very aware of the power its product wielded, the Hollywood film industry in the postwar era was able to cut an extremely advantageous deal with the U.S. government, achieving a guarantee that all foreign costs would be repaid in Marshall Plan dollars and that Washington would pay an additional $25,000 for every film exported to European markets.[35] The film industry had very strong ties to the State Department and was frequently not loath to cooperate on specific issues, such as rereleasing Ernst Lubisch's *Ninotchka* on the eve of the Italian election in order to discourage Italian voters from supporting the communists, removing scenes and withholding films from export that were deemed not to portray the United States in the best possible light, and producing a series of explicitly cold war films in the early 1950s. On the other hand, as Paul Swann observes, it was for the most part very difficult to use Hollywood films to promote specific U.S. policies abroad: "In practice, the only thing that was certain was that the effects of American motion pictures overseas were uncertain and unpredictable."[36]

It is, of course, quite impossible to determine how deliberately Hollywood might have promoted a new model of domestic femininity and to what degree factors exterior to Hollywood might have influenced the film industry's decisions. Certainly, American businessmen were quite aware that the housewife marriage was highly beneficial to the postwar capitalist order. Friedan herself cites a 1945 marketing study that determined that the "Balanced Homemaker" was, "from the market standpoint, the ideal type. . . . Since the Balanced Homemaker represents the market with the greatest future potential, it would be to the advantage of the appliance manufacturer to make more and more women aware of the desirability of belonging to this group."[37] It is clear, however, that beginning around 1940 the portrayal of women in Hollywood film changed quite suddenly, with a new emphasis on domesticity emerging at the very time when real American women were following the example of Rosie the Riveter. Susan Hartmann has maintained that the war decade represented "the greatest assault on female careerism" ever, with films of that era favorably portraying women who give up a career for marriage while condemning women who try to combine the two.[38] In his study "Hollywood and the Politics of the American Way," Lary May discerns a new category of female figure in his movie plot samples from the war years, a "woman who identified her personal goals with realizing the dream of 'patriotic domesticity,'" a formula that increased from zero in 1940 to over 35 percent of all plots by 1948.[39] May also shows that other films of the same period "tame" mass consumption by making it "the locus of a new dream of private freedom" (147). Many of the films of the early to mid-1940s that May examines were also included among the relatively small group of films (only 112 by September 1948) that Heide Fehrenbach cites as approved for exhibition in the U.S. zone in the first postwar years.[40] Carter identifies film as a crucial medium that "not only provided a forum for the articulation of collective and/or national identities; more than this, through tie-ins, for example, between film, fashion, advertising, and the women's magazines, it acted as a symbolic vehicle for new models of consuming femininity."[41] Doubtless this is entirely true, but the examples she gives—three melodramas that address "a crucial postwar feminine transition . . . of the female protagonist from luxury consumer to bourgeois housewife"—are all German-made films. Interwoven in each of those films, Carter tells us, is the narrative of national transformation that is the topic of her book, "the story . . . of West Germany's transition to a proto-American society of mass consumption." But what Carter leaves entirely out of her story may be one of its most important aspects, the role that a variety of American influences played in turning the FRG into that "proto-American society of mass consumption," with Americanized German women as its consuming subjects.[42]

So let me ask the question posed in Carter's title: "How German *is* she?" Carter intends the title of her book to highlight the tension between female conformity to a national ideal of domestic femininity in the service of economic recovery *and* possibly more subversive desires not so easily accommodated within the narrative of the *Wirtschaftswunder.* That may well be the case, but to me the book's title strikingly evokes the topic of this collection—How American is it?—and points toward the non-German pressures that induced West German women to embrace this construction of femininity rather than some other. As the FRG was urged, encouraged, and also compelled to conform to the economic principles of what, to put the best face on it, one might term its American benefactor, so were individual West Germans, in the smaller realm of the family and everyday life, to decide for themselves that, as in America, the possession of ever more consumer items was the road to happiness and that forming themselves into the subjects and citizens likely to reach that goal was the optimal path to pursue, for women as well as for men. The *Wirtschaftswunder,* with women at the household helm, is, of course, the German version of the American Way of Life. How American is she? If "America" is taken to signify the American Way of Life, the model of domesticated modern consumerism that the *Wirtschaftswunder* tried to emulate, we might wish to answer in the following way: mutatis mutandis, very.

NOTES

1. Betty Friedan, *The Feminine Mystique* (New York: Dell, 1970), 61.
2. Robert M. Collins, *More: The Politics of Economic Growth in Postwar America* (New York: Oxford, 2000), 38–39.
3. Collins, 22.

4. Collins, 39, xi.

5. Gary Cross, *An All-Consuming Century: Why Commercialism Won in Modern America* (New York: Columbia University Press, 2000), 1, 5.

6. Lawrence Glickman, "The 'Ism' That Won the Century," *Nation,* December 4, 2000, 33–38.

7. Elaine Tyler May, *Homeward Bound: American Families in the Cold War Era* (New York: Basic Books, 1988), 11.

8. Lesley Johnson, "'As Housewives we [*sic*] Are Worms': Women, Modernity, and the Home Question," in *Feminism and Cultural Studies,* ed. Morag Schiach (New York: Oxford University Press, 1999), 477.

9. Johnson, 488–89.

10. Erica Carter, *How German Is She? Postwar West German Reconstruction and the Consuming Woman* (Ann Arbor: University of Michigan Press, 1997), 9.

11. Cited in Robert G. Moeller, *Protecting Motherhood: Women and the Family in the Politics of Postwar West Germany* (Berkeley: University of California Press, 1993), 139–40.

12. Carter, 65.

13. Elaine Tyler May, 8–9.

14. Cited in Elaine Tyler May, 17–18.

15. Emily Rosenberg, *Spreading the American Dream: American Economic and Cultural Expansion, 1890–1945* (New York: Hill and Wang, 1982).

16. Mary Nolan, "America in the German Imagination," in *Transactions, Transgressions, Transformations: American Culture in Western Europe and Japan,* ed. Heide Fehrenbach and Uta G. Poiger (New York: Berghahn, 2000), 13.

17. Cf. Hans Dieter Schäfer, *Das gespaltene Bewußtsein: Deutsche Kultur und Lebenswirklichkeit, 1933–1945* (Munich: Carl Hanser, 1981), and Rainer Zitelmann, *Hitler: Selbstverständnis eines Revolutionärs* (Stuttgart: Klett-Cotta, 1987).

18. Victoria de Grazia, "Nationalising Women: The Competition between Fascist and Commercial Cultural Models in Mussolini's Italy," in *Cultural Transmissions and Receptions: American Mass Culture in Europe,* ed. R. Kroes, R. W. Rydell, and D. F. J. Bosscher (Amsterdam: VU University Press, 1993).

19. Nolan, 16.

20. Michael Wildt, "Changes in Consumption as Social Practice in West Germany during the 1950s," in *Getting and Spending: European and American Consumer Societies in the Twentieth Century,* ed. Susan Strasser, Charles McGovern, and Matthias Judt (Washington, DC: German Historical Institute and Cambridge University Press, 1998), 313.

21. See also Michael Wildt, *Am Beginn der "Konsumgesellschaft": Mangelerfahrung, Lebenshaltung, Wohlstandshoffnung in Westdeutschland in den fünfziger Jahren* (Hamburg: Ergebnisse, 1994).

22. Elizabeth D. Heineman, *What Difference Does a Husband Make? Women and Marital Status in Nazi and Postwar Germany* (Berkeley: University of California Press, 1999); and "The Hour of the Women: Memories of Germany's 'Crisis Years' and West German National Identity," *American Historical Review* 101, no. 2 (April 1996): 354–95.

23. Uta G. Poiger, *Jazz, Rock, and Rebels: Cold War Politics and American*

Culture in a Divided Germany (Berkeley: University of California Press, 2000); Maria Höhn, *GIs and Fräuleins: The German-American Encounter in 1950s West Germany* (Chapel Hill: University of North Carolina Press, 2002).

24. Rosenberg, *Spreading the American Dream*, 191.

25. Reinhold Wagnleitner, "Propagating the American Dream: Cultural Policies as Means of Integration," in *Exporting America: Essays on American Studies Abroad*, ed. Richard P. Horwitz (New York: Garland, 1993), 329.

26. Cf. Hinrich Becker, *Das Beste aus* Reader's Digest*: Ideologische Grundzüge in der Zeitschrift* Das Beste aus Reader's Digest*: Untersucht an den Jahrggängen 1949/50, 1973, 1979/80* (Kiel: n.p., 1984); and Paul Swann, "The Little State Department: Washington and Hollywood's Rhetoric of the Postwar Audience," in *Hollywood in Europe: Experiences of a Cultural Hegemony*, ed. David W. Ellwood and Rob Kroes (Amsterdam: VU University Press, 1994), 185.

27. Hans-Jürgen Schröder, "Marshall Plan Propaganda in Austria and Western Germany," in *The Marshall Plan in Austria*, ed. Günter Bischof, Anton Pelinka, and Dieter Steifel, Contemporary Austrian Studies 8 (New Brunswick: Transaction, 2000), 213–19.

28. Michael Hoenisch, "Film as an Instrument of the U.S. Reeducation Program in Germany after 1945 and the Example of 'Todesmühlen,'" *Englisch Amerikanische Studien* 4 (June 1982): 201.

29. Schröder, 221.

30. Cited in David W. Ellwood, *Rebuilding Europe: Western Europe, America, and Postwar Reconstruction* (London: Longman, 1992), 227.

31. Hoenisch, 204.

32. Reinhold Wagnleitner, *Coca-Colonization and the Cold War: The Cultural Mission of the United States in Austria after the Second World War* (Chapel Hill: University of North Carolina Press, 1994), 229.

33. Cited in Wagnleitner, *Coca-Colonization*, 227.

34. Cited in David W. Ellwood, "Introduction: Historical Methods and Approaches," in *Hollywood in Europe: Experiences of a Cultural Hegemony*, ed. David W. Ellwood and Rob Kroes (Amsterdam: VU University Press, 1994), 6.

35. Reinhold Wagnleitner, "American Cultural Diplomacy, the Cinema, and the Cold War in Central Europe" in *Hollywood in Europe: Experiences of a Cultural Hegemony*, ed. David W. Ellwood and Rob Kroes (Amsterdam: VU University Press, 1994), 203.

36. Swann, 180–81.

37. Friedan, 200–201.

38. Susan Hartmann, *The Home Front and Beyond: American Women in the 1940s* (Boston: Twayne, 1982), 189–205.

39. Lary May, *The Big Tomorrow: Hollywood and the Politics of the American Way* (Chicago: University of Chicago Press, 2000), 163.

40. Heide Fehrenbach, *Cinema in Democratizing Germany* (Chapel Hill: University of North Carolina Press, 1995), 261–64.

41. Carter, 176.

42. Carter, 179.

Part II

Gender, Race, and Marginal Identities in Pop Music and Literature

Searching for Proper New Music: Jazz in Cold War Germany

Uta G. Poiger

Since the 1920s, American popular music has generated heated debates in Germany, with opponents and defenders fighting over styles ranging from jazz to rock 'n' roll to hip-hop. While the anti-Americanism evident in these battles has attracted considerable scholarly attention, we still know less about the ways in which forms of American music and culture have become part of the official self-representations of Germans. In this essay, I explore how one form, namely jazz, became increasingly acceptable in 1950s cold war Germany. Focusing on the understandings of culture, respectability, and race that made jazz largely uncontroversial, I examine the multivalent political meanings of U.S. culture abroad.

During the Weimar and Nazi years opponents of jazz described the music as overly sexualized, created by unrespectable African-Americans, and marketed by Jews. In the 1930s and 1940s the Nazis attempted to ban jazz and persecuted jazz fans, but, caught between their desire to realize a racist utopia and the need to keep the German population entertained, even the Nazis allowed some forms of swing on the airwaves. Many musicians and fans saw their support for the music as an apolitical act, although some on the left and very few on the right thought jazz to be compatible with their respective political causes.[1]

After 1945, when jazz experienced a renaissance in both Germanies, jazz music remained in the political cross fires, this time of the cold war. Initially, East German authorities harassed jazz fans, while critics in West Germany publicly disdained them. Both sides were particularly worried about dancing jazz fans and jam sessions in the so-called hot clubs in East and West Germany. Such concerns were exacerbated when growing numbers of German rock 'n' roll fans began to dance to the music of Bill Haley and Elvis Presley after 1956. By 1960, however, the West German minister of defense, Franz-Josef Strauß, declared jazz to be a music for the new West German army, and jazz could be widely heard on state-sponsored television and radio stations and in state-supported youth clubs. East German authorities, too, allowed some jazz concerts, although they continued to be more worried about American music than their West German counterparts. This changing place of jazz in the postwar German cultural landscape was linked to efforts in both states to newly define Germanness in the aftermath of national socialism and in the face of the cold war.[2]

Jazz in West Germany

Until the 1950s Europeans usually referred to all American popular music as jazz. In both Germanies it was only after 1955 that narrower definitions of "authentic" jazz as different from "lighter" popular hits—and especially from rock 'n' roll—gained widespread currency. In West Germany, radio host, writer, and producer Joachim Ernst Berendt became the most influential person to shape positive reevaluations of jazz. In East Germany, Reginald Rudorf, a social scientist, radio host, and writer, was the leading proponent of the music.

Berendt—in his West German radio broadcasts, publications, and lectures—defined jazz as a serious artistic and philosophical enterprise. He asserted emphatically that the popular hits broadcast on American and European radio stations or played at most concerts were not jazz. Authentic jazz, according to him, was not simply a dance music; it distinguished itself from popular hits through complex rhythmic variety, unique tones, and improvisation.[3]

Berendt sought to sanitize, desexualize, and decommercialize what he considered true jazz and proper jazz fan behavior. Thus he discredited those jazz fans who were dancing and romping around at jam sessions in postwar German jazz joints. His ideal jazz connoisseurs were at once antiauthoritarian and respectable. In 1953, for example, Berendt made a distinction between serious fans and the so-called Swing-Heinis—a term that the Nazis had likewise used in their persecutions of jazz fans. He described Swing-Heinis as youths with striped socks, shorter pants, and longer hair. Although he acknowledged that they stood in direct opposition to the soldier ideal, he did not like them. Rather, he urged serious, respectable (*seriöse*) jazz fans to teach these Swing-Heinis about the true meaning of jazz. In his validations of jazz as noncommercial, antiauthoritarian music, Berendt thus relied on a certain gender conservatism.

This vision was also reflected in Berendt's treatment of different jazz styles. Not surprisingly, Berendt liked best the spartan, and less danceable, music of bebop and cool jazz. Bebop had been developed by black musicians such as Charlie Parker and Dizzy Gillespie in Harlem jazz clubs around 1945. Consciously turning their backs to their audience, the bebop musicians countered stereotypes of black performers, and their new styles made evaluations such as Berendt's possible. Perhaps it was not by chance that Berendt seemed to like cool jazz even better than bebop. Played by both black and white musicians, and combining "white" and "black" musical styles, cool jazz quickly became the symbol of successful racial integration. Berendt likened cool jazz to European classical music and claimed that, together with Stravinsky's music, cool represented an adequate understanding of the contemporary era. Berendt made jazz into a universalizing experience and stressed that jazz had gone beyond its African and African-American roots to gain appeal around the world.

In the aftermath of intense German nationalism and racism prior to 1945 and in the context of West German efforts to erect the Christian West as a cultural and political ideal in the first half of the 1950s, Berendt's stance was in many ways radical. He validated jazz as a serious artistic tradition and insisted that neither jazz nor African-American jazz musicians were primitive. But at the same time he made European music the standard against which the "progress" of jazz was to be judged. His validations focused, on the one hand, on improvisation, that is, the unmanipulated aspects of jazz, and, on the other hand, on the respectability of authentic jazz musicians and their audience. Berendt made jazz compatible with the bourgeois notion of (high) culture and with a bourgeois gender system.[4]

Berendt's ideas were attractive: his 1953 *Jazzbuch* sold 75,000 copies within months. Upon its publication, Berendt became the single most powerful jazz critic in West Germany, who also spread his ideas in radio broadcasts and lectures. By 1955 the new type of more intellectual jazz fans whom Berendt championed became widely visible in West Germany. For many of them Berendt's *Jazzbuch* became a bible.

At the same time other critics used Berendt's arguments to encourage respectable behavior among jazz musicians and fans. In March 1956 the West Berlin youth magazine *Blickpunkt* (published by the West Berlin association of public youth organizations) criticized the behavior of Lionel Hampton and his audience at a Berlin concert. The audience had "no idea about jazz," yet it was able to influence Hampton's performance negatively. Hampton allegedly turned into a mere "showman" spurred on by the wishes of his noisy audience. Those who knew Hampton from records could, according to *Blickpunkt,* hardly enjoy his performance or the brass players of his "gang" who were rolling around on the stage. The "true enthusiast" did not get to see the "true Lionel Hampton," whose music, according to the article, had almost as many nuances as chamber music. Exactly following Berendt's logic, *Blickpunkt* asserted that Hampton drew his powerful style from his connection with Harlem, the "steamy Negro part of New York," measured Hampton's achievements against European music, and demanded restrained seriousness from his audience.[5]

In West Berlin the "respectable" fans organized in the newly founded New Jazz Circle Berlin, a club that held jazz concerts and regular lectures. Here the audience listened intently to recordings, which "jazz experts"—either guest speakers or club members—interpreted. The emphasis on respectability and the dedication to an intellectual experience of jazz actually discouraged lower-class and female jazz fans: 90 percent of the audience at lectures were male, and a majority came from the middle and upper classes.

It was in the context of youth riots and the adolescent consumption of rock 'n' roll that these respectable jazz fans gained widespread attention after 1955. The West Berlin *Tagesspiegel* reported in 1957 on the respectable jazz fans who attended lectures of the New Jazz Circle Berlin in work or office clothes and who rarely wore jeans. The paper applauded that their behavior was far different from the disturbances that adolescent rowdies were causing in Berlin (and other East and West German cities) during the same period; according to the paper, one could hardly imagine that others of their age would roar, jump on benches, and make loud noise with bells during public "so-called jazz concerts."[6]

In these years the lines between jazz and rock 'n' roll were still fluid in the minds of most Germans, but people like Berendt and members of the New Jazz Circle Berlin stepped up their efforts to divorce jazz from commercial dance music and stressed that rock 'n' roll was not jazz and that jazz fans were respectable, engaged members of society.[7] Indeed, "true" jazz increasingly seemed a remedy against youthful unruliness. More and more voices argued that jazz associations directed adolescent protest into appropriate channels and that their work was therefore worthy of state support.[8] West German bureaucrats began to follow these suggestions. In 1956–57 city officials in West Berlin put on ten jazz lectures and one jazz concert as part of their youth protection efforts.[9] Such state-sponsored events marked the growing acceptance of jazz in West Germany.

Jazz in East Germany

The positive redefinition of jazz in West Germany happened against the background of the suppression of jazz in East Germany. Around 1950, East German authorities, following their Soviet counterparts, had started an outright campaign against jazz, and jazz remained highly controversial in the following years. Not surprisingly, jazz fans in East Germany found it more difficult than West German fans to pursue their interests. Frequently, they smuggled records and Western publications on jazz into the German Democratic Republic (GDR) and listened to Western radio stations.[10] Yet some East German voices existed that sought to make jazz officially acceptable, the most outspoken of which was Reginald Rudorf.

From 1952 to 1957 Rudorf, a member of the East German Socialist Unity Party (SED), published articles and gave lectures, where he indicted what he called "unauthentic" jazz and urged officials to support the proliferation of "authentic" jazz. His definitions were somewhat inconsistent, but he usually praised blues, Dixieland, and spirituals as authentic and rejected bebop and other forms of modern jazz.[11]

Rudorf's efforts on behalf of jazz were somewhat successful, as long as he located his arguments within the official cultural doctrine of the East German SED. In March 1951 the SED's Central Committee had called for a search for an authentic German national culture. East German officials denounced all cultural expressions that put more stress on form than content; such art allegedly lost its humanist and democratic character and was characteristic of the imperialism of late capitalist systems, particularly the United States. Considerably earlier than the New Left in the West, East German officials followed Soviet propaganda in labeling U.S. culture a tool of imperialism. Like their Soviet counterparts, East German officials leveled accusations of "decadence," "cosmopolitanism," and "formalism" against, for example, the literature of Kafka, against abstract painting, and also against undesirable music, such as jazz.[12] In distinguishing between good authentic jazz, on the one hand, and commercial dance music and modern jazz, on the other, Rudorf employed this same language. For example, he indicted swing music and the bebop of Charlie Parker as decadent. At the same time that he derided certain aspects of jazz, Rudorf stressed that African-American folk music, including some forms of jazz such as blues and Dixieland, could fruitfully stimulate the development of a new "clean" German dance music.[13]

In his rejections of musical forms such as swing and boogie, Rudorf linked the absence of male and female respectability to threats against proper German national identity. "The ecstatic jumps of the deplorable brushheads and their *Amizonen,*" quipped Rudorf, "are at their worst when the orchestra plays louder, when a saxophone begins to squeak in a vulgar way or when shrill trumpet solos ring." By identifying male jazz fans merely by their bouffant hairstyles and speaking of them, derogatorily, as "brushheads" (*Bürstenköpfe*), Rudorf associated them with fashion and thus with femininity. Furthermore, playing with the words "Amazons," "Amis" (Americans), and "American Zone," Rudorf portrayed Americanized German women as sexual aggressors and as masculinized. ("*Amizonen*" was a term Germans used to describe women who had sexual relations with U.S. soldiers.)[14] Rudorf thus warned against the dangers of popular jazz in terms that connected a proper Germanness to respectable gender mores.

In his promotion of blues and Dixieland, Rudorf proposed that authentic jazz could help to counter the dangerous effects of American commercial music in East Germany and elsewhere. Just as East Germans could learn from the lively folk music of the Soviet Union and the other people's republics, so too, Rudorf suggested, could East Germans learn from authentic jazz.[15]

Rudorf's validation of jazz, like Berendt's in West Germany, rested on distinguishing authentic from commercial music and on separating authentic jazz from any associations with decadence or unbridled sexuality. Yet in spite of similarities in their logic, Berendt and Rudorf came to different conclusions. In contrast to Berendt and many of the West German jazz associations that found bebop and modern jazz most valuable, Rudorf rejected such forms of jazz as decadent. Secretly, however, Rudorf applauded modern jazz in letters to his acquaintance Siegfried Schmidt in Halle.[16]

Rudorf's use of official terminology allowed him to carve a space for jazz in East Germany, and it contributed to the confusion in both his own efforts and official responses to him. Within his framework of distinguishing authentic from commercial and modern "formalist" jazz, Rudorf was able to broaden the range of officially acceptable tunes, and in 1955 he briefly gained official recognition for an association of mostly male Leipzig jazz fans.[17] But in spite of Rudorf's efforts, many East German officials continued to be suspicious of *all* jazz and *all* jazz fans.

Because GDR officials positioned themselves as champions of civil rights in the United States and generally believed in the revolutionary potential of the authentic folk music of the oppressed, their attacks on jazz required that jazz be denied the status of authentic African-American music. One official, Ludwig Richard Müller, declared that it did not matter whether jazz contained elements of "Negro folk music"; rather, it mattered to what ends jazz was being used. Another official, Georg Knepler, director of the Berlin Music Academy, stressed that East German composers and musicians greatly admired both the cultural creativity of African-Americans and the fight for equal rights against the barbarian racial policies of the ruling class in the United States. Indeed, in order to prove that he was not a racist, Knepler acclaimed the work of African-American actor and singer Paul Robeson, who during these years, because of his involvement in the U.S. Communist Party, was fighting to retain his U.S. citizenship. At the height of Soviet attacks in jazz, Robeson himself had published an article directed against jazz in the major Soviet music journal in 1949. In words that Rudorf had picked up in a 1952 article on jazz, Robeson argued that spirituals and blues were the only true Negro music in the United States. Commercial jazz, whether played by whites or African-Americans, "prostituted and ruthlessly perverted the genuine expressions of folk life." Knepler followed Robeson in refuting Rudorf's thesis that jazz was the music of the Negro proletariat in the American South. Blues and spirituals—which Robeson had sung—were indeed true folk music, according to Knepler, but jazz was not. Both Müller and Knepler supported this rejection of jazz with references to its sexualizing effects. Knepler spoke of the marks that brothels and gangster hangouts had left on jazz, while Müller was especially worried about the "public display of sexual drives" among jazz fans who danced.[18]

In critiquing *all* jazz, both Knepler and Müller employed a vocabulary similar to Rudorf's rejections of commercial jazz. Elements of "decadence," lamented Knepler, had intruded into the so-called true jazz. In jazz the "exuberance" of "Negro dances" turned into "hysteria," intense expressiveness "degenerated" into empty clownery. Müller bemoaned the attempts of composers and musicians to satisfy the tastes of "Swing-Heinis" through "sexual groans" and unacceptable "decadent" dances.

The racist undertones of these attacks came to the surface when

Müller repeated SED leader Walter Ulbricht's words that the "'ape culture' [*Affenkultur*] of decadent jazz" had to be countered with a new, healthy German dance culture. And using anti-Semitic vocabulary, officials indicted Rudorf and jazz fans in Germany and abroad as followers of "cosmopolitan" dance music and "internationalism." They found their suspicions confirmed when the Leipzig jazz club did not endorse East German rearmament, and in May 1955 they dissolved the group.[19]

Cold War Conflicts

The back and forth between Rudorf and other jazz fans and East German authorities continued. In times of greater leniency—that is, after the June 1953 uprising and in the aftermath of Khrushchev's attacks on Stalinism in 1956—jazz fans were able to pursue their interests more openly and even with state support. Rudorf, however, stretched the limits too far when he organized jazz concerts in Protestant churches and gave lectures in West Germany. In 1957 he was arrested and convicted for slandering the Freie Deutsche Jugend (FDJ) and the SED and for having used jazz as a cover for political crimes.[20]

On the other side of the Iron Curtain, press and officials in West Germany and the United States were watching closely what was happening in East Germany.[21] The suppression of jazz in East Germany and other countries of the Warsaw Pact made jazz into an attractive messenger for American and West German democracy. Many of the West German jazz clubs, such as the New Jazz Circle Berlin, met in American cultural centers. After many requests from the field and positive press reports about respectable European fans, jazz became an official part of the cultural programs that the United States Information Agency and the State Department sponsored after 1956, but not without major complaints from Southern segregationists.[22]

West Germans, for their part, used jazz against youthful rebelliousness at home and to set themselves apart from the Nazi past and the cold war enemies to the East. This multiple function of jazz—as an alleged tamer of young rebels and as a representative of Western democracy—contributed to its astounding proliferation through books, festivals, radio, and television in West Germany in the second half of the 1950s.[23] In August 1958 West German defense minister Franz-Josef Strauß suggested that he too saw jazz positively and indeed as the appropriate music of the West German army: "the community-building powers" of jazz converged with the efforts of this new army. He explicitly used jazz to show that West Germany and the West German army differed from both its German cold war enemy to the East and the Third Reich.[24] Officials in West Berlin successfully attracted young people to a state-sponsored youth club called Jazz-Saloon, and by 1964 the West German Goethe Institutes used West German jazz bands in their mission to portray German culture abroad.[25] In this logic, jazz came to symbolize the new pluralist, post-fascist, antitotalitarian society that West German politicians in the second half of the 1950s were increasingly espousing.

In East Germany, state officials continued to be more repressive. After a phase of confusion and leniency, they ultimately accepted only narrow concepts of "authentic negro music." In the late 1950s, they allowed only spirituals and blues, and in this increasingly repressive climate, some jazz musicians and jazz club members, including Rudorf after finishing his prison term, left East for West Germany.[26] At the same time East German officials sought to suppress the "open" dancing associated with boogie and rock 'n' roll, and they continued to dissolve any independent clubs that jazz fans attempted to form.

For East and West German officials, who were trying to make a break with the racist German past, jazz likely had some attraction because of its roots in African-American culture and because it had been attacked by the Nazis (and perhaps also because many white American jazz musicians were Jewish, although that was never an explicit topic). In the context of a cold war pro–civil rights agenda designed to counter criticisms of the United States, many U.S. politicians likewise considered African-American musicians important figures in portraying the United States as a country that had overcome racism.[27] However, tolerance also had clear limits. Neither in Strauß's promotion of jazz nor in the West Berlin Jazz-Saloon were the African-American roots of jazz a theme. Jazz, in order to be acceptable, clearly had to be deracialized and even "whitened." And in the debates over jazz, both East and West Germans asserted visions of culture that rendered conservative gender mores and respectable Germanness interdependent. In both countries in the 1950s, jazz also needed to be desexualized before it could become respectable.

Nonetheless, important differences emerged: on the defensive against Western imports and commercial culture, East German authorities were far more repressive. In this context jazz fans and officials in East Germany continued to see jazz as a potential vehicle for political resistance, a possibility that West Germans had successfully contained. We know much about German hostilities toward

America and American popular culture, but my brief exploration shows how some forms of American culture became part of a cold war liberal West German self-presentation. By the 1960s the West German magazine *Twen* added an image of jazz similar to the promotion of the music to American whites in *Downbeat* and *Playboy:* jazz was associated with the leisure and pleasure of a masculinist culture that included pre- and extramarital sex for men.[28]

This account of the changing reception of jazz in cold war Germany reveals the complex processes involved in the German reception of American culture. For 1950s German adolescents, jazz frequently felt transformative, as an act of rebellion against parents, dominant cultural norms, and remnants of the Nazi past. As jazz aficionados succeeded in making the music more respectable, jazz also was compatible with maintaining class or gender stratification and became attractive to U.S. and West German authorities. We still need to learn more about the interpretive horizons that U.S. and German jazz musicians have opened with changing musical forms, and at the same time we need to look carefully at the social and political contexts in which various forms have been received, rejected, and institutionalized.[29]

Work on American culture abroad ideally needs to begin by paying attention to both sides in these transmissions, the United States and the receiving countries. American culture certainly has not been a uniform or unifying tool of U.S. imperialism. While jazz lost some of its controversial edge in the 1950s as West Germany became more liberal and as the U.S. government recognized the music as a legitimate cultural expression, the music continued to broadcast multiple messages. And changing forms of U.S. culture continue to generate lively and even acerbic discussions in both the United States and Germany. The processes by which national and subnational cultures have been shaped in mutual engagement, attraction, and opposition, often within highly asymmetrical power relations, remain an important focus for the analysis of all international interactions, including German-American encounters.[30] Thus it is crucial to recognize the diversity and contested character of cultures on both sides of the Atlantic and even to think beyond a strict German or U.S. focus in locating the contexts in which these contests happen. In the case of jazz these include, for example, developments in the Soviet Union or challenges to U.S. power by nonaligned states. With all this in mind, histories of U.S.-German cultural and political interactions promise to get only more complex.[31]

NOTES

1. On jazz in the Weimar Republic and the Third Reich, see especially Michael Kater, *Different Drummers: Jazz in the Culture of Nazi Germany* (New York: Oxford University Press, 1992).

2. For more extensive discussions of the postwar German reception of jazz, see Uta G. Poiger, *Jazz, Rock, and Rebels: Cold War Politics and American Culture in a Divided Germany* (Berkeley: University of California Press, 2000), chaps. 1, 4, and epilogue, and "American Jazz in the German Cold War," in *Music and German National Identity*, ed. Celia Applegate and Pamela Potter (Chicago: University of Chicago Press, 2002), 218–33.

3. This discussion draws on the following studies by Joachim-Ernst Berendt: *Der Jazz: Eine zeitkritische Studie* (Stuttgart: Deutsche Verlagsanstalt, 1950); "Zum Thema Jazz," *Frankfurter Hefte* 7 (October 1952): 768–79; "Americana: Erlebnisse und Gedanken von einer US-Reise," *Melos* 18 (March 1951): 78–82; "Für und wider den Jazz," *Merkur* 7 (1953): 887–90; *Das Jazzbuch: Entwicklung und Bedeutung der Jazzmusik* (Frankfurt am Main: Fischer, 1953).

4. On the problems of constructing jazz as a universal experience and the challenges to this view, see Scott DeVeaux, "Constructing the Jazz Tradition: Jazz Historiography," *Black American Literature Forum* 25 (fall 1991): 525–60; Ingrid Monson, "The Problem with White Hipness: Race, Gender, and Cultural Conceptions of Jazz Historical Discourse," *Journal of the American Musicological Society* 48 (fall 1995): 396–422.

5. "Jazz," *Blickpunkt*, March 1956.

6. "Jazz-Freunde ohne Klamauk," *Tagesspiegel*, June 16, 1957.

7. See, for example, Joachim Ernst Berendt, "Haleys Musik ist kein Jazz," *Die Welt*, July 21, 1958.

8. H. W. Corten, "Kann der Jazz unserer Jugend schaden?" *Die Welt*, July 21, 1957.

9. Minutes of the 28. Sitzung, Jugendwohlfahrtsausschuss, Bezirksamt Kreuzberg, May 2, 1957, Landesarchiv Berlin, Kalckreuthstr (LAB), Rep. 206, Acc. 3070/3582.

10. See Reginald Rudorf, *Jazz in der Zone* (Cologne: Kiepenheuer und Witsch, 1964).

11. Reginald Rudolf (*sic*), "Für eine frohe, ausdrucksvolle Tanzmusik," *Musik und Gesellschaft* 2 (August 1952): 247–52; Reginald Rudorf "Die Tanzmusik muß neue Wege gehen," *Musik und Gesellschaft* 4, pt. 1 (February 1954): 51—56, pt. 2 (March 1954): 92—95. See also the autobiography by Reginald Rudorf, *Nie wieder links: Eine deutsche Reportage* (Frankfurt am Main: Ullstein, 1990).

12. See, for example, Günter Erbe, *Die verfemte Moderne: Die Auseinandersetzung mit dem "Modernismus" in Kulturpolitik, Literaturwissenschaft und Literatur der DDR* (Opladen: Westdeutscher Verlag, 1993). On the repression of jazz in East Germany and in the Soviet Union, see also Michael Rauhut, *Beat in der Grauzone: DDR-Rock, 1964–1972—Politik und Alltag* (Berlin: Basisdruck, 1993); Rudorf, *Jazz in der Zone*; S. Frederick Starr, *Red and Hot: The Fate of Jazz in the Soviet*

Union, 1917–1980 (New York: Oxford University Press, 1983); Timothy Ryback, *Rock around the Bloc: A History of Rock Music in Eastern Europe and the Soviet Union* (New York: Oxford University Press, 1990).

13. Rudolf (*sic*), "Für eine frohe, ausdrucksvolle Tanzmusik"; Rudorf, "Die Tanzmusik." For similar arguments, see Hermann Meyer, *Musik im Zeitgeschehen* (Berlin, 1952), quoted in Rauhut, *Beat in der Grauzone,* 19.

14. Rudorf, "Die Tanzmusik."

15. Rudolf (*sic*), "Für eine frohe, ausdrucksvolle Tanzmusik"; Rudorf, "Die Tanzmusik." See also Rudorf, *Jazz in der Zone,* 37–39; Horst Lange, *Jazz in Deutschland: Die deutsche Jazz-Chronik 1900–1960* (Berlin: Colloquium, 1966).

16. Rudorf, "Die Tanzmusik," and *Jazz in der Zone,* 43–44.

17. See Rudorf and Lukasz, letter to the Zentralrat der FDJ, Kulturabteilung, April 12, 1955, JA-IzJ A392 (Institut für zeitgeschichtliche Jugendforschung—Jugendarchiv). My thanks to Raelynn Hillhouse for pointing me to this file. Copy of letter Thomas to Abteilung Kultur, Zentralrat der FDJ, May 10, 1955, JA-IzJ A392; Sekretariat, "Abschrift," Leipzig, January 26, 1956, JA-IzJ A392: Lange, *Jazz in Deutschland;* Rudorf, *Jazz in der Zone.*

18. Ludwig Richard Müller, "Dekadenz und lebensfroher Neubeginn," *Musik und Gesellschaft* 5 (April 1955): 114–17; Georg Knepler, "Jazz und die Volksmusik," *Musik und Gesellschaft* 5 (June 1956): 181–83; Paul Robeson, "Pesni moega naroda," *Sovetskaia muzyka* (July 1949), quoted in Starr, *Red and Hot,* 221–22.

19. Müller, "Dekadenz"; "Jazzdiskussion," April 7, 1955, Berlin; copy of letter Thomas to Abteilung Kultur, Zentralrat der FDJ, 10 May 1955; Kurt Knoblauch, FDJ Bezirksleitung Leipzig, to FDJ-Zentralrat, August 3, 1955; Lamberz (FDJ-Zentralrat, Kultur) to Knoblauch, January 1, 1956; Rudorf, Lukasz, Thomas to Karl Namokel, FDJ Zentralrat, December 27, 1955, all JA-IzJ A392.

20. See Rudorf, *Jazz in der Zone,* 116–25; "Die Tätigkeit des Ministeriums für Kultur, insbesondere der HA Musik auf dem Gebiete des Jazz," n.d., ca. September 1957, Barch P (Bundesarchiv Abteilungen Potsdam) DR1 Nr. 243; Poiger, *Jazz, Rock, and Rebels,* chap. 4.

21. "Gefahr für den Stehgeiger," *Der Spiegel,* October 26, 1955; "Zonen-Jazzexperte in Ungnade," *Der Tag,* February 24, 1957; "Prügel für Jazzanhänger," *SBZ-Archiv* 8, April 25, 1957; U.S. Mission Berlin, Despatch 983, May 7, 1957; RG 59, 762b.00/5–757; Despatch 388, December 16, 1957, RG 59, 762.00/12–1657; Despatch 489, January 31, 1958, RG 59, 762b.00/1–3158; Despatch 575, March 10, 1958, RG 59, 762.00/3–1058, National Archives (NA).

22. See Charles A. Thomson and Walter H. C. Leaves, *Cultural Relations and U.S. Foreign Policy* (Bloomington: Indiana University Press, 1963), 123; Penny M. Von Eschen, "'Satchmo Blows Up the World': Jazz, Race, and Empire during the Cold War," in *"Here, There, and Everywhere": The Foreign Politics of American Popular Culture,* ed. Reinhold Wagnleitner and Elaine Tyler May (Hanover, NH: University Press of New England, 2000), 163–78, 165.

23. See Horst Koegler, "Jazz—theoretisch," *Der Monat* 12 (October 1959): 58–64. See also Kaspar Maase, *BRAVO Amerika: Erkundungen zur Jugendkultur der Bundesrepublik in den fünfziger Jahren* (Hamburg: Junius, 1992), 179–85.

24. "Bundeswehr pflegt reinen Jazz," *Tagesspiegel,* August 8, 1958, quoted in

Rauhut, *Beat in der Grauzone,* 21; "Jazz-Begeisterung in der Truppe," *Die Welt,* August 9, 1958.

25. Poiger, *Jazz, Rock, and Rebels,* chap. 4, epilogue.

26. See Rudorf, *Jazz in der Zone.*

27. Von Eschen, "'Satchmo,'" 167.

28. For the United States, see Von Eschen, "'Satchmo,'" 165.

29. For a similar approach, see Monson, "Problem with White Hipness," and Von Eschen, "'Satchmo.'"

30. Frederick Cooper and Ann Laura Stoler have made a similar point related to histories of empire. See "Between Metropole and Colony: Rethinking a Research Agenda," in *Tensions of Empire: Colonial Cultures in a Bourgeois World,* ed. Cooper and Stoler (Berkeley: University of California Press, 1997), 1–56.

31. See, for example, Von Eschen, "'Satchmo'"; Gerd Gemünden, *Framed Visions: Popular Culture, Americanization, and the Contemporary German and Austrian Imagination* (Ann Arbor: University of Michigan Press, 1998); Reinhold Wagnleitner, "The Empire of Fun, or Talkin' Soviet Union Blues: The Sound of Freedom and U.S. Cultural Hegemony in Europe," *Diplomatic History* 23 (summer 1999): 499–524.

Hip-Hop Made in Germany: From Old School to the Kanaksta Movement

Sabine von Dirke

The November 2000 issue of the German weekly *Focus* reads as follows:

> Whether hamburger, Hollywood stars, or hip-hop—what young people love and buy, obviously, needs to come from across the Atlantic. The United States is the role model for our youth. Whatever comes from over there is simply cool.[1]

The *Focus* article goes on, however, to give a measured assessment of the perceived threat to "German" culture and "German" youth by U.S. popular culture imports. It questions the notion of "Americanization" typically defined as the most pernicious form of cultural imperialism, where U.S. popular culture products invade and taint authentic cultures, if not wipe them out altogether. Defining Americanization as cultural imperialism is not particularly helpful in analyzing transatlantic transfers of popular music culture.[2] The binary opposition of an economic and cultural power center versus an economically weak and therefore powerless margin does not correctly describe the relationship between the United States and Europe. Of the "big five" transnational record companies, only one is in U.S. hands—Time-Warner-WEA. One belongs to a Japanese multinational company, Sony-CBS, and the others are in European hands with one of the largest conglomerates, BMG-RCA, headquartered in Germany.[3]

The transformation of the U.S. music channel MTV, whose show *Yo! MTV Raps* helped to disseminate hip-hop to a broad audience, serves as another example that contests the cultural imperialism theory. MTV was forced to adjust to local contexts in today's global but highly fragmentized media landscape. In order to stay competitive, it became necessary for MTV to offer local programming instead of the global Anglo-American one that it initially aired. In Germany, Viva, which started in 1993, successfully challenged the monopoly of MTV and its monolingual policy (i.e., the use of English lyrics only) that excluded indigenous German rock, pop, and hip-hop music.[4] These examples show that the assumption that economic power translates into an unmediated cultural effect is just as problematic as the jargon of authenticity and globalization that the cultural imperialism thesis employs. Arjun Appadurai's approach to cultural transfers represents a more adequate conceptualization of the messy processes that are going on globally. He maintains that

> the new global cultural economy has to be seen as a complex, over-lapping, disjunctive order, which cannot any longer be understood in terms of existing center-periphery models (even those which might account for multiple centers and peripheries). . . . at least as rapidly as forces from various metropolises are brought into new societies they tend to become indigenised in one or another way: this is true of music and housing styles as much as it is true of science and terrorism, spectacles and constitutions.[5]

When attempting to understand the U.S.-European relationship, Rob Kroes and others have argued in a similar vein that the transatlantic transfer of popular culture is more usefully conceptualized as a form of "creolization" or hybridization, that is, an appropriation via negotiation of the incoming pop culture products based on the specific structure, traditions, and needs or interests of the indigenous culture(s) rather than the one-way street paradigm implicit in the term "Americanization."[6] This holds true for the reception and adaptations of hip-hop culture in Germany as well. I want to emphasize the plural, "adaptations," since there is not just one single adaptation of the U.S. model. Both gender and socioethnic positions were and are determining variables in the way hip-hop was and is received.

In spite of the diversity found in German hip-hop culture, three dominant strains of adapting the U.S. model can be distinguished. The Old School, that is, the pioneers of hip-hop active since the early 1980s, developed a vague idea of a transnational hip-hop community that was still strongly indebted to the U.S. model of message rap. The New School, which emerged almost concurrently with unification and became the focus of the music industry's attention, saw itself as stepping out of the shadow of U.S. popular culture. Hip-hop was for them *Die letzte Besatzermusik.* In fact, Die Fantastischen Vier (also known as Fanta 4), the commercially most successful rap crew to date, titled their (auto)biography with this neologism.[7] Finally, the second and third generation of immigrants adopted rap music in order to forge an alternative identity in opposition and outside of the confines of ethnicity, race, and nationality.

The Old School: Postnational Identity in the Age of Global Hip-Hop

From the perspective of the Old School, hip-hop today is a story of the betrayal of its origins, ideals, and community or, in other words, of hip-hop's fall from grace for commercial reasons. The memories of Old Schoolers such as Cora E. or members of Advanced Chemistry, Fresh Familee, King Size Terror, and Rock da Most conjure up images of tight-knit communities of local practitioners well versed in and insisting on hip-hop's trinity of rap music (DJ-ing/MC-ing), break dancing, and graffiti.[8] In the Old School narratives—whether in raps or interviews—hip-hop features itself as saving its practitioners and German youth in general from drifting into delinquency and as giving their lives meaning and purpose. One of the most well-known raps on this topic is perhaps Cora E.'s "Schlüsselkind" (Latchkey kid), which is a tribute to the transformative power of hip-hop culture and directly refers to the country of its origin, the United States:

> I almost drowned but was lucky the wave from the United States
>   threw me back onto land
> Started to live, became active, and dreamed for the first time
>   without being asleep
> There was something waiting for me and I went for it
> Something I could get and I stayed on it and that's how it began
> that I was able to achieve something
> I wanted to rap like Shante.[9]

The key words in the discourse of the Old School are those on which the Old School in the United States was built: respect, doing one's own thing, active participation and not just passive consumption, peace and nonviolence, education, independence, community, and realness. The

Old School did not equate "realness" with "street credibility" as defined by U.S. hip-hop. Quite to the contrary, the German Old School was aware of the differences between the situation in the United States and their own. "Realness" was a synonym for being true to oneself or, in other words, for a concept of authenticity. Many raps of the Old School address this issue and reject unreflected imitation of U.S. hip-hop as clichés and as the betrayal of the concept of realness. MC René, for instance, intones:

> I cannot relate to street violence, so it would be fake to
> have a gun go off, many love the topics that are trendy,
> the themes that fly by on MTV, but where is your
> personality collective clichés, will claim victory over facts,
> no, 'cause rap is communication, expression, modern
> conversation. A rapper who copies others is a copy for whom
> I will never have respect.[10]

Whether diss rap, brag rap, or message rap, language plays an important role in rap music. Initially, during the 1980s, many German MCs rapped in English though not exclusively. To equate the use of English raps by homegrown rappers with Americanization is a reductive reading of the complicated process of transatlantic cultural transfers. It forgets about German history, namely, that there was no untainted German folk traditions left after Nazism on which an alternative popular music and youth culture could have been built. U.S. popular culture, especially those examples originating from African-American musical traditions, was the only valid tune that held the promise of liberation. In this context, the predominance of English within popular culture makes sense as a distancing device from the Nazi past and as an attempt to participate in a global intercultural community of dissent challenging mainstream culture. As to the latter, the function of English for popular music culture is comparable to the use of English in the international scientific community.

Furthermore, when hip-hop was adopted in Germany it was the Old School of U.S. hip-hop that was appropriated, that is, the message rap of Grandmaster Flash and the Glorious Five and the idea of the Zulu Nation developed by Afrika Bambaata. This school, however, represented a critique of white America.[11] U.S. message rap, therefore, precluded an easy identification with mainstream white America—or, to be more precise, with the myth that the United States is the land of freedom, prosperity, and equal opportunity for all. Under the sign of the Zulu Nation, U.S. hip-hop functioned like other adaptations of artistic expressions of African-Americans by white audiences.[12] Hip-hop was read and embraced as a genuine articulation of dissent or resistance to mainstream culture and was imagined to transcend the specific national and social situation. In other words, hip-hop inherited the rebel image of rock 'n' roll.

As previously pointed out, the German hip-hop scene was from the beginning aware of the differences between the social situation in the Federal Republic of Germany (FRG) and in the United States and understood that a simple identification with disenfranchised African-Americans would be untenable. Yet, the inner city as presented by U.S. hip-hop culture through music, videos, and film became the metaphor of oppression and resistance with which the German Old School identified and from which it constructed its vague self-understanding as a transnational, multicultural community in opposition to everything that is reminiscent of mainstream. As one Old Schooler, DJ Cutfaster, put it in lamenting the decay of hip-hop into commercial pop: "Most people have forgotten that hip-hop functions as a mouthpiece against violence and oppression and ultimately against the ghetto, which has become the metaphor for the deplorable state of our world."[13]

The Old School had an ideological investment in hip-hop that precluded a crossover into the mainstream. Its practitioners envisioned and propagated hip-hop as an underground community that needed to keep its distance from and to create resistance to mainstream culture in order to avoid co-optation. This hip-hop culture was defined in an inclusive rather than exclusive manner, with the big exception of gender. The recollections of the Old School, therefore, emphasize that hip-hop in its early golden years transcended national, ethnic, racial, and linguistic identifications. In the words of a rap by Cora E., one of the few female rappers,

> nationalities come together as a subculture
> in spite of the different languages there is understanding
> no matter where you come from, hip-hop grants you asylum.[14]

Many hip-hop crews were indeed multiethnic or multiracial and multilingual. Advanced Chemistry—with its members of Italian, Haitian-German, and Ghanese-German family background—or Fresh Familee—with Tachi from Turkey, Suli from Macedonia, and Higgi from Morocco—may serve here as examples. Many insiders refer to the importance of break dancing for immigrant youth and their strong numbers among the B-Boys during the 1980s.[15] Hip-hop was learned by doing, that is, by watching and copying from the short break-dance sequence in the movie *Flashdance* or the U.S. documentaries *Wild Style* and *Beat Street*. All of these creative expressions did not require taking expensive lessons. As fresh imports, break dancing, graffiti, rapping, and DJ-ing created a free-for-all because they were not yet coded in terms of ethnicity or nationality and social class like most other after-school activities.[16] Hence, articulating the relationship between U.S. hip-hop and hip-hop made in Germany in terms of an analogy between the situation of specific social groups, then, makes sense to a certain extent.[17] Yet, it is important to remember that this is only one facet of the complex transatlantic transfer of hip-hop culture; the adaptation of hip-hop by German middle-class kids is a different story.

The New School: Commercialization and Nationalization

Even when using the Old School's notion of authenticity or sense of realness as a measure for authentic or valid appropriation, the happy-go-lucky party rap music of the New School (for which the Stuttgart-based, solidly middle-class crew Fantastische Vier functioned as a midwife) cannot be chided as inauthentic. The music critic Günther Jacob convincingly argues that, in the global pop culture arena, artistic, especially musical, forms can be rightfully appropriated by various groups around the globe. Hence he rejects the critique of white European hip-hop artists as engaging in pure posturing because they have not experienced racial discrimination as black rap musicians have. Jacob maintains: "They [white hip-hops] engage in posturing only if they imitate contents and attitudes that have no relationship to their own life world or are only aesthetically mediated."[18]

Like the Old School, the middle-class party hip-hops of the 1990s appropriated the musical forms of U.S. hip-hop in their own way. Nevertheless, the New School was also most critical of the one-to-one equation of the United States and Germany, emphasizing instead the differences between their own social situation and that of African-American youth. Already in 1991, Fanta 4 realized the imitation of U.S. hip-hop as clichéd and intoned:

It has nothing to do with hip-hop
to rest on one's old ghetto image

for one it makes sense for me to tell who I am and where I
    come from
and there indeed it is not that bad."[19]

However, New and Old School were at odds in their understanding of
how hip-hop and mainstream culture should relate to each other—it is
the ever recurring problem of selling out to the mainstream for commercial gain. The New School crew Fanta 4 admits in its (auto)biogra-
phy that they had no political agenda but were only interested in
becoming popular, to go mainstream from the very beginning, and to
pursue this goal strategically.

Fanta 4's and other hip-hop crews' switch to rapping predominantly, if not exclusively, in German was motivated by several factors,
including the crossover potential. Another reason could be simply
insufficient knowledge of English. In fact, one member of Fettes Brot,
a New School crew, bluntly admitted that to be the case.[20] More
importantly and within the logic of rapping, the switch to German
made sense since rap wants to communicate with its audience. The
desire to be understood by the audience, in terms of both conveying a
message and showing off one's rhetorical skills, was therefore the primary motivating factor. Rapping in German was not an issue until
Fanta 4's German party rap stormed the charts in 1991, after which the
music industry realized that the resurgence of national sentiment in the
wake of the fall of the Berlin Wall "opened up the space for the commercialization of a new nationally coded youth culture."[21] As one of
the recent historiographers of hip-hop pointed out bitterly, "nationalities and language did not play a role in the hip-hop scene until Fantastische Vier turned being German into a brand."[22]

As much as the Old School rapped against nationalism and racism
and attempted to hold on to its ideal of a transnational, multicultural
hip-hop identity of dissent,[23] the music industry's commodification
strategies led to the differentiation of popular music and youth culture
along national or ethnic lines. The year 1991 saw the arrival of the first
sampler under the music industry's new national flag of "Deutsch
Rap," whose title *Krauts with Attitude* clearly refers to the U.S. crew
NWA (Niggers with Attitude). The cover of the record utilized Germany's national colors of black, red, and gold. The liner notes include
a call for opposing the strong influence of English, meaning the Anglo-
American influence of popular culture. Oddly enough, of the fifteen
songs, only three were in German, one was in French, and the rest were
in English.[24]

Even if the switch to rapping in German was initially made to facilitate the genuine adaptation of African-American music culture to the German situation (as well as to attempt to step out of the shadow of U.S. hip-hop), the music industry's marketing strategies reinforced the ethnic differentiation and politics of exclusion typical for postwar West German society. Adegoke Odukoya, who defines himself as Afro-German and was a member of the multiethnic crew Weep Not Child, summed it up: "All of a sudden, there was a definition of German hip-hop that no longer included many crews. All those who rapped in English or told their story in Turkish or Yugoslavian no longer felt at home and also were no longer welcome."[25]

From Oriental Hip-Hop to Kanakstas

The ethnonational differentiation in hip-hop was dubbed "Oriental Hip-Hop" to designate and market those multinational or multiethnic crews who used their other language(s), which was frequently, but not exclusively, Turkish. At the same time when *Krauts with Attitude* was released, the Nuremberg crew King Size Terror released their first vinyl with a Turkish language rap called "Bir Yabancimin Hayati" (The life of the stranger). Both of these releases represent examples of how hip-hop got caught up in this market-driven ethnic labeling. As a *taz* article on the Turkish rap crew Cartel points out, rapping consistently in Turkish was not necessarily a choice but rather the result of being defined by mainstream culture as different, more precisely defined within the framework of Orientalist discourse as the exoticized other and marketed as such.[26]

In light of this discourse and politics of exclusion, it is perhaps not surprising that U.S. hip-hop gained significance for immigrant youth again in the 1990s. This sociopolitical situation invited drawing, in particular, on the gangsta rap genre that was at the same time popular and controversial in the United States.[27] The most striking similarity between U.S. gangsta rap and hip-hop made in Germany is the reappropriation of ethnic slurs such as *Kanake* or *Kümmel* hurled at the immigrants by Germans. Already in 1994, the band Fresh Familee, for instance, problematized the derogatory term *Kanake* and German stereotypes about immigrant men with their rap "Sexy Kanake," and the MC Afrob has several raps in which he uses the equally insulting term *Kaffer* for people of Black-African or Caribbean descent. Today many young immigrants, primarily young Turks who grew up in Germany, refer to themselves as Kanakstas. The name *Kanaksta* likens itself to the U.S. hip-hop model by combining the German slur for immigrant—*Kanake*—with U.S. slang ("gangsta").

In the introduction to his book *Kanak Sprak*, Feridun Zaimoglu, who positioned himself as a spokesperson for the Kanaksta concept in the public sphere, articulates the parallel between the United States and Germany:

> The foundation of this community is still a negative self-confidence as it articulates itself superficially in the seeming self-recrimination: Kanake! This derogatory term becomes a word of recognition and for identification that binds these "*Lumpenethnier*" together. Analogous to the black-consciousness movement in the United States, the various subidentities of immigrants recognize the broader thematic contexts and connections.[28]

In Zaimoglu's two anthologies—*Kanak Sprak*, which features only men, and *Koppstoff*, which features only women[29]—several Kanakstas give their position on the situation of the second and third generation of immigrants in Germany. They maintain that hip-hop is a means to reassert themselves against both the politics of exclusion and the multicultural discourse that often assigns the immigrants an exoticized ethnic identity. The language used in these anthologies indeed resembles rapping and serves a dual purpose: to give voice to the anger and frustration of the second and third generation of immigrants and to codify a new vernacular, "Kanak Sprak," that is, a "metropolitan jargon" as Zaimoglu calls it himself.[30] At the same time, however, it is important not to lose sight of the fact that the African-American vernaculars emerged in a historically very different situation from the "Kanak Sprak" used by parts of the immigrant community in Germany. The two should therefore not be equated with one another.

The question arises as to how to evaluate this appropriation of the gangsta rap postures by or for the Kanaksta concept. On the one hand, the Kanaksta concept is eager to shatter the media's infatuation with the immigrant as an inner-city kid torn between two cultures.[31] On the other hand, the Kanaksta concept adopts the slang and posturing of the U.S. gangsta rap, that is, the ghetto image, as a provocation of mainstream society, including the contemporary German multicultural peaceniks. Yet, instead of reading the Kanaksta phenomenon as a form of unreflected Americanization, I contend that it is a deliberately marked adaptation in direct response to mainstream culture's paranoid invocation of U.S. race relations, for which the inner city has become a negative symbol of social decay and of the failure of the multicultural society.

A *Spiegel* cover story may serve here as one concrete example. In this article on the socioethnic disparity of German society, *Der Spiegel* repeatedly compared the situation in German cities with its increasing ethnic differentiation and clashes between immigrant and German youth to the "gang wars in the slums of the big cities in the United States."[32] In addition, *Der Spiegel* connected German inner-city youth, that is, immigrants, with hip-hop and violence by inserting an interview with a Turkish rapper into the title story.[33] The most visible articulation of the Kanaksta movement to date, the group Kanak Attak,[34] founded in 1998, responded to the *Spiegel* article directly by using the cover on its first Web site. Not only are Kanak Attak events accompanied by hip-hop music, but the group relies on the hip-hop concept of sampling as the guiding principle for their attempts to escape the politics of ethnic identification, or rather stigmatization, as clearly stated in its manifesto:

> Kanak Attak is a community of different people from diverse backgrounds who share a commitment to eradicate racism from German society. Kanak Attak is not interested in questions about passport or heritage, in fact it challenges such questions in the first place. . . . Our common position consists of an attack against the "Kanakisation" of specific groups of people through racist ascriptions which denies people their social, legal and political rights. Kanak Attak is therefore anti-nationalist, anti-racist and rejects every single form of identity politics, as supported by ethnic absolutist thinking.[35]

While appropriating the language and posture of U.S. gangsta rap, this group does not, however, pick up on separatist tendencies, that is, the black nationalism of some U.S. hip-hop artists. To the contrary, the Kanakstas appear to return to the idea of a transnational and transethnic identity that was in a far less articulated way the foundation of the Old School's self-understanding in the 1980s. Being a Kanaksta is therefore not tied to ethnicity or nationality, that is, being an immigrant to Germany, but instead defined as an attitude expressing opposition to mainstream culture, including the left-liberal concept of multiculturalism, and as an attitude that embraces difference. As one early member of the Kanak Attak put it in an interview: "This moment of difference that we propagate is not simply one that can be ethnicized. Instead it is a political difference, a difference to the mainstream. Or perhaps an opposition against conformity."[36]

In spite of this embrace of difference and the fact that the Kanak Attak group in Berlin thematizes issues of gender and sexual preferences, the larger context of hip-hop made in Germany shares with the U.S. hip-hop scene a problematic approach to gender, with respect to both the content of the lyrics and the limited number of female hip-hop artists. Without exonerating hip-hop culture on the issue of gender, it is important to remember that popular music culture did not start the exclusion of women from certain cultural activities and also did not invent misogyny but rather represents a reflection of these prevalent features in patriarchal societies around the globe.[37] The limited German discussion on hip-hop and gender is split into two camps: In the one camp are those who reject misogynist raps as indecent, either from a moral or from a feminist perspective. In the other camp are those who argue that these lyrics and machismo postures should not be taken literally or seriously since they are nothing but a game. While these two main positions cut across gender lines, this should not obscure a fact that Holly Kruse has highlighted in her discussion of gender in popular music culture, namely, that "the power relationships in production and consumption" of all popular music have "attempted to limit the roles and meanings available to women" in the popular music world.[38]

The patriarchal power relationships in production and consumption are generally, though not uniformly, hostile to women who seek to deviate from their prescribed gender role. Hip-hop culture is no exception. While many raps rearticulate gender stereotypes and sexist attitudes, others confront them critically, such as Fischmob's "4'55," which speaks out against rape and the widespread stereotype that women wearing sexy clothes are actually asking for it.[39] A consensus exists, however, across most genres of popular music culture that female artists' looks are as important as, if not more important than, their music, reinforcing a predominantly male expectation that women should wear sexually titillating outfits no matter their musical talents. This was most recently documented in an on-line magazine, *www.hiphop.de,* which calls itself "The Hip Hop Community on the Internet." In one of the chatrooms, entitled "Hip Hop Girlz," the following statement triggered an ongoing exchange on women and hip-hop: "Here anything can be posted from people who feel that girls should wear nothing but baggys (okay, almost nothing else) to those who think that females have no clue about hip-hop."[40] This statement was accompanied by a photo of a scantily clad woman showing off her cleavage titled "HipHopBunny." The contributions to this chatroom rearticulate the notion that hip-hop is still a male-dominated music genre in which women represent a minority and can occupy only a narrowly defined set of roles.

Interestingly, the few female hip-hop artists who seem to have made it refrain from addressing these issues; that is, they appear oblivious to the long tradition in the music world of prescribing women's role within it by either marginalizing their contributions or excluding them altogether as performers. At least one female hip-hop artist, Sabrina Setlur, has attempted to capitalize on male fantasies for her own advantage. Although opinion as to whether Setlur's music qualifies as hip-hop is divided, she started out as a part of Moses Pelham and Thomas Hofmann's rap crew, Rödelsheimer Hartreim Projekt, whose marketing strategy was to present itself as the evil and violent counterpart to the squeaky clean party hip-hop of the Fantastische Vier.[41] Setlur initially used the stage name "Schwester S," with obvious reference to the African-American hip-hop vernacular. The bi-racial Setlur shares with female U.S. rappers the darker hue of her skin and (with some of them) a penchant for glamorous and sexy fashion. Since her first CD *S ist soweit* (S. is ready) was released in 1995 on Pelham Power Production's label, Setlur has gained notoriety in the press not for her music but for her looks and her private life. The media's infatuation with Setlur serves as an example of how female rappers and hip-hop fans are still under the spell of the male gaze, which reduces women to their physical appearance.

The two other leading women of German hip-hop—Cora E., especially in her rap "And the MC is female," and the newcomer from East Germany, Pyranja, who released her first CD in the fall of 2000—fault their own gender for the situation for lacking the courage and drive to make it in the hip-hop world.[42] Based on these examples, it appears that some of the leading female rappers in Germany do not want to dwell on the gendered nature of the music business as long as they can be successful, even if it means reinforcing stereotypes or accepting the status of a novelty act. One is left to wonder why rap music, which has won recognition for its ability to thematize ethnic and racial inequalities, falls silent when confronted with the problem of gender.

How gender and ethnic or national identity intersect represents a complex issue that requires more research, especially for the German context. For instance, the extent to which Setlur's bi-racial heritage plays a role in the hip-hop community's and the media's preception of her would be an interesting case in point. Without such detailed research and because of the minority status of women in German hip-hop, it is hard to assess whether and, if so, how gender affects transatlantic transfers of music culture. For now, it is only possible to answer the question—How American is hip-hop made in Germany?—in more general terms.

While popular music and youth culture in Germany might respond to the impetus of U.S. popular music models, this transatlantic transfer cannot adequately be described as a form of cultural imperialism but rather as a reworking of U.S. models in response to domestic constellations. At the same time, the adaptation of hip-hop in Germany shows that the United States still functions as the foil and/or projection screen for conceptualizing a multiethnic/multiracial, multilingual, and transnational hip-hop community for both the Old School and the Kanakstas. Yet, different aspects of hip-hop culture in the United States became relevant depending on the socioethnic position of the hip-hop practitioners and the current sociopolitical situation. German hip-hop started out as a transnational and cosmopolitan youth subculture that was indebted to Afrika Bambaata's idea of the Zulu Nation and employed, at first, predominantly English raps. It became, however, enmeshed in the discourse on national identity in the wake of unification. With the marketing categories "Deutsch-Rap" and "Oriental Hip-Hop," the music industry articulated and utilized these growing national sentiments for its reintegration of rap music into mainstream culture. Whereas the Old School's switch to German was analogous to the U.S. Old School's idea of message rap, that is, edutainment, the signifying practices from appropriation of derogatory terms to a minority street vernacular was more important for the Kanaksta concept. U.S. popular culture may still be the primary point of reference for both mainstream and dissident youth cultures. Yet, the various youth subcultures that appropriate U.S. popular culture show themselves to be aware of the differences between their own situation and that in the United States. The three strains of hip-hop made in Germany are therefore good examples of the process of creolization or hybridization that characterizes transatlantic transfers of popular music culture, and they challenge the negative notion of Americanization as cultural imperialism.

NOTES

1. Alex Wolfsgrubern, "We want you, and you . . ." *Focus* 46 (November 2000): 50. "Ob Hamburger, Hollywoodstar oder Hip-hop, was von der Jugend geliebt und gekauft wird, muss offenbar von jenseits des Atlantiks kommen.

Amerika ist für die Jugend Vorbild. Was von dort kommt ist einfach cool." All translations in the essay are my own.

2. For a discussion of the concept and theory of cultural imperialism, see John Tomlinson, *Cultural Imperialism* (London: Pinter, 1991). For a critique of the cultural imperialism theory's usefulness for popular music culture, see Tony Mitchell, *Popular Music and Local Identity: Rock, Pop, and Rap in Europe and Oceania* (London and New York: Leicester University Press, 1996), esp. chap. 3.

3. Mitchell, *Popular Music and Local Identity,* 52.

4. See Gerald Traufetter, "Die Vermischung der Weltkulturen," *Der Spiegel* 44 (2000), 234–38, and "'Ich bin die Mama, die Schwester mit dem Hammer.' Der Musikkanal Viva bring MTV in Zugzwang," *Die Welt,* February 10, 1996. On-line archive: http://www.deldaten/1996102/10/0210Ku99270.htx

5. Arjun Appadurai, "Disjuncture and Difference in the Global Cultural Economy," *Public Culture* 2, no. 2 (spring 1990): 5–6.

6. Rob Kroes, "Americanisation: What Are We Talking About?" in *Cultural Transmissions and Receptions: American Mass Culture in Europe,* ed. R. Kroes, R. W. Rydell, and D. F. J. Bosscher (Amsterdam: VU University Press, 1993), 302–18. After completion of this essay, Mark Pennay's article "Rap in Germany," which also emphasizes the significance of the specific local context for understanding German hip-hop, was published in the fall of 2001 in *Global Noise: Rap and Hip-Hop outside the USA,* ed. Tony Mitchell (Middletown, CT: Wesleyan University Press, 2001), 111–32.

7. Die Fantastischen Vier, *Die letzte Besatzermusik: Die Autobiographie,* ed. Ralf Niemczyk (Cologne: Kiepenheuer and Witsch, 1999).

8. See, for example, Sebastian Krekow and Jens Steiner, *Bei uns geht einiges: Die deutsche Hip hop-Szene* (Berlin: Schwarzkopf and Schwarzkopf, 2000), 12–13, as well as statements by several hip-hop artists in this historiography.

9. Cora E., "Schlüsselkind," *Corage* (EMI, 1996).

> ich ertrank fast sank doch hatte Glück die Welle aus Amerika
> spülte mich wieder an Land zurück begann zu leben wurd
> aktiv und hab zum ersten Mal geträumt ohne daß ich schlief
> da war Etwas das auf mich wartete also ging ich
> Etwas das ich bekomm' kann bleib ich dran also fing es an
> dass ich Etwas erreichen kann . . . ich wollte rappen wie Shante.

10. MC René, "Untergrundunterhaltung," *Renevolution* (MZEE, 1995).

> Ich habe keinen Bezug zu Gewalt auf Asphalt, deshalb
> wäre es Betrug, wenn die Waffe losknallt, viele lieben die
> Themen, die im Trend liegen, Rigidimigdi-Schemen, die
> über MTV fliegen, aber wo ist die Persönlichkeit geblieben,
> kollektive Klischees, die über Tatsachen siegen, nein, denn
> Rap ist Kommunikation, Ausdrucksform, moderne
> Konversation. Ein Rapper, der kopiert, ist nur eine Kopie,
> Respekt für 'ne Kopie bekommst Du von mir nie."

See also MC Réne, "Nur im Original," on the same CD, as well as Advanced Chemistry, "Alte Schule," *Advanced Chemistry* (360 Degree Records, 1995), and Hardkor Kingxz, "Sprengt die Brücken," <http://www.epoxweb.de/lyrics/hiphoplyricsesk.htm>.

11. See the following historical accounts of U.S. hip-hop culture: Alan Light, ed., *The VIBE History of Hip-hop* (New York: Three River Press, 1999); Tricia Rose, *Black Noise: Rap Music and Black Culture in Contemporary America* (Hanover: Wesleyan University Press, 1994); and, as a German resource, Ulf Poschardt, *DJ-Culture: Diskjockeys und Popkultur* (Reinbek: Rowohlt, 1997).

12. For a discussion of this reappropriation within the United States, see Russell A. Potter, *Spectacular Vernaculars: Hip-Hop and the Politics of Postmodernism* (Albany: SUNY Press, 1995); for the earlier German context, that is, the adaptation of jazz and rock 'n' roll, see Uta Poiger, *Jazz, Rock, and Rebels: Cold War Politics and American Culture in a Divided Germany* (Berkley: University of California Press, 2000).

13. Quoted in Sascha Verlan and Hannes Loh, *20 Jahre Hip-hop in Deutschland* (Höfen: Hannibal, 2000), 84: "Die meisten haben vergessen, dass Hip-hop ein Sprachrohr ist gegen Gewalt und Unterdrückung, letztlich gegen das Ghetto, das zur Metapher für Missstände in der Welt wird."

14. Cora E., "Könnt ihr mich hör'n?" *Könnt ihr mich hör'n?* (Buback, 1993).

> natonalitäten komm' zusamm' in einem untergrund
> trotz verschied'ner sprachen herrscht verständigung
> egal woher du kommst, hip-hop gibt dir asyl.

15. See, for example, the rap "Eski Okul" (Old school) by Boulevard Bou, which like many other raps can be found on this Web site: <http://www.epoxweb.de/lyrics/hiphoplyricsesk.htm>:

> Anfang 80 als alles begann,
> brachten viele meiner Brüder die Breakdancebewegung voran . . . .
> Soviele Türken und Kurden waren dabei, . . .

16. See Annette Weber, "Du kannst es dir nicht aussuchen," *die tageszeitung,* June 27, 1995, 16.

17. On this issue see, for example, Andreas Welskop, who was the initiator of the government-sponsored SWAT Posse in Berlin, in Krekow and Steiner, *Bei uns geht einiges,* 138–49.

18. Günther Jacob, *Agit-Pop: Schwarze Musik und weiße Hörer* (Berlin and Amsterdam: Edition ID-Archiv, 1993), 206. "Zu Posern werden sie [white hip-hops] erst, wenn sie Inhalte und Haltungen imitieren, die in ihrer eigenen Lebenssituation keine oder nur ästhetisch vermittelte Voraussetzungen haben."

19. Fantastische Vier, "Hip-hop Musik," *Vier gewinnt* (Sony, 1992).

> es hat ein für allemal mit hip-hop nichts zu tun
> sich auf seinem alten ghettoimage auszuruhn
> zum einen hats für mich den sinn zu sagen wer ich bin
> zu beschreiben wo ich herkomm und da ists halt nicht so schlimm.

See also Smudo, who is a member of Fantastische Vier, and Torch of Advanced Chemistry in Krekow and Steiner, *Bei uns geht einiges,* 40 and 52f.

20. Schiffmeister in Krekow and Steiner, *Bei uns geht einiges,* 154: "Mein Schul-Englisch hat nie dazu gereicht, in einer anständigen Rap-Band zu sein oder das zu tun, was ich mir unter Rap vorgestellt habe. Das hätte ich nie auf englisch machen können. Deshalb fand ich den Schritt relativ logisch."

21. Dietmar Elflein, "From Krauts with Attitudes to Turks with Attitudes: Some Aspects of Hip-hop History in Germany," *Popular Music* 17, no. 3 (1998): 257.

22. Verlan and Loh, *20 Jahre Hip-hop in Deutschland,* 44: "In der Hip-hop-Szene hatten Nationalitäten und Sprachen nie eine Rolle gespielt, die Fantastischen Vier machten Deutschsein zu einem Markenzeichen."

23. Some of the most striking examples of opposing xenophobia and nationalism from the early 1990s are Fresh Familee, "Ahmet Gündüz," *Coming from Ratinga* (1991); Advanced Chemistry, *Fremd im eigenen Land* (MZEE, 1992), and "Operation §3," *Advanced Chemistry* (360 Degree Records, 1995); State of Departmentz, "Auf der Jagd nach 3. Oktober" and "Mach meinen Kumpel nicht an!" *Reimexplosion* (Rap Nation, 1994); "Weep Not Child," *From Hoyerswerda to Rostock* (Buback, 1993), and *Halt keine Gewalt! Hip-hop Aktivisten Gegen Gewalt* (Juiceful, 1994); and Toni L., *Dummerweise* (360 Degree Records, 1996).

24. See also Elflein, "From Krauts with Attitudes to Turks with Attitudes," 258.

25. Quoted in Verlan and Loh, *20 Jahre Hip-hop in Deutschland,* 143: "Plötzlich kam eine Definition von 'deutschem Hip-hop' zustande, wo viele Gruppen nicht mehr drin vorkamen. Alle jene, die auf Englisch gerappt haben oder ihre Story auf Türkisch oder Jugoslawisch erzählt haben, fühlten sich da nicht mehr zuhause, waren auch nicht mehr willkommen."

26. On Orientalism see Edward Said, *Orientalism* (New York: Random House, 1978), and *Culture and Imperialism* (New York: Knopf, 1993). See also the comments by Alper in Weber, "Du kannst es dir nicht aussuchen,"16: "Irgendwann wird klar, daß du es dir nicht aussuchen kannst, daß das die andern für dich tun."

27. Verlan and Loh date this orientation toward gangsta rap from the United States at the end of 1995 in their *20 Jahre Hip-hop in Deutschland,* 282; see also Akay in Feridun Zaimoglu, *Kanak Sprak: 24 Mißtöne vom Rande der Gesellschaft* (Berlin: Rotbuch, 1995), 25. On the controversy surrounding U.S. gangsta rap, see Rose, *Black Noise,* esp. chap. 4.

28. Zaimoglu, *Kanak Sprak,* 17.

Noch ist das tragende Element dieser Community ein negatives Selbstbewußtsein, wie es in der scheinbaren Selbstbezichtigung seinen oberflächlichen Ausdruck findet: Kanake! Dieses verunglimpfende Hetzwort wird zum identitätsstiftenden Kennwort, zur verbindenen Klammer dieser "Lumpenethnier." Analog zur Black-consciousness-Bewegung in den U.S.A. werden sich die einzelnen Kanak-Subidentitäten zunehmend übergreifender Zusammenhänge und Inhalte bewußt.

29. Feridun Zaimoglu, *Koppstoff: Kanaka Sprak vom Rande der Gesellschaft* (Hamburg: EVA/Rotbuch, 1998).

30. Zaimoglu claims in Verlan and Loh, *20 Jahre Hip-hop in Deutschland,* 156, that this vernacular is authentic, that is, that he simply recorded it. See, on this claim, Petra Fachinger's chapter, "Writing Back to Liberal Discourse: Feridun Zaimoglu's Grotesque Realism," in her monograph *Rewriting Germany from the Margins: "Other" German Literature of the 1980s and 1990s.* (Montreal and London: McGill-Queen's University Press, 2001), 98–111.

31. See Kanak Attak, "Manifesto: Kanak Attak and Basta!" which can be found on the following Web site: <http://www.passagiere.de/ka/manifest_dt.htm>; see also Tachi and Ade on this issue, both in Verlan and Loh, *20 Jahre Hip-hop in Deutschland,* 138–42.

32. "Zeitbomben in den Vorstädten," *Der Spiegel* 16 (1997): 79.

33. "'Ich muß blöd gewesen sein': Rapper Hakan Durmus über seine Zeit in der Kreuzberger Türken-Gang *36 Boys, "Der Spiegel* 16 (1997): 88.

34. On Kanak Attak, see their Web site: <http://www.kanak-attak.de>; Verlan and Loh, *20 Jahre Hip-hop,* 155–65; and Thomas Jahn, "Türksun = Du bist Türke: HipHop, House und Pop: In den türkischen Ghettos von München, Köln, Berlin pocht ein neues Wir-Gefühl," *Die Zeit* 3 (January 19, 1996), 21. See also the respective entry in Carmine Chiellino, ed., *Interkulturelle Literatur in Deutschland: Ein Handbuch* (Stuttgart and Weimar: Metzler, 2000), 445–46.

35. Kanak Attak, "Manifesto."

36. Laura in "Dieser Song gehört uns! Interview mit Imran Ayata, Laura Mestre Vives and Vanessa Barth von Kanak Attak," *diskus: Frankfurter StudentInnen Zeitschrift* 1 (May 1999).

37. For a detailed history of the difficulties women had to break into rock music and rock-related genres, see Lucy O'Brien, *She Bop: The Definitive History of Women in Rock, Pop, and Soul* (London: Penguin Books, 1995).

38. Holly Kruse, "Gender," in *Key Terms in Popular Music and Culture,* ed. Bruce Horner and Thomas Swiss (Malden, MA, and Oxford: Blackwell, 1999), 85.

39. Fischmob, "4'55," *Männer können ihre . . .* (Plattenmeister, 1995).

40. Here is the entire entry to the chatroom: "Wie sieht's aus mit einem kleinen Topic ueber Maedchen, Hip-hop und wie die beiden zusammenpassen . . . ?!? Hier kann alles rein, von Leuten, die finden, dass Maedels nix anderes tragen sollten als Baggys (na ja, FAST nix anderes) bis zu denen, die meinen das die weibliche Seite keine Ahnung von Hip-hop hat . . . !!! Ich fange dann mal an und lasse Bilder sprechen." Bild: "HipHopBunny04.jpg."

41. On Moses P. and the Rödelheimer Hartreim Projekt, see Verlan and Loh, *20 Jahre Hip-hop,* 187–89, 249–51.

42. Cora E., "Und der MC ist weiblich," *Corage* (EMI, 1996). See also Pyranja's statements in Krekow and Steiner, *Bei uns geht einiges,* 284–85, and in Verlan and Loh, *20 Jahre Hip-hop,* 258–67.

"In Case of Misunderständig, Read On!" Pop as Translation

Eckhard Schumacher

In an essay with the strange, ostensibly misspelled title "Wort Auf!" Diedrich Diederichsen, one of the most influential pop music critics since the early 1980s, relates an anecdote that could be regarded as a prototypical model for the self-guided introduction of German-speaking youngsters to a foreign language:

> When my brother and I were four and six respectively, we met in front of the radio every Sunday to listen to the hit parade, as if it were a revelation, even though, of course, we couldn't understand a word the Beatles sang. Still, we had to give the songs names, had to get our lips and tongues to form something when we sang them. So a kind of English came into being that had absolutely no meaning whatsoever, or at least, it consisted of a few intelligible words—after all, you learn pretty quickly at that age—and lots of nonsense words. Sometime later, when we started learning English as a totally normal foreign language, we couldn't get rid of our own version; we could already speak a kind of English, which a second one could never equal. At some point, I could translate a Dylan song, but I already knew it by heart and enjoyed the linguistic effects, which I loaded with half-knowledge, paranoid interpretation, and desire.[1]

Diederichsen's anecdote precisely points out "the great advantage and the great peculiarity"[2] Germans experience when they hear Anglo-American pop music and its lyrics. When they are first confronted with foreign pop music, the problem is one of more or less complete incomprehensibility. In hindsight, however, not understanding the new, strange, yet, at the same time, oddly familiar and exceedingly attractive language does not appear to be a deficiency. Instead, this incomprehension opens up a form of understanding and a way of dealing with what you can call a foreign language—in this case, one named "pop," which owes its productivity to the aspect of incomprehension, inscrutability, or, at least, misunderstanding. Appropriating the foreign language is like "speaking in tongues," writes Diederichsen, and produces "endless chains of digressions occurring at every second somewhat clear-cut word."[3] This happens because the appropriation is overdetermined by pop-specific coding and laden with meanings that "totally normal English"[4] can never attain. We are thus speaking about a way of receiving pop music that is not about learning English, as Andreas Neumeister writes, in order to "listen to T. Rex in the original."[5] Instead, when you listen to pop music, you learn a language that seems to be a foreign language in a dual sense. It is as different from the so-called mother tongue as it is from the foreign language that you later learn in school as "totally normal English." Yet nevertheless it seems astonishingly close to both.

These thoughts refer to a way of dealing with pop that was characteristic for certain German magazines in the 1980s and 1990s, such as *Sounds, Mode & Verzweiflung,* and *Spex,* and for different German bands such as The 39 Clocks and Freiwillige Selbstkontrolle (FSK). Around 1980, The 39 Clocks, a band from Hanover, invented an American-English dialect earmarked by a penetrating German accent, deliberately dilettantish imitations of American role models like The Velvet Underground, and apparently misspelled song titles like "Pain It Dark" or "Twisted and Shouts."[6] In contrast, members of FSK, the Munich band started by Thomas Meinecke and others, have been singing in German since 1980. However, they sing in a German constituted of "transatlantically misinterpreted Americanisms,"[7] of linguistic deformations, mixtures, and hybrids, recognizable in song titles such as "(I Wish I Could) Sprechen Sie Deutsch," "Pennsylfawnisch Schnitzelbank," or "Mein Funky Ballantine's."[8] Meinecke, who is responsible for the lyrics, comments on FSK's use of the German language: "We don't discover our identity in the lyrics of our mother tongue, but our difference; we don't write songs in German because it is understandable, but to constructively create friction in the language."[9]

If we are talking about examining and appropriating American pop phenomena from a German and German-speaking perspective, then this friction can be as productive as Diederichsen's mixture of "half-knowledge, paranoid interpretation, and desire."[10] In both cases, one simultaneously understands too little and too much. One literally sticks to the words and cares little for the possibly correct meaning; one adapts found material—newly processed or newly discovered—and aims to de-form, to mix languages, to produce effects without worrying about which convention, essence, or identity might be present. One not only then realizes that one's distance to what is supposedly strange is shrinking but also comprehends the distance to one's own familiar mother tongue. Thus pop can be understood as a form of entertainment that is also a form of dissidence, since it culls a "chance to be different," as Meinecke writes regarding Diederichsen, from an "incorrect remake," by trusting to "productive misunderstandings . . . to renew genres and exceed identities."[11] When dealing in this way with what is regarded as either one's own or a foreign language, one can produce a particular form of "ambivalence" that, says Diederichsen, makes "dissidence" possible when "misunderstandings hover in the air" and "essences are deconstructed."[12] All of this, I would suggest, can be understood by means of the anecdote cited previously as well as through the title of Diederichsen's essay—"Wort Auf!"—which can only be translated improperly as "Word Up!" In the German original, the title is already an almost literal, interlinear, and thus incorrect (in terms of conventional standards) translation of the phrase prominent in the Anglo-American and African-American pop discourse, "Word Up!"[13] In other words, "Wort Auf!" can be read as a form of translation that not only points out the difficulties of understanding the idiom of the foreign language called "pop" but also presents possible ways of productively appropriating it—ways that are in no small part constituted by misreadings, purposeful or not, and "fruitful misunderstandings."[14]

As I will show, those different strategies of dealing with pop not only open up connections to concepts like "resignification" or "signifyin(g)," popularized by Judith Butler and Henry Louis Gates Jr.,[15] that have increasingly become part of the discussions over the past years in the pop discourse.[16] They also recall Rolf Dieter Brinkmann's earlier approach, which can be seen as a blueprint for the popularization of Anglo-American pop culture in Germany in the late 1960s and early 1970s. In retrospect we can even say that it also prefigured some of those writing strategies that came up in the wake of punk and new wave music in the late 1970s and early 1980s, for instance, Diederichsen's and Meinecke's. And in the context of the rise of "pop literature" in the late 1990s, several writers and critics again referred to Brinkmann as a historical role model for trash aesthetics and subversive pop literature.[17] From this perspective, despite their differences,

Diederichsen's and Meinecke's concepts of "pop" can also be understood as references to Brinkmann's attitudes and his ways of writing— as an adjusted citation, as a repetition with a difference, as a form of shifting translations.

"Misunderstandings are not," Brinkmann writes in 1969 in his "Notizen" for the anthology *Silver Screen,* which contains translations of new American poetry, "instead, they expand the understanding of something that is 'incorrectly' understood—they're guided digressions, they blast holes through the usual associations (it's so cool to read: 'Über allen Gipfeln zieht es!')."[18] This plea for misunderstandings and errors is a tactic guiding Brinkmann's perception and translation of what he calls the "new American scene." At the end of the 1960s, Brinkmann published translations in the anthologies *Silver Screen* and *ACID,*[19] as well as the volume *Lunch Poems,*[20] a collection of poems by Frank O'Hara—all of which were received with great acclaim in Germany. According to Ralf Rainer Rygulla, the co-editor of *ACID,* it was through new American literature—that is, through translating it[21]—that Brinkmann first discovered a type of English beyond school English. Supporting this claim is the fact that, in this case, Brinkmann's appropriation of a foreign language also led to a recognizable change in his own style of writing. The poetological essays, which Brinkmann added to the anthologies as prefaces, are much more than mere introductions to the new American literature scene. Brinkmann unfolds what turns out to be a literary program, which he himself attempts to carry out in a different form in his poems, prose, and essays. As Agnes C. Mueller writes in *Lyrik "made in USA,"* Brinkmann did not seek out American poetry "because it fit into an already existing program or concept, but rather, his program developed from the inspiration he received from the American poets' new techniques of writing."[22]

At the same time, a significant instigation for Brinkmann's excitement about the "new American scene" is his polemic turn against those German-speaking "poets," who, as "living dead," claim "the cultural words for themselves."[23] Brinkmann opposed what he called the "spooky German cultural business," turned against skeptical cultural criticism, against abstraction, theory, and any type of cultural politics that—as in the 1968 *Kursbuch*—called for the "death of literature."[24] So the starting point for his euphoric approach to America is his distance to his own context, to his own language. This distance also leads to a skepticism toward the usual methods of producing meaning, to mistrust of the "feedback system of words and meanings in the common order of grammatics," which, according to Brinkmann, "has for a long time had nothing to do with daily sensory experience."[25] Yet it is exactly sensory experience and "ordinary details" that are the decisive aspects of Frank O'Hara's poetry, says Brinkmann. In his poetry, "the only real time is the present."[26] This sensibility, oriented toward the present, has "no previous, settled, internalized pattern, no cosy, much-loved prejudices to lose when it gets involved with the present."[27] And this is precisely what Brinkmann attempted to carry out in his own texts, as, for example, in the 1968 volume of poetry *Die Piloten.*[28] He made an issue of the tense relation between subjectivity and the world of objects, since he did not merely attempt to reproduce so-called reality in the sense of a "pure copy."[29] As Karl Heinz Bohrer writes, he was a "skeptical phenomenologist," "an observer attracted to objects," who set reality in motion in and through language.[30] "The surprising aspect," writes Brinkmann, "lies in the unusual collection of details that have not lost all reference to reality, as the conventions of the avant-garde will have it, yet have not been abandoned to reality or slipped into musty preoccupation with the inner self."[31] Beyond the triple dissociation from the conventional avant-garde, tautological realism, and musty preoccupation with the inner self, Brinkmann created space for his own work, where it became possible for him to do exactly what he ascribed to the American literary scene: "to take what is at hand and do something with it, other than what was intended . . . to spread out, to scatter—to break through existing patterns of associations."[32] Only in this way, and not through political content, writes Brinkmann, can literature also become a political issue that opens up a free space in which "possibility becomes concrete," where "a bit of liberated reality" can be created.[33] Starting with Ted Berrigan's suggestion to "redo it and sign your name to it," Brinkmann summarized in his "Notizen" for *Silver Screen* some of the central writing methods in the American scene, which he reports upon and simultaneously uses as a program for his own writing:

> To make one out of several existing, written texts (poems), to "polish up" old poems . . . surprisingly, one's own poem emerges by putting together several foreign texts, through *surface translation,* etc. One's own expression lies in the way the ready-made pieces are arranged, as long as the arranger's psychic dimension is kept! These procedures *empty* the given meaning, long accepted as "natural," which binds one and leads the individual away from himself. Moreover, through such methods, we become conscious that we live in

the *age of photocopy* (Xerox), the time of unlimited possibilities of reproduction, which qualitatively alters the copied object.[34]

From these lines, it is possible to almost effortlessly discern methods and paradigms that, to this day, are still associated with the concept of "pop": the work with ready-made material that uses repetition to dissolve the previously existing structures of meaning and, through this repetition, simultaneously shifts, alters, and resignifies. According to Brinkmann, at the end of the 1960s, a "general style" emerged from this procedure, for which, as he writes in 1968, "the term 'POP' is only valid for the time being." It is about a "sensibility that refuses to accept cheap, intellectual alternatives for creative products of every kind of art—writing, painting, filmmaking, playing music."[35] Replacing those established cultural dichotomies, which Brinkmann calls "cheap, intellectual alternatives," is a "mixture of various fields and categories,"[36] which avoids categorization: "the new products don't allow themselves to be annexed to what already exists. . . . they have left behind the old categories of understanding."[37]

Like many other writers and theorists at the end of the 1960s,[38] Brinkmann is repeatedly involved in "*dismantling the cultural definitions of* 'author' and 'reader,'" in "dissolving the strict definition of the *work*" and "of a unified style."[39] The dissolution of the "existing systems of reference and interpretation,"[40] which Brinkmann not only demanded but also pursued, corresponded to the "dissolution of hitherto accepted rigid divisions of genre," which have to be "seen in the context of the dissolution of inflexible roles of sexual behavior." Brinkmann writes that the structures of existing *Gattungen* (genres, gender, or genus) must be "taken apart and rearranged," so that "the clichéd roles of sexual behavior" can no longer have an effect. "And it is precisely the degree to which things are taken apart and rearranged that also changes the good old question about the 'meaning' of a poem, a novel, etc."[41] Therefore, as Brinkmann writes, matters have gone beyond the topic of whether it's "a joke when someone asks if Shakespeare was a woman."[42] New literature is concerned with producing an "order, which can no longer understand itself in the traditional patterns of expression"; it's about mixtures, in which "the entire text becomes a stream of voices flowing into each other—voices that cannot be clearly distinguished according to their gender."[43]

It is not only the process of distinguishing genre and gender but also the strict division of thinking in terms of national poetry and national poets that is, for Brinkmann, one of the "categories of understanding" undermined by the new American scene. At the end of the 1960s, in the pop as well as the student movement, Brinkmann noted what he called a "unified sensibility," a "global sensitivity" in place of the "isolation, which began with the molding of a literature bound to a particular language and nation."[44] One of Brinkmann's examples for this development has to do with the problem that is nowadays once again a topic in the debate about the protection of the German language.[45] Brinkmann writes: "Take all of the Americanisms that were in the German language in 1955 and compare them with the Americanisms in the language today, in 1968. Today's share will be incomparably higher." Even though Brinkmann leaves the question open, the consequences he sees are significantly different from those seen by the language defenders of today. "Nowadays, we can deal with 'American' material and the signals it contains more confidently than we did ten years ago. The question is, can there still be rigid national divisions?"[46] However, the reason for Brinkmann's insistence upon pursuing this question is based not just in the writing methods of the American role models. Their attitude comes close to Brinkmann's disposition, which he still emphasized in the mid-1970s, a few years after his pop phase: "Again and again, it did me good to forget my own origins. I've felt this freedom physically every time, as soon as I left the border—which was at the same time the ordained border of language and comprehension."[47] In the poem "Westwärts, Teil 2," Brinkmann describes another way to leave behind the systems of order and categories of understanding. Being distant to what is supposed to be one's own language opens up space to play—and this space can be expanded even further by the confrontation with a foreign language. "It's good that I don't understand everything when I'm in Italian surroundings"[48]—that was Brinkmann's comment on his decision not to learn Italian during his sojourn in Rome at the beginning of the 1970s. And on his stay in the United States, described in *Westwärts,* he says: "the less I understood the language, the clearer the things at hand became in my consciousness."[49] A few lines later, in his description of his return to the borders of his own language, Brinkmann countered the possibilities (and not just the linguistic ones) opened up by the double distance from his own and the foreign language: "'Einsteigen bitte! 1 Befehlston / in deutsch. War das einmal / meine Sprache? Das ist noch nie / meine Sprache gewesen! Die / Sprache hat immer anderen gehört."[50]

As Hans-Thies Lehmann writes, Brinkmann's texts escape "monolingualism, the linguistic determination" through "polylingualism."[51] This polylingualism can be regarded as a consequence of the dissolution of national boundaries, as are his various experiments with translations. While translating Frank O'Hara's poetry, Brinkmann rather cautiously attempts to keep the syntax, form, and rhythm of the American, and in his own poems he radicalized the process of interlinear translation in a peculiar way: "Roll über, Beethoven! Die Jungen / sind richtig gewesen. Sie haben Kilo / Meterweit gesehen."[52] In this poem, Brinkmann lines up titles from the pop music canon next to each other: "Roll Over Beethoven" (Chuck Berry), "The Kids Are Alright" (The Who), and "I Can See for Miles" (The Who). As in the case of "und wie fällt man in / die Liebe,"[53] this interlinear translation seems to be incorrect, at least according to conventional standards. Yet it is actually the starting point for a new tone, for new styles and writing procedures, which are hallmarks of Brinkmann's poetry, even when he is not directly, obviously translating. Repeatedly, Brinkmann uses or invents words that sop up foreign as well as German particles and phonetic structures but do not belong entirely to one language or the other.

The so-called surface translations produce similar effects. Brinkmann strewed these throughout his texts or used them as a writing strategy in his collaborations with Ralf Rainer Rygulla. They can be understood not only as another consequence of crossing the language borders but also in other ways, as transposition or translation of inspirations from American literature. Inspired "by a writing method especially popular in the New York poetry scene," the poem "Der joviale Russe," for instance, was an "incorrect" translation of Apollinaire's "La jolie russe." It was the attempt to convey the "surface understanding" of a poem a moment after reading it, "without knowing the foreign language (in this case, French)."[54] Brinkmann used a similar method with comparable effects in his poem "Fragment zu einigen populären Songs." In a letter, Brinkmann explained the lines "Wer reitet auf / der Schnecke?"[55] this way: "'Who rides on the snail': a totally incorrect translation of a line from a Doors' song called 'The End,' which says: ride this lane. But from the way it sounds, it could also be 'ride this snake.' Transposed via a surface translation into the German language, just using the sound, that is, the sound of a word, the word changes from snake to snail [*Schnecke*] (after all, we aren't very familiar with snakes here any more)."[56]

In another kind of translation, one he refers to in *Rom, Blicke* by (mis)quoting a phrase taken from Alfred Korzybski, this method of mixing languages appears to be part of Brinkmann's reading program at the same time: "In case of Misunderständig, read on! (Korzybski)."[57] This reading program is not only a plea for productive misunderstandings but also a method of writing that lastingly marks Brinkmann's poetology. Neither his attention to ordinary things nor his ceaseless emphasis on directness and simplicity should lead to the impression that the texts are also easy to understand. Turning the "existing categories of understanding" into an issue can easily produce false conclusions, as Brinkmann shows in the "Notiz" to *Die Piloten:* "The people to whom I show my things often say that they're actually not poems any more. . . . They say everything's easy, you can understand it, and that, in turn, makes my poems incomprehensible to them."[58] Despite his polemic opposition to the equalization of poetry and obscurity, which was canonized in the 1950s and early 1960s,[59] Brinkmann doesn't simply sign up with the other side, doesn't wager without further ado on accessibility and simple comprehensibility. In Brinkmann's texts, there is more of that characteristic of pop art that, in the 1960s, art theorist Max Imdahl called the "dismantling of the self-evident"—"Entselbstverständlichung des Selbstverständlichen."[60] Just as supposedly obvious things suddenly can seem incomprehensible when removed from their "musty context" and deprived of "the usual interpretations,"[61] so can mass compatibility and hermetics, comprehensibility and incomprehensibility, make direct contact with each other or collapse into each other. "*When a disturbance appears* on the scene, it is possible for a moment to see through what is familiar and therefore what has not been transparent for a long time."[62] When Brinkmann writes, "This disturbance *is* the American poem,"[63] he refers to the methods of mixing genres, categories, and languages in American poetry as well as to those perturbations that first arise from his perspective, that is, out of his confrontation with a foreign language. The emphasis on the aspect of disturbance underscores that the concern here is not to replace obscurity with clarity in the name of directness and simplicity. Even in Brinkmann's own texts, the opposite seems to be the case. In the process of writing, even the most familiar things are removed for moments from the "existing categories of understanding": "the surroundings / become, as I look up, look around, / incomprehensible."[64] In reverting to American role models, Brinkmann replaces hermetics not with undisguised clarity or another phantasma of comprehensibility, but instead by disturbingly deleting the opposition between comprehensibility and incomprehensibility. "The question of meaning is superfluous—the narrative is simply 'there.' It is its own argument," writes Brinkmann about a story by Ron Padgett.[65] Brinkmann's goal is to eliminate the predominant category of hermeneutic-oriented understanding, a logic fixated on sense and meaning. Just as Padgett's story makes the question of meaning irrelevant for Brinkmann, in his own writing he tries to distance himself from an attitude that always requires and forces comprehensibility: "it would be great if you didn't understand it. That also goes for the attempt to understand a poem."[66] Brinkmann does not take so much a position against comprehension as he questions its premises: "Why do you want to understand poetry? Why do you want to understand? Doesn't that mean the triumph of the belief in a compulsory order?"[67]

Overall correlations of meaning do not appear to be unavoidable standards for orientation but are a totalitarian system of order that artificially, compulsively makes a scheme out of what is "*simply just there.*"[68] Brinkmann questions the assumption that contexts can comprehensively and sensibly be established by understanding. "Comprehension in general is a very snappy thing! What gets cut off there?"[69] Comprehension does not appear to provide the possibility of restoring a lost fullness of sense. Instead, it is assumed that comprehension is dominated by logical editing and cutting, which determine daily perception—"after all, gazes are constantly producing cut-ups!"[70]—as well as Brinkmann's ways of writing. Even if a phantasma of sensory totality permeates Brinkmann's texts, he defends himself against every attempt to completely grasp reality and language. From this perspective, Brinkmann develops the demand that poets should write in protest against the formulations of "those who believe, madly enough, that they have totally understood the terms and the language."[71] With this, he also opposes an attitude that desires clarity without any residue: "How I hate the apparent clarity of language, and how I like things to line up, as they are right here,"[72] he writes in a text in which he has—"right here"—directly lined up quotations from lyrics, song titles, descriptions of everyday life, biographical details, and poetological thoughts, without any hierarchical order. In this case, too, genres, styles, and language levels are intertwined; here, too, that "mixture" takes place, which leaves behind the "existing categories of understanding." Precisely because of the apparent self-evidence of the objects, this form of writing differentiates itself from an environment where everything has always already been and is always already supposed to be understood. "Why quotations? Because I don't understand them! Why a poem? Because after writing it, I don't understand it any more."[73] This "dismantling of the self-evident" is seen again in Brinkmann's desire to dissolve the words from their functional contexts and thus to protect them from "clear, univocal interpretation."[74]

"I'd like to use words that / can't be used, I thought. I'd like to speak to those, whom I / love, / . . . I like simply / just simply to be without explanation."[75]

Although there are many similarities between Brinkmann's texts and Diederichsen's or Meinecke's, this quote also shows the equally clear (and not solely historical) differences that separate their texts. Both Diederichsen and Meinecke, I guess, would seldom like to be "without explanation." At least both are far from joining in with Brinkmann's furor against abstraction and theory. But these differences should not overshadow potential similarities. Diederichsen's and Meinecke's concepts of "mixture" and their way of dealing with "misunderstandings" and "ambivalences" can be read as references to Brinkmann as well as to their approach to American pop culture. Diederichsen writes that Brinkmann had, "on a literary level, given the injection of North American culture that made life in the FRG tolerable (and because of this double foreignness, he made more of this American culture than they did in the USA)."[76] In this sense, Diederichsen describes Brinkmann as one of those authors for whom "the German language was also a means to escape from themselves" and who accordingly "created a German literature that was on the run from the German and the Germans."[77]

The question of how "American" German pop culture is will not be answered this way. Rather, because of this double foreignness, Brinkmann's methods of writing open up the possibility of discussing the relationship in other ways. Because Brinkmann understood "pop" to be a form of translation with a difference, a method of "reproduction that qualitatively alters the copied object,"[78] he undermines the possibility of clearly differentiating between "German" and "American." From a position of cultural pessimism, one could attempt to denounce this kind of mixture as a symptom of "Americanization." But one could just as well view it as part of an equally esthetic and political project, whose aim is to dissolve assigned identities, conventional categories of understanding, and outdated language barriers—and thus to produce a constellation in which the question posed in the title of the present volume can no longer be answered: German pop culture: how "American" is it? On the other hand, this title could be regarded as a possible answer. If we take the quotation marks around the word "American" seriously, then the "America" we talk about is already a quotation—or, in Brinkmann's words, a "reproduction that qualitatively alters the copied object." What I have tried to show here is that, at least from the perspectives of Brinkmann, Diederichsen, and Meinecke, we should add quotation marks to the word "German" as well.

Translated by Allison Plath-Moseley

NOTES

1. Diedrich Diederichsen, "Wort Auf!" *Spex* 9 (1988): 34: "Als mein Bruder und ich im Alter von 4 bzw. 6 Jahren anfingen, uns Sonntag für Sonntag vorm Radio einzufinden, um wie eine Offenbarung die Hitparade entgegenzunehmen, konnten wir natürlich kein einziges Wort der Beatles verstehen. Dennoch mußten wir die Titel bezeichnen, mußten unsere Lippen und Gaumen zu irgendwas formen, wenn wir die Songs sangen. So entstand ein Englisch, das keinerlei Bedeutung hatte, bzw. das aus wenigen bedeutenden, man lernt ja ziemlich schnell in dem Alter, und vielen nicht-bedeutenden Wörtern bestand. Als wir Englisch irgendwann auch als ganz normale Fremdsprache lernten, war das schon nicht mehr wegzukriegen, wir konnten bereits ein Englisch, das sich mit diesem zweiten niemals decken würde. Ich konnte irgendwann einen Dylan-Song übersetzen, aber ich konnte ihn immer schon vorher auswendig und mich an den sprachlichen Effekten freuen, diese zusätzlich mit Halbwissen, paranoischer Interpretation und Begehren . . . aufladen." (All translations are by Allison Plath-Moseley; in case of longer quotations and significant phrases, the original German will be added in the footnote.)

2. Ibid.

3. Ibid.

4. Ibid.

5. Andreas Neumeister, "Pop als Wille und Vorstellung," in *Sound Signatures: Pop-Splitter,* ed. Jochen Bonz (Frankfurt am Main: Suhrkamp, 2001), here 20: "Englisch gelernt, um T.Rex im Original hören zu können."

6. The 39 Clocks, *Pain It Dark* (Hannover: No Fun Records, 1981).

7. Thomas Meinecke, "Alles Mist," *Spiegel Spezial* 2 (1994): 83: "transatlantisch fehlinterpretierte Amerikanismen."

8. See Freiwillige Selbstkontrolle, *American Sector* (York: Ediesta Records, 1987); *FSK in Dixieland* (Hamburg: ZickZack, 1987); *Original Gasman Band* (Hamburg: ZickZack, 1989).

9. Meinecke, "Alles Mist," 83: "Nicht unsere Identität finden wir in den muttersprachlichen Texten, sondern unsere Abweichung, nicht ihrer Verständlichkeit, sondern der konstruktiven Reibung am Formalen halber schreiben wir Songtexte auf deutsch."

10. Diederichsen: "Wort Auf!" 34.

11. Meinecke, "Alles Mist," 83.

12. Diedrich Diederichsen, *Freiheit macht arm: Das Leben nach Rock'n'Roll, 1990–93* (Cologne: Kiepenheuer und Witsch, 1993), 89–90.

13. In *Black American English,* a glossary for German students of English, one reads: *"word or word up*—affirmative response: 'Really!' 'Right!' 'I'm telling you!' /—response asking confirmation: 'Really?' 'Is that right?'" Ed. Herbert Graf et al. (Straelen: Straelener Manuskripte, 1994), 165.

14. Diederichsen, *Freiheit macht arm,* 62: "fruchtbare Mißverständnisse."

15. See Judith Butler, *Gender Trouble: Feminism and the Subversion of Identity* (New York and London: Routledge, 1990); Henry Louis Gates Jr., *The Signifying Monkey: A Theory of African-American Literary Criticism* (New York and Oxford: Oxford University Press, 1988).

16. For further references, see my essay "'Re-make/Re-model'—Zitat und Per-formativität im Pop-Diskurs," in *Zitier-Fähigkeit,* ed. Andrea Gutenberg and Ralph Poole (Berlin: Erich Schmidt, 2001), 271–91.

17. See, for example, Heiner Link, ed., *Trash-Piloten: Texte für die 90er* (Leipzig: Reclam, 1997); Johannes Ullmaier, *Von Acid nach Adlon und zurück: Eine Reise durch die deutschsprachige Popliteratur* (Mainz: Ventil, 2001).

18. Rolf Dieter Brinkmann, "Notizen 1969 zu amerikanischen Gedichten und zu der Anthologie 'Silverscreen'," *Der Film in Worten* (Reinbek: Rowohlt, 1982), 262–63: "Mißverständnisse sind keine, sondern erweitern das Verständnis einer Sache, die 'falsch' verstanden worden ist—es sind gesteuerte Abweichungen, ein Durchschlagen gängiger Assoziationen (wie schön irre ist es zu lesen: 'Über allen Gipfeln zieht es!')."

19. Rolf Dieter Brinkmann and Ralf-Rainer Rygulla, eds., *ACID: Neue amerikanische Szene* (Frankfurt am Main: März, 1969); Rolf Dieter Brinkmann, ed., *Silver Screen: Neue amerikanische Lyrik* (Cologne: Kiepenheuer und Witsch, 1969).

20. Frank O'Hara, *Lunch Poems und andere Gedichte,* ed. Rolf Dieter Brinkmann (Cologne: Kiepenheuer und Witsch, 1969).

21. See Gunter Geduldig and Marco Sagurna, "'Es genügten ihm seine Empfindungen der Welt gegenüber': Ein Gespräch mit Ralf-Rainer Rygulla," in *too much: Das lange Leben des Rolf Dieter Brinkmann,* ed. Geduldig and Sagurna (Aachen: Alano, 1994), 99.

22. Agnes C. Mueller, *Lyrik "made in USA": Vermittlung und Rezeption in der Bundesrepublik* (Amsterdam and Atlanta: Rodopi, 1999), 138.

23. Rolf Dieter Brinkmann, *Standphotos: Gedichte, 1962–1970* (Reinbek: Rowohlt, 1980), 185: "jetzt halten sie die Kulturellen Wörter besetzt . . . , lebende Tote."

24. See Hans Magnus Enzensberger, "Gemeinplätze, die Neueste Literatur betreffend," *Kursbuch* 15 (November 1968): 187–97; and Mueller, *Lyrik "made in USA,"* 129–31.

25. Rolf Dieter Brinkmann, "Der Film in Worten," in *Der Film in Worten* (Reinbek: Rowohlt, 1982), 223: "Das Rückkopplungssystem der Wörter, das in gewohnten grammatikalischen Ordnungen wirksam ist, entspricht längst nicht mehr tagtäglich zu machender sinnlicher Erfahrung."

26. Rolf Dieter Brinkmann, "Die Lyrik Frank O'Haras," in *Der Film in Worten* (Reinbek: Rowohlt, 1982), 211, 213: "daß für Literatur die einzig reale Zeit die Gegenwart sei."

27. Brinkmann, "Der Film in Worten," 224: "keine alteingenisteten, verinnerlichten Muster, keine heimeligen, liebgewonnenen Vorurteile zu verlieren, wenn sie sich auf Gegenwart einläßt."

28. Rolf Dieter Brinkmann, *Die Piloten* (Cologne: Kiepenheuer und Witsch, 1968), rpt. in Brickmann, *Standphotos*.

29. Brinkmann, "Die Lyrik Frank O'Haras," 213.

30. Karl Heinz Bohrer, "Was alles fraglich ist: Rolf Dieter Brinkmanns erster Gedichtband," *Frankfurter Allgemeine Zeitung,* November 11, 1967.

31. Brinkmann, "Die Lyrik Frank O'Haras," 215: "Das überraschende Moment liegt in der ungewohnten Zusammenstellung der Details, die trotzdem nicht jeden Bezug zur Realität verloren haben, wie es die Konvention des Avantgardistischen will, andererseits sich aber auch nicht der Realität ausliefert oder ausgleitet in muffige Innerlichkeit."

32. Brinkmann, "Der Film in Worten," 231: "mit Vorhandenem etwas anderes als das Intendierte zu machen . . . sich auszubreiten, zu verstreuen—vorhandene Assoziationsmuster zu durchbrechen."

33. Ibid., 231, 228: "ein Stückchen befreite Realität."

34. Brinkmann, "Notizen 1969," 265: "Aus mehreren vorhandenen, ausgeschriebenen Texten (Gedichten) einen zu machen, alte Gedichte 'aufzumöbeln' . . . das eigene Gedicht ergibt sich überraschend aus dem Zusammenführen mehrerer fremder Texte, aus *Oberflächenübersetzungen* etc.: die Möglichkeit des eigenen Ausdrucks liegt im Arrangement der Fertigteile, sobald die psychische Dimension dessen, der das macht, darin enthalten ist! Diese Vorgänge *entleeren* den vorgegebenen und längst als 'natürlich' hingenommenen Bedeutungsgehalt, der unfrei macht und den Einzelnen nur von sich wegführt. Darüber hinaus wirkt sich in solchen Methoden konkret das Bewußtsein aus, im *Zeitalter der Ablichtungen* (Xerox) zu leben, der unbegrenzten Vervielfältigungsmöglichkeit, die den abgelichteten Gegenstand qualitativ verändert."

35. Rolf Dieter Brinkmann, "Angriff aufs Monopol. Ich hasse alte Dichter," in *Roman oder Leben: Postmoderne in der deutschen Literatur,* ed. Uwe Wittstock (Leipzig: Kiepenheuer, 1994), 71: "jene Sensibilität, die den schöpferischen Produkten jeder Kunstart—Schreiben, Malen, Filmen, Musikmachen—die billigen gedanklichen Alternativen verweigert." Brinkmann's connection to American pop art is analyzed by Gerd Gemünden, "The Depth of the Surface, or, What Rolf Dieter Brinkmann Learned from Andy Warhol," *German Quarterly* 68 (1995): 235–50.

36. Brinkmann, "Der Film in Worten," 228, 232.

37. Ibid., 228: "die neuen Produkte lassen sich nicht mehr ohne weiteres dem Bestehenden zuschlagen . . . —sie haben die bestehenden Verständniskategorien hinter sich gelassen."

38. See, for example, Roland Barthes, "The Death of the Author," in *Image, Music, Text,* trans. Stephen Heath (New York: Hill and Wang, 1977), 142–48; and Michel Foucault, "What Is an Author?" In *Textual Strategies: Perspectives in Poststructuralist Criticism,* ed. Josué Harari (Ithaca: Cornell University Press, 1979), 141–60.

39. Brinkmann, "Notizen 1969," 255, 257: "*Abbau der kulturellen Definition*

'Autor' und 'Leser'," "Auflösung des strengen *Werk*-Begriffs," "Auflösung eines einheitlichen Stils."

40. Ibid., 253: "die vorgegebenen Bezugs- und Interpretationssysteme."

41. Brinkmann, "Der Film in Worten," 241–42: "von einem Autor zerlegt und neu arrangiert werden muß, so daß das Klischee sexuellen Rollenverhaltens . . . sich nicht mehr auswirken kann—und genau das, der Grad des Zerlegens und Arrangierens, verändert auch die alte, hübsche Frage nach dem 'Sinn' eines Gedichts, Romans etc."

42. Ibid., 241: "ist es eben kein Witz, wenn gefragt wird: War Shakespeare eine Frau?"

43. Ibid., 243–44: "Ordnung, die in tradierten Ausdrucksmustern sich nicht mehr verstehen kann . . . so daß der Gesamttext zu dem Ineinandergerinnen von Stimmen wird, die sich nicht in ihrer Geschlechtszugehörigkeit eindeutig herausheben lassen."

44. Brinkmann, "Notizen 1969," 250: "Isolation, die mit der Ausprägung einer an eine bestimmte Sprache und Nation gebundenen Literatur begonnen hat."

45. See, for example, Eckart Werthebach, "Die deutsche Sprache braucht gesetzlichen Schutz," *Berliner Morgenpost,* December 31, 2000; Ulrich Noller, "'Man muss das Deutsche stark machen': Interview mit Georg Klein," *die tageszeitung,* March 22, 2001; Jens Jessen, "Schicksal Denglisch: Gegen Hegemonie hilft kein Sprachgesetz," *Die Zeit,* March 8, 2001.

46. Brinkmann, "Angriff aufs Monopol," 72: "Man nehme einmal nur die Amerikanismen in der deutschen Sprache im Jahr 1955 zusammen und vergleiche sie mit den Amerikanismen, die heute, 1968, aufgefunden werden können. Der heutige Anteil wird ungleich höher sein. . . . Man geht mit 'amerikanischem' Material und den darin eingelagerten Signalen heute selbstverständlicher um als noch vor zehn Jahren. Die Frage ist, ob es noch starre nationale Einteilungen geben kann?"

47. Rolf Dieter Brinkmann, "Westwärts, Teil 2," *Westwärts 1 & 2: Gedichte* (Reinbek: Rowohlt, 1974), 52: "Gut tat, immer von neuem die eigene Herkunft zu vergessen. Diese Freiheit habe ich jedesmal körperlich gespürt, sobald ich die Grenze, die zugleich die Grenze der Sprache und des Verständnisses war, das verordnet wurde, verließ."

48. Rolf Dieter Brinkmann, *Rom, Blicke* (Reinbek: Rowohlt, 1979), 193: "Sehr gut ist, daß ich nicht alles in der italienischen Umgebung verstehe."

49. Brinkmann, "Westwärts, Teil 2," 52: "je weniger ich in der Sprache verstanden habe, desto klarer sind mir die vorhandenen Dinge in das Bewußtsein getreten."

50. Ibid., 53 (in English): "'All aboard, please!' 1 peremptory tone / in German. Was that once / my language? That was never / my language! This / language has always belonged to others."

51. See Hans-Thies Lehmann, "SCHRIFT / BILD / SCHNITT: Graphismus und die Erkundung der Sprachgrenzen bei Rolf Dieter Brinkmann," in *Rolf Dieter Brinkmann: Literaturmagazin Sonderheft 36,* ed. Maleen Brinkmann (Reinbek: Rowohlt, 1995), 196.

52. Brinkmann, "Im Voyageurs Apt. 311 East 31st Street, Austin," *Westwärts 1 & 2,* 76.

53. Brinkmann, "Westwärts," 42; since there is no exact German equivalent for the idiomatic expression "to fall in love," Brinkmann's "und wie fällt man in / die Liebe" sounds as strange as FSK's "Wenn Du einmal in Liebe fällst." See FSK, "Venus im Pelz # 2," *Goes Underground* (Hamburg: ZickZack, 1984).

54. Ralf Rainer Rygulla and Rolf Dieter Brinkmann, "Der joviale Russe," in *Mammut: März Texte 1 & 2, 1969–1984,* ed. Jörg Schröder (Herbstein: März, 1984), 304: "ohne Kenntnis der Fremdsprache (in diesem Fall des Französischen) ein Gedicht zu übertragen nach dem im Augenblick des Lesens sich einstellenden *Oberflächenverständnis.*"

55. Rolf Dieter Brinkmann, "Fragment zu einigen populären Songs," *Literaturmagazin* 2 (1975): 116.

56. Rolf Dieter Brinkmann, *Briefe an Hartmut, 1974–1975* (Reinbek: Rowohlt, 1999), 198: "Wer reitet auf der Schnecke: eine total falsch übersetzte Zeile aus einem Doors-Song, Titel The End, wo es heißt: ride this lane, aber vom oberflächlichen Gehör her könnte das auch heißen, ride this snake—und weiter oberflächlich umgesetzt in die deutsche Sprache, und zwar nur über den Klang, also vom Laut eines Wortes her, geht die Übertragung von snake zuerst zu Schnecke (Schlangen kennt man ja hier kaum noch)."

57. Brinkmann, *Rom, Blicke,* 199 (deliberately misspelled English/German!); in a letter to Harmut Schnell, Brinkmann drops another quotation from Korzybski: "when in perplexity, read on" (Brinkmann, *Briefe an Hartmut,* 142). Presumably, Brinkmann here refers to Alfred Korzybski, *Science and Sanity: An Introduction to Non-Aristotelian Systems and General Semantics,* 4th ed. (1933; reprint, Lakeville, CT: International Non-Aristotelian Library Publishing, 1958), xxv.

58. Brinkmann, *Standphotos,* 186: "Häufig höre ich von Leuten, denen ich meine Sachen zeige, daß dies nun eigentlich keine Gedichte mehr seien. . . . Sie sagen, das hier sei ja alles einfach, man könne es ja verstehen, und das wiederum macht ihnen meine Gedichte unverständlich."

59. See my chapter, "The Wake of Modernism: Paradigmen der Unverständlichkeit," in *Die Ironie der Unverständlichkeit: Johann Georg Hamann, Friedrich Schlegel, Jacques Derrida, Paul de Man* (Frankfurt am Main: Suhrkamp, 2000), 57–81.

60. Max Imdahl, "'Op', 'Pop' oder die immer zu Ende gehende Geschichte der Kunst," in *Die nicht mehr schönen Künste: Grenzphänomene des Ästhetischen* [= Poetik und Hermeneutik 3], ed. Hans Robert Jauß (Munich: Fink, 1968), 697.

61. Brinkmann, "Notizen 1969," 251.

62. Ibid., 258: "Für einen Augenblick wird durchschaubar, was vertraut und daher längst nicht mehr durchschaubar ist, *wenn Irritation eintritt.*"

63. Ibid.: "Diese Irritation *ist* das amerikanische Gedicht."

64. Brinkmann, "Rolltreppen im August," *Westwärts 1 & 2,* 71: "die Umgebung / wird, als ich aufblicke, um mich schaue, / unverständlich."

65. Brinkmann, "Der Film in Worten," 236: "Die Frage nach der Bedeutung erübrigt sich—die Erzählung ist einfach 'da', sie ist ihr eigenes Argument."

66. Rolf Dieter Brinkmann, "Ein unkontrolliertes Nachwort zu meinen Gedichten," *Literaturmagazin* 5 (1976): 232: "am besten ist, du verstehst das nicht.' Das gilt auch für die Versuche, ein Gedicht zu verstehen."

67. Ibid., 244: "Warum wollen Sie Dichtung verstehen? Warum wollen Sie verstehen? Schlägt da nicht ein Glaube durch, daß eine verbindliche Ordnung besteht?"

68. Brinkmann, "Notizen 1969," 248: *einfach nur da.*"

69. Brinkmann, *Rom, Blicke,* 193: "Überhaupt ist das Verstehen eine sehr schnittige Sache! Was wird da abgeschnitten?"

70. Ibid., 93: "die Blicke machen ja ständig cut ups!"

71. Brinkmann, "Ein unkontrolliertes Nachwort," 246: "denen, die glauben, wahnhaft, sie hätten die Formulierungen und die Sprache restlos begriffen."

72. Ibid., 247: "Wie hasse ich die scheinbare Klarheit der Sprache, und ich mag das Nebeneinander wie hier, an dieser Stelle."

73. Rolf Dieter Brinkmann, "Anmerkungen zu meinem Gedicht 'Vanille'," in *Mammut: März Texte 1 & 2,* 144: "Warum Zitate? Weil ich sie nicht verstehe! Warum ein Gedicht? Weil ich es nach dem Schreiben nicht mehr verstehe."

74. Brinkmann, "Der Film in Worten," 239.

75. Brinkmann, "Westwärts, Teil 2," 50: "Ich möchte Wörter benutzen, die / nicht zu benutzen sind, dachte ich. Ich möchte sprechen zu denen, die ich / liebe, / . . . ich möchte einfach / nur einfach nur ohne Erklärung sein."

76. Diederichsen, *Freiheit macht arm,* 151: "auf literarischer Ebene die Spritze nordamerikanische Kultur injiziert, die das Leben in der BRD erträglich gemacht hat (und teilweise aus amerikanischer Kultur wegen doppelter Fremdheit mehr machte als die USA)."

77. Ibid.: "für die die deutsche Sprache auch ein Mittel war, ihr selbst zu entkommen . . . und die entsprechend eine deutsche Literatur auf der Flucht vor dem und den Deutschen entwarfen."

78. Brinkmann, "Notizen 1969," 265: "Vervielfältigungsmöglichkeit, die den . . . Gegenstand qualitativ verändert."

Part III

German Writers Today:
Literature in the Age of Pop

The American Dead End of German Literature

Matthias Politycki

After his best-selling Weiberroman *(1997), the fictional record of a male protagonist's views on gender issues in Germany's 1970 and 1980s, Matthias Politycki entered the debate on contemporary German literature by staking out new territory for the '78ers generation (as opposed to that of the '68ers). Politycki's essays echo his generation's call for a new aesthetics in German literature, one that neither sells out to the "trivial" best-seller narratives influenced by (American) creative writing schools nor remains aloof from its contemporary German readership. Instead, German literature needs to find its own voice by inventing both a language and a narrative technique that is entertaining, yet sophisticated. A trained "Germanist," Politycki is often attacked for his polemics against the current literary scene, which also target high-profile critics and publishing houses. His similarly controversial position on the "Americanization" of German language and literature should be read within the context of his call for a new European aesthetics.*

Is it not doing well, the most recent German literature, now that we don't even know how to keep up with all those trendy new movements (such as pop literature, the renaissance of the narrative, New German Readability, and the so-called *Frolleinwunder*)? Oh yes, German literature is finally doing well again, the only question is, how long will this last? Today's German literature faces immediate extinction, since there seems to be a lack of new themes and since its language, the German language, is becoming increasingly estranged from that which it is trying to depict, from "reality." We now lack vocabulary for significant portions of our lives, because we have become too complacent to invent new terminology and because we render our own vocabulary senselessly into Anglo-sized or Americanized idioms, whose rich, century-old meanings and connotations we cannot fully comprehend let alone use effectively. This is why we receive "reality" as a second-hand commodity, a commodity crafted by someone else, for someone else, while our own linguistic identity slowly begins its descent into oblivion.

Meanwhile, we are well beyond just assimilating a few words or expressions. It now has to be a full phrase or sentence—thereby slowly abolishing our grammatical structures, as well as, more importantly, the very core of our language, which determines the way we think and feel. Our self-manipulation has grown so sophisticated that, I submit, in most cases we are completely unaware of it.

One small example: "Das *macht* Sinn" swept over Germany like an epidemic a few years ago, as a direct translation of "it makes sense." Within months, the centuries-old "Das *hat* Sinn" was completely erad-icated. Is this a purely arbitrary process? Certainly not. "Es hat Sinn" carries the slight connotation of something positively "German." It *has* sense, all by itself, completely without our intervention, just as the idiomatic lamp in Mörike's poem: Whether or not we gaze at it, whether or not we imply any sense or meaning for it, it carries its mean-ing in itself, it rests within itself, perhaps it just *seems* to rest within itself, by just shining for itself—we'll never know for certain. In any case, there seems to be some deeper force at work, justifying the mean-ing of a thing or a process in itself. You may consider this an eccentric overinterpretation. But perhaps you'd like to take the opposite, the clear-cut, simple phrase "it makes sense," and ask yourself: Who is this person supposed to be, he or she who first has to make, or create, sense or meaning? Can it be us, who inspect a matter for as long as it takes us to logically dissect it into its individual units? What hypocrisy! And if it is not us, in any case someone or something has first to become active in order to create sense or meaning—some fateful "it"! Whoever or whatever "it" is that "makes" sense, we see here the full extent of the discrepancy between Anglo-American rationalism and German romanticism. I consider the functionalist-operative term of "making" sense completely lacking the modesty of "having" sense or meaning, and no matter how cool I'd like to be, something in me revolts.

The sum of those individual examples of linguistic deindividualiza-tion, however, constitutes a whole paradigm. And this is what I am concerned with, as someone who not only depends on the German lan-guage but also loves it. If this, my, our language loses its power to assimilate, it will expire, just as when Latin slowly dissolved—and something very beautiful emerged, that is, Italian. In our case, it'll be "Anglogerman-Newhighpidgin," which also means no less than the beginning of an "Anglogerman-Newhighpidgin" literature. However, the necessary by-product, the end of a German literature, seems less desirable to me, which has nothing to do with any kind of reactionary nationalism, quite the opposite. Let's not leave this highly problematic subject to those who could misuse it, let's instead claim it for ourselves!

But, of course, the problem never was a purely linguistic one. With the end of World War II, Europe (and, actually, most parts of the world, with the possible exception of Bhutan or Burundi) was recolonized by the United States, which at first was probably good and necessary. After a few decades of cultural imperialism, however, the face of Europe has changed radically. We now know this face of ours much less than ever before, whereas we know the American Midwest not only up to the last corner of its living room furniture but also down to the bottom of its bowls of popcorn, which are being consumed in those living rooms, while the living room of, let's say, a Finnish peasant is as foreign to us as the interior core of the individual popcorn. But who knows, perhaps there would be more to discover in the interior of a popcorn than in the entire popcorn bowl, and certainly more than in the Midwestern living room, where those popcorn bowls are being emptied by us and for us—the audience of TV soaps—exactly the same way, day in and day out. By now, we can even simulate a Midwestern living room scenario when we're at the movies, where we, eating popcorn, watch others in their Midwestern living rooms, eating popcorn, watching movies.

But the fact that we find ourselves at the beginning of the end of not only a German *speaking* but also a *German*-speaking culture seems well established by now. A certain Natan Sznaider even claimed recently in an article entitled "Amerika, Du hast es besser" (America, you're better off) that the United States had made certain after 1945 "that we all [and he means all Europeans] were able to become Americans"[1]—*were* able to, past tense! And since this seems to be a fait accompli for the sum of our culture, it certainly cannot be kept out of literature. Even as readers, as writers, and as novelists, we are in a constant process of self-"Americanization." In German bookstores, the creative-writing imports from the United States abound, and according to several influential critics at home, our German literature would do much better if only we'd learn to use those same proven techniques. But what if German literature is not incapable of learning, but rather just doesn't want to go down this road? To deliver an entertaining one-way novel where, after one quick read-through, nothing remains—is this the kind of literature worth writing for a non-American?

So they come across the Atlantic in their cream-colored suits, the

Tom Wolfes, usually not offering more than the forced facade of their dandy-like appearance, and in German feuilletons aren't even embarrassed to lecture us on European literature! But who the hell is Tom Wolfe? Certainly not someone whose writing I'd miss for one day, either as a reader (who likes to be skillfully entertained) or as a writer (who likes to learn about new techniques).

It's time to counteract this trend. U.S. literature by Wolfe, Boyle, Auster, etc., which for years now has dominated sales in Germany (and I am here not speaking of writers such as DeLillo, Gaddis, or Brodkey), is terribly boring in its calculated state of continued excitement. We already know all of these stories from TV soaps and the advertising industry, so why read them, since they have nothing to do with our lives? Because of their highly rated entertainment value? But entertainment is now available in German literature for the same price, and besides, as Martin Hielscher, editor of Kiepenheuer & Witsch, once remarked, "entertainment value is more a side effect of an interesting text; the real question is whether or not it can provide us with an actual experience."

No, literature in Germany is certainly not in any kind of danger, and I'm not concerned with the "world status" of any kind of German literature. Only individual authors reach world status, and on this level it really doesn't matter where they're from. But if the world is interested in them, it may actually be their regional origin that makes them so interesting, and this is what annoys me: Not only do we want to be the "better" Americans, but we also voluntarily give up our so-called national identities, not in order to foster an international synthesis of world culture, as some people claim, but in order to foster the worldwide imperialism of a U.S. monoculture.

Now, don't think of me as a proponent of some kind of either leftist or rightist anti-Americanism, but what seemed appropriate yesterday may be wrong today and, returning to German literature, may tomorrow be a death sentence. In the meantime, we are not only deciding on the concept of "Germanness," however that may be defined, we are also dealing with our identity as Europeans, as the entire "old world" turns into a pseudo–United States. We have begun to neglect each other, ceased to be interested in one another, to engage with each other, we have recently become ignorant of each other. Translations today usually favor mediocrity, texts written in an ordinary, easily digestible, and cheaply translatable style. From such books, no longer conceived in an original way, and thus no longer capable of conveying the unique world of an author, or of an entire culture, from such books we only learn what we already know. I am referring here to the absence of "learning" (in terms of an aesthetic experience), drastically interfering with a reader's curiosity about other, neighboring, cultures. Some publishers even go so far as to say that we now have a harder time understanding our immediate neighboring cultures than U.S. culture and thus more often than not decide against contracting a translation. Something fundamental seems to have been lost here, the idea that it is precisely the specific "otherness" of a book, even if it is difficult to translate, that makes it attractive and that inspires us to read in order to find out about something different from our own experience. Because of this confusion, the non-German speaking world today is under a gross misconception concerning contemporary German literature, the conception of some sort of Grass-Süskind-Schlink literature. And who knows what misconceptions our image of French literature may contain, not to mention Finnish literature. We probably only perceive those non-German texts that might as well be from the United States—I am here, of course, speaking in general terms only—and wouldn't it be important to counteract those trends with a new pride as Europeans? Otherwise, we may soon be not only at the end of a German literature but rather at the end of *any* non-U.S.-type literature.

My counterproposal envisions a European aesthetics, which imagines itself on equal footing with that of the United States. Once we have reached the era of postnational literatures, our aesthetic judgment based on contemporary German literature will at any rate no longer be sufficient, and we won't have a choice except to go with a European vision. A European vision, however, that reaches beyond Cape Gibraltar and the Ural Mountains, since "European aesthetics" should not simply be equated with a new form of regionalism but is meant to serve as a new model. But if we continue to avoid the question of our own perspective, an attitude easily camouflaged as progressive liberalism, we German writers should at least be consistent and should engage *Faust II* using creative-writing techniques and then translate it into Anglogerman-Newhighpidgin, so that people will still be able to understand it. And we should, of course, always turn up in cream-colored suits, so people may still recognize us as writers.

So what could this be, what I'd call "European aesthetics" for lack of a better expression, though I am aware that it may sound single-mindedly? At any rate, it is not meant as a geographic category—I am thinking of Nabokov here as an example. And, of course, it cannot be about the introduction of a unifying normative aesthetics to foster European unification as a sum of all the specific national characteristics. It is rather about the opposite, about the discovery of deeply rooted "European" characteristics within all the national specifics. Why not start by looking at France, which has always proven productive for Germans! With this, we may just as well have reached the end of German literature, but I'd consider a fully "Europeanized" end to be far preferable to the impending partially Americanized end now quietly under way. Thus, what could we propose as cultural common denominators to combat the dominance of the creative-writing aesthetics? Here are a few suggestions.

1. Commitment to *detail* instead of an exclusive commitment to plot. Narrative strategies that are not just functional but are ends in themselves that do not require any particular reason—as, for example, with respect to the construction of the plot as a whole.

2. A feeling for *atmosphere* instead of maximizing the amount of information that is being mediated. An atmospheric concentration, not as a retarding element that impedes the narrative flow but as pleasure, a pleasure that adds to the narrative itself.

3. The art of the *nonnarrative* rather than always insisting on stories, stories, stories. Now that even the Germans have learned the American lesson, the nonnarrative should again be understood as an important part of the narrative, the seemingly purposeless beyond any kind of story line.

4. *Multiply coded texts* instead of just textual surface. The story line of a narrative may be sufficient for 90 percent of readers, but it can only be the surface of a "European" text. The other 10 percent are moved by the thing itself: the stimulation of allusions, the choice of metaphors, the use of aphorisms, the playful reconfiguration of established narrative structures, characters, scenes, motives, rhetorical figures, even individual words. In a European text, a long tradition is embedded, not as a burden or barrier for readers but as an additional pleasurable offering for those who know the rules of the game and feel inclined to participate.

5. *Indirect* fulfillment of expectations. To not immediately satisfy reader expectation is more interesting, more productively unsettling, and forms a more lasting impression. When someone buys a ticket for a buggy ride but in the end returns from a roller coaster ride, he will probably have had an important experience.

6. Mediation of an *experience* instead of pure entertainment, in order to deliver more subtle pleasures than just the suspense of a

good story. A book can transform its readers, a book can provide an experience of intense joy, well beyond its entertainment value. Of course, entertainment is a prerequisite to draw a reader in.

7. A *slow-paced* unfolding of the narrative rather than creating suspense from the very first line. If you invest in a broader scope at the outset, you can really speed up later on. A slow pace is also—contrary to assumptions—the opposite of boring or draining reading, whereas the hysterical and artificial creation of suspense (a dead body on the first page, then another one every thirty pages) is indeed uninteresting, since it's usually done much better in film.

8. An emphasis on *style,* instead of using words purely for their narrative function, a rhetorical structure that may also appear disturbing. Every book conceived using European aesthetics is by definition unique, whereas a product of a creative-writing school is always a copy of other success stories, a product of a compromise designed to draw in as many readers as possible. Perhaps we could agree that a certain amount of friction and initial obscurity is characteristic for European literature?

Obviously, such suggestions are not exactly met with enthusiasm these days. Eurocentrism in times of multiculturalism? In times of a weak euro dollar? In times of a general weariness of all things European fueled by the empty jargon of our so-called political leaders? Admittedly, the thought of a European aesthetics seems rather annoying, especially now that German publishers are, astonishingly enough, finally focusing on German literature again. But it is necessary, nevertheless. Till now, the eternal debates on the current state of German literature have barely managed to go beyond the prejudices linked to an outdated aesthetics mainly centered on the Gruppe 47. This housecleaning has been more than necessary. And now? We're more or less empty-handed, since current literary criticism has been reduced to judgments of taste. A new phase in the debate would be crucial, a phase in which new criteria are suggested.

Whoever wants to misunderstand me may do so. Yes, indeed, the buzzword of a "European aesthetics" is nothing but a cover name and meant to sound like really old hat, something that may already have existed in ancient Greece. This old hat seems to have gone out of fashion with all the craze about baseball caps (or tailored suits, but that is a different story, the story of those who say, "hi, I do pop literature," and will be told some other time). My entire appeal for a European narrative comes down to that which has always been expected of great literature—because we are about to abandon those expectations.

In the end, our choice is between a hostile or a friendly takeover, since German literature as we know it will no longer exist in the near future. We are thus living in a time that will soon come to an end. For those who do not just want to enjoy this end, for those who desire to retain some of what is about to expire for a new beginning, for those it may be worthwhile to think along the lines of a new European aesthetics.

Translated by Agnes C. Mueller

NOTES

"Der amerikanische Holzweg: Am Anfang vom Ende einer deutschsprachigen Literatur" first appeared in *Frankfurter Rundschau* 66 (March 18, 2000): ZB2. This is the first publication in English.

1. Natan Sznaider, "Amerika, Du hast es besser," *Süddeutsche Zeitung,* October 29, 1999.

Myself as Text (Extended Version)

Thomas Meinecke

Thomas Meinecke (b. 1955) lives and works in a small Bavarian village. He is the founding member of the band FSK (Freiwillige Selbstkontrolle), which has so far released twenty records, and he worked as a DJ for the major public radio station in Bavaria. His 1998 novel Tomboy, *a great success with critics and audiences alike, records the interconnectedness of pop music, critical theory, gender, and literary discourses. Both his music and his writings are committed to decoding verbal and nonverbal cultural signals that permeate contemporary life. Accordingly, his latest novel,* Hellblau (2001), *is concerned with the complexities of ethnic identities in a German-American setting, written from the perspective of a fictional "reader." For Meinecke, as for Warhol, "pop" brings the past into the present. Consequently, in Meinecke's intrinsically present-oriented texts, "pop" serves as a tool to transverse boundaries, not only connecting the United States and Germany but also Germany's "East" and "West."*

In 1987 I had a scholarship for the Literary Colloquium Berlin, which was in the western half of the former capital of the German Reich. Or is (more on that later). Most of the scholarship recipients were supposed to come from West Germany, the FRG. Our scholarships were part of an expanded cultural project meant to give artificial respiration to the ex-metropolis that had existed for a good forty years in a geographic as well as political shadow. Our assignment was to delve into this place's so-called state of emergency. Once back in our hometowns (as impressed as we could possibly be, of course), it was expected that we would print our testimonies in book form. A task that, after some initial inner struggle, I obediently carried out, since no other alternative requiring me to stay in Berlin occurred to me at the time. And actually, I'd always written about things I was currently involved with or surrounded by. Finally, my motto was and is "never make something up," never put yourself in a position where you have to invent something.

So I delivered a somewhat eccentric Berlin story titled "Wood," which actually appeared as a book in 1988, one year before the so-called reunification (of which there was not the slightest sign before 1987). Never one to defend Berlin, I wrote my text in a rather mannered style, remaining aloof from everything, as if I were writing a report about a remote situation many decades past. I wrote set phrases such as there was the wall. There was no-man's-land. We called the other part of Germany the GDR. And things like that. Everything in the simple past tense. This bothered my former editor; it was actually the only disagreement we had about my manuscript. I just couldn't express things that way, he remarked. Things that had to do with the plot might be allowed to disappear into this logical past, so to speak, but the wall could not. The two Germanies could not. Of course, I had no objections to the divided nation, and yet I insisted upon my reticent method, which circled in spirals around its subjects; and a very crucial part of that method was the use of the simple past for everything. And so I triumphed over the editor. Ultimately, the reviews tore the book apart for its first-person perspective. For instance, they said, this narrator "I" had not known how to use his half-year Berlin scholarship more sensibly than to try (stubbornly as well as unthankfully) to kill the mayor then in office, Mr. Diepgen. And furthermore, they said, German tax money, even in the form of a scholarship, is not meant for such things. Another mark of the fatal problem of literary reception: the simple-minded craving of bourgeois literary critics for so-called plots.

In 1989 the Berlin Wall fell for real, but in my book it did not say here is the wall. Here is the no-man's-land. We call the eastern part of Germany the GDR. At that moment, I belatedly regretted my stylistic decision; my editor, however, could breathe more easily, because now everything was finally correct. Just as it was in reality. The situation became even more piquant when "Wood" appeared once again, in paperback, with a 1999 publication date. The wall stood here. No-man's-land ran from here to there. And so on. In that year the government moved from Bonn to Berlin. Ten years after the GDR joined the FRG. This is something that the German public has grammatical trouble with, even today, for instance, when people say that Erich Honecker was the head of state of the former GDR. It now appeared to me that the reader might think that the grotesque reticence of my text, at least in some places, was the self-assurance of an author who is master of his material. But, even acknowledging the advantages of productive misunderstanding, I never wanted to be that kind of an author.

My publisher and I agreed that a note on the first page of the book should point out the original publication date. At any rate, I am writing my new novel in the present tense.

ACTUALLY, ALL OF my writing has been about the present. The reaction of my former editor ultimately reflects the expectations of many readers who assume that authors generally put their current level of knowledge on paper. However, to arrive at an agreement with a reader about a common present can also mean agreeing on a common past, which may include having enthusiastically listened to an ABC record in the pop music summer of 1982. Of course, this is not particularly productive. More on that later, too. At the same time, however, there cannot be an absolute "now" in a text. The moment I turn in my manuscript, it obviously becomes a yesterday, a little while ago, a moment ago. The electronic speed of new media, such as the Internet, merely hides this fact. Radio, on the other hand, clearly confronts our ears with the fleetingness of listening. On the radio, you can casually talk about "sending" a text. And as someone who has for a long time worked with this medium, the transmission into the ether, as well as the obvious temporariness of being on the air, have always been welcome to me. Paper, on the other hand, suggests patience, the longest possible stretch of time, immortality, eternity. None of that interests me. Paper leads to the biggest mess. And is thus naturally the most attractive challenge for writers. The fact that Rainald Goetz's Internet diary *Abfall für alle* not only functioned later as a book but also once again revealed all its greatness comforts me somewhat about that tiresome yet widespread crop of Internet literature, which, from the start, has wanted nothing more than to be printed as soon as possible—on sublime sheets of paper.

When a writer composes a "now," it should not be about a rather journalistic delusion of actuality. It should be more like the unattainable ideal of capturing a moment in time. The productive paradox of keeping a diary. About the lovely contradiction of an asymptomatic fixation, so to speak, which makes the beloved inadequacy of language constructive. And thus deconstructs language. Which is why literature obsessed with the "now," with its often uncompromising attitude, sound, and groove (let's call it pop literature for the next fifteen minutes)—even the kind that is reviled by the bourgeois camp with an almost desperate vehemence—occasionally stands out from most traditional narratives that seek remembrance and usually aim at reconciliation. If you're going to reminisce, then make it current. Write stories about the present. Write the history of the present. Which reflects upon the process of writing history. And immediately reveals its expiration date along with it.

Since the "now" is not an exact point in time, but one that marks the pitch, so to speak, of flexible, dynamic stretches of time, I can show this by way of two great writers who impressed me at a very early age— Henry Miller and Andy Warhol. The gist of Miller's writing was that he was constantly at the heels of his own death: each second of his life was like his last. Warhol, on the other hand, for whom every day was like the first day of the rest of his life, claimed to have no memories at all. Warhol, of course, said this as the greatest pop figure of all time. With his profound trust in repetition and monotony. And his revolutionary expansion of European dialectics, based on the past, deficit, and sorrow, by adding thoroughly euphoric, American tautologies, confronting us with the present, with totals, and with mere profit. Coming from Walt Whitman, the first great American enumerator, Warhol's aesthetic observations are completely nonironic appreciations of the surface. Having learned from him that the surface is the core. With his signed Brillo boxes, raising the copy to the status of the original, finally rendering the reference itself essential.

This way, pop really does bring the past into the present: through citation. Through sample. Whereby a sample also releases memory. I don't understand the techno-oriented theoretician's idealized notion, according to which there ought to be totally reference-free samples. Pop (to which, this time, I will add techno in order to separate them both from rock) cannot be pop when it is completely without references. For instance, the music by the grand Detroit-based techno group Drexciya, with its Afro-diasporic, submarine superstructure, is, of course, anything but free of references or apolitical. Even Andy Warhol, who, as is well known, made the citation the productive center of his art, continually attempted to get as close as possible to the nirvana of referencelessness without becoming completely abstract. Whereby even the abstract is, of course, an abstraction of something concrete. There are quasi-objectless Rorschach images by Warhol that, however, still allude to the psychology of the Rorschach test. There are pictures that, at first glance, seem to be abstract but actually contain the contours of Warhol's shadow. And there are the piss pictures, upon whose surfaces the artist's stream of urine has drawn lines that don't form to anything immediately recognizable but that suggest countless connotations as soon as you find out about the technique with which they were created. Even if you don't know that Warhol had already fixed many of his famous portraits with his own urine.

Techno means text. The instrumental teaches me how to write. It repoliticizes my consciousness. I can find my way to political reality through techno modulation. Rock, on the other hand, has no texture; it can't tell us anything right now. Apart from the great phallocentric subject. Rock doesn't want to do anything except ejaculate. Traditional narratives, before techno, before pop, often wanted that, too: they were built on washed-out bridges of tension, the climax, the plot on page 200. It's just too bad that ninety out of a hundred writers still work that way. And others, who, I wrongly believed, stood with me for twenty years in bohemian, strategic, and aesthetic solidarity against this type of work, also claim to have grown up, joined society, and immediately began to demand the heroic restoration of the autonomous subject, the strong individual (a reactionary development that can be compared only to Joschka Fischer's fatal maneuver). Recently seen on a poster in Berlin: the stage as dance floor. Much too early to permit the revival of the traditional author, a figure that has died a well-deserved death. There's no reason for this revival. As before, there is still great mistrust of the supposed genius and his so-called God-given talent.

I want to continue for the time being, probably forever, not writing about myself but away from myself. Around myself. Mark distance. The rest of everything that has been described, that which is left over, could then be called the subject, as far as I'm concerned. The place where it starts. As the rest, outside of my text. My prophylactic working hypothesis remains: the autonomous subject is gone. And with it, the author. Most of my contemporaries haven't even noticed it yet, anyway. Not to mention understood. No trace of that understanding in the collective consciousness of the hybrid subject, no common sense regarding the artificial construction of so-called identity. The progressive, political work under these conditions has just begun. Naturally, the deconstruction of the subject is a much more lengthy, troublesome project than its easy reinstatement as an ear-splitting, strident representative of well-known social constraints and collusions that actually can be overcome through deconstructive analysis.

Deconstruction is, for me, the same as deconstructive feminism, which pulverizes the location of language, the phallic center of power, takes it apart down to its smallest particle. I think it will be a long time before this work is done. Why should it be ended prematurely, then, in favor of an undead, essentialist chimera known as the autonomous subject? Whose political interest will then, ultimately, be served? Mine won't, at any rate. I think it is especially fatal that those who rave about the renewed introduction of the subject refer to the same objects of study as the deconstructivist Judith Butler. For instance, to transsexuals. There is no longer any talk of how they are victims of the dichotomy of hierarchical gender roles, how they symbolize this disparity, but instead they are glorified as strong, active individuals who were simply able to overcome socially assigned idiosyncrasies. This way the reactionary change of paradigms described previously can, very subliminally, carry the day: both sides can propel the same theme forward, with completely different political intentions.

My first novel, *Tomboy,* published in 1998, revolves around Butler and her theories from the perspective of an adoring fan. More to the point, it's about the construction of all gender identities. Since I've been traveling around and reading from the book, mostly men (who have no interest whatsoever in exploring this complex subject in the first place) take the trouble to let me know that they've heard that Judith Butler is long since passé: her theses have nothing to do with political reality; in America they're now talking about completely different matters. But, in fact, none of the social problems expounded upon by deconstructive feminists has even come close to being solved. A British writer who considers herself a feminist recently tried to persuade me that the entire gender discourse is nothing more than the intellectual palaver of the elite. If she wanted to, she could, of course, simply use her royalties to pay for a penis transplant. And become a man. In reality, however, countless transsexuals become prostitutes and die of AIDS before ever having their desperately envisioned and, at any rate, tragic alignment operation, as it's called. Often on a dance floor called the stage.

When, equipped with two record players and a mixing board, I deejay in public, I bring with me a certain pool of sound files, which in English are appropriately enough called records. But I don't know beforehand in which order I will play them. I do know that they will relate to each other in a logical way, that they will fuse together to make a good idea, an intelligent order, at whose gradual creation I am present, standing at the controls, a participating observer. Watching not so much the reaction of the dancers as the signals that come out of the board. Whenever it's possible, I let two different records run synchronically, their impulses upliftingly embracing and intertwining. The excitement builds at moments when it can no longer be clearly determined from which source which piece originates. By mixing supposedly disparate pieces so that they form a synthesis. When the citation loses its quotation marks.

As a result of various defensive maneuvers against dominant literary concepts, I've learned to write my texts not as an author but as a reader, so to speak. To reproduce my reading process in writing. To take randomly found material, which I did not necessarily properly understand, over which I am not the lord and master, and to let it flow through me. And then to pass it on to other readers. To display the complicated as—complicated. The constructed as constructed. To allow the book to write me, as it were. For once, to let it be more clever than the author. To let the author, the supposed subject, become the object. Myself as text. A boundless horror of the original idea. So I sit in my workplace, between towers of books, which are also records, and, following the musical logic of a DJ set, successively extract my material from myself. Naturally, just like a good DJ, I want to deliver a narrative. And I also usually try to avoid letting the records diverge, although that can occasionally be a highly welcome effect. See the language of the writer fall on its face, as in a slapstick movie. I'm always glad to let that happen. I definitely want to tell a completely different story than the rocker's and therefore do not tolerate narrative distractions such as plot, arcs of tension, and climax, beginnings and endings, resolutions or even redemptions. Instead, I try to re-create what I find in techno—an expanse of text whose modulation is as complex as possible. Which isn't masterfully concerned with pop, but, instead, is pop itself. Dynamic, hypnotic, discursive: a record. Disco, house, and techno DJs have given my writing wings, just as the beat generation might have been influenced by Charlie Parker's soulful, deconstructive alto saxophone playing.

Hubert Fichte was pop; he even recorded a live LP in the Star Club. Rolf Dieter Brinkmann was pop. As were many other books published at the time by März Verlag. But pop literature as such doesn't exist. There also is no pop movement. At the most, an attitude. Pop is not an entity that strategically reacts to, for instance, the penetrating attributes ascribed to it. Something that can defend itself against these things. Echoing Rainald Goetz: pop doesn't have a problem. Even when Tony Blair suddenly wants to be pop. I think pop pieces itself together out of innumerable, fast, unpredictable, individual processes, which seem chaotic from the outside and have, as we often hear, arbitrary effects. Which is why pop should not have any manifesto. Pop is a practice. A means. An analytical procedure for dealing with politically productive methods available on the surface. A means of perception. Pop is reading. Diagnosis, but not prognosis. Not knowledge, but questions. In the standardized system of coordinates not masculine, but feminine. A code accessible to all. And definitely self-referential.

So anyone who is involved with pop is susceptible to all kinds of nostalgic stirrings. The social dangers of dealing with pop are less grounded in its notorious mechanisms of exclusion, but in their opposite: the untimely, rapidly progressing process of aging, usually starting around thirty, involving an emphatic farewell to all things grounded in the present and a deeply sentimental understanding of common past experiences; cannonized pop socialization. This process can only once again become pop if it radically turns round and looks toward the future, postulates something new, or finds a new way, as Roxy Music managed to do in 1972. This was a way that did not exist before, a way that can only be described as postmodern, and it gave birth to a new bastard: re-make/re-model. Wolfgang Voigt was equally innovative in the 1990s in Cologne, with polkas, T Rex, and Juliane Werding. Pop is indeed interested in the popular, but pop itself doesn't have to be popular. That is why so much of what is described as pop literature—self-satisfied, backward-looking texts that have fallen prey to the reminiscent gesture—is not pop but, instead, stale literature seeking sympathetic understanding. The new Berlin.

Translated by Allison Plath-Moseley

NOTE

"Ich als Text (Extended Version)" was first published in *Zuerst bin ich immer Leser: Prosa schreiben heute*, ed. Ute-Christine Krupp and Ulrike Janssen (Frankfurt am Main: Suhrkamp, 2000). This is the first publication in English.

Part IV

Local Stories in Global Idioms: German Cinema at the Turn of the Twenty-first Century

Popular Cinema, National Cinema, and European Integration

Marc Silberman

German cinema in the 1990s is a story of structural changes responding to audiovisual diversification and to the global networking that has come to play a major role in the European Union. The infrastructural shifts in the movie industry and the discourse about the significance of national cinema(s) that has accompanied those shifts over the past ten years will concern me here. I propose to set out some of the parameters that have given rise to the complaints and hype surrounding developments in the past ten years and then to conclude with some speculative comments on the implications of the new media landscape in Germany and Europe.

In the two decades prior to 1990, cinema critics, historians, and funding agencies in both East and West Germany as well as the foreign audience for international films regarded German contributions as artistically sophisticated works representing the liberal and cosmopolitan spirit of postwar Germany, the products of a personal, subjective, and committed view of reality transformed into a meaningful social dialogue. Such a perspective assumed a selective view of what counted as quality in the cinema, a view shaped by considerations derived from or legitimated by "high culture" characteristics of authorial control, authenticity of voice, formal complexity, and the artist's public role in mediating social critique. For example, the strict physical distinction within the East German Deutsche Film-Aktiengesellschaft (DEFA) studios between television production located in the Adlershof studios and feature film production in the Babelsberg studios mirrored the division between personnel and resources directed toward popular culture and art. Although the Babelsberg facility also produced "popular" fare such as children's movies and topical comedies, these were considered to be finger exercises for younger directors either to prove their mettle or to punish those who had pushed the ideological limits too far in developing material for more "serious" productions such as historical films, adaptations of literary texts, or dramas. The membership of several DEFA directors in the Academy of Arts of the German Democratic Republic (GDR) with their selected "Meisterschüler" might be seen as symptomatic for the status the cinema had achieved in the GDR as a legitimate artistic endeavor, a status bought at the price of political quiescence or marginalization that was sometimes apostrophized as poetic realism during the 1980s.

The New German Cinema in the Federal Republic had meanwhile established its reputation as the most successful European new wave of the 1970s through its orientation toward the *Autorenfilm*, a concept emphasizing the individual creativity and genius of the director who controls and is responsible for all aspects of the filmic work of art. The ongoing laments and eulogies for the artistically ambitious New German Cinema throughout the 1980s did not arise because the aging mavericks of the 1960s and 1970s stopped making films but because the funding and distribution market for their vision of film production was shrinking. Never commercially viable in West Germany (the box-office market share for these features vacillated between 4 and 10 percent annually into the 1980s), the mature New German Cinema, like its DEFA counterpart, was drawing ever closer to a kind of state-sponsored stagnation. At the same time, the commercially successful West German contributions of the 1980s—those that are rarely mentioned in film histories or by film critics and that are never exported—were dominated by television comics like Otto Waalkes, Loriot, Didi Hallervorden, and Gerhard Polt.

This was the situation, then, in 1990. While the DEFA studios had built a solid reputation for craftsmanship coupled with conservative aesthetic and political judgment, DEFA's domestic audience had been eroded by competition from imported films, increasingly from the West, and from television programming received from both East and West German broadcasters. In West Germany the New German Cinema directors, who in any case had never constituted a unified movement, were drifting toward more commercial filmmaking, while others dropped out or emigrated and still others tried to establish a niche existence. Meanwhile the younger generation considered the New German Cinema by this point to be an extension of "Papas Kino." The year 1990 reconfigured the playing field in a number of significant ways. Reunification suddenly pitted a large pool of talent from the East against colleagues in the West, who were all competing for state and local subsidies as well as for public television cofinancing, including from the two new regional public television stations in the newly constituted eastern federal states. In addition, television deregulation opened the door to private broadcasters with an enormous appetite for new (cheap) talent and with great potential as a secondary market for feature films. Moreover, import/export strategies of the American majors adapted to the new European landscape with investments in multiplex cinemas and moves to protect their traditionally high share in the German market by investing in local production with distribution guarantees.[1] Finally, the political agenda for European integration introduced new audiovisual policies and a new vision of European cultural identity.

The movie industry in the united Germany continued through the year 2000 to produce between sixty and seventy cinema features annually, but more than half of those launched sold too few tickets at the box office to amortize the production costs. The real news in the 1990s was the success of a series of comedies. These included the familiar television crossover products that had already established a following in the 1980s, as well as comedies aimed at the younger audience by a new generation of filmmakers. The absolute leader of the pack was Sönke Wortmann's *Der bewegte Mann,* which gained a 30 percent market share when it opened in 1994 and went on to sell an unprecedented 6.5 million admissions in Germany during its commercial release.[2] This was followed in 1995 by Detlev Buck's *Männerpension* (3.5 million admissions), Michael Schaak and Udo Beissel's *Werner—Das muß kesseln* (5 million admissions in 1995–96), and Wortmann's *Das Superweib* (2.3 million admissions). The trend peaked in 1996–97, when the market share for domestic productions maintained itself at around 17 percent, the highest since the early 1980s, but the truly historic figures for the first quarter of 1997—a solid 31.5 percent of the market share—were attributable to the release of only three extremely popular comedies, Helmut Dietl's *Rossini,* Thomas Jahn's *Knockin' on Heaven's Door,* and Michael Schaak and Veit Vollmer's animated feature *Das kleine Arschloch.*[3] After that the trend receded, with only four comedies surpassing the watershed of 2 million tickets sold: *Lola rennt* by Tom Tykwer in 1998; two features in 1999, *Asterix und Obelix gegen Caesar* and the animated film *Werner—Volles Rooää!!!;* and *Sonnenallee* by Leander Haussmann in 2000.

Although there was a constant stream of comedy successes during these ten years, with more features than ever breaking the symbolic barrier of 1 million admissions, the average German market share—

excluding that one unusual peak in 1997—ranged between a modest 8 and 13 percent.[4] Indeed, more relevant is the fact that many of these comedies, like the artistically ambitious features of the New German Cinema, were produced originally as television films or at least with television cofinancing. A major difference of this recent cinematographic cheerfulness, however, is the synthesis of visual and structural aesthetics from film and television. Thus, one finds conventional television-type narratives using familiar recipes and genre resolutions with amusing twists but characterized by well-crafted cinematography and editing techniques derived from cinematic know-how.

While it has been clear in Germany since the early 1960s that statistically comedies have a better chance for domestic audience acceptance than any other genre, the reason for the abundance and extraordinary success of comedy fare in the 1990s would need a more multifaceted explanation. First and foremost, generational issues and shifts in youth culture have changed the cinema landscape. All statistics indicate that the cinema is overwhelmingly a young people's medium. About 60 percent of the audience consists of viewers under thirty years old; 89 percent of the fourteen to nineteen year olds and 76 percent of the twenty to twenty-nine year olds go to the movies at least once a week in Germany, while those over thirty tend to stay at home and watch television.[5] Television programming, especially among the private broadcasters, has played a major role in popularizing life-style issues around sexuality, gender role reversals, and romance. In addition, the (re-)discovery of movies as vehicles for stars has created a powerful synergy with television talk shows, sitcoms, soaps, and detective serials. Since private television is dependent on advertising revenues, the commercialization of the cinema based on audience expectations, formulaic plots, and stereotypical characters becomes more explicit and helps explain the copycat quality of this comedy boom. At the same time the movie industry itself is concerned that the comedy wave is only that, a temporary high that cannot be expected to strengthen the industry's position on a long-term basis. As is usually the case with comedy, it is rarely exportable, so these domestic successes have not translated into international distribution.[6] Possibly more significant is the fact that domestic audiences have been attracted back to the cinemas to watch German movies, and this may prove to be the foundation upon which in the years to come the German movie industry can build its audience with other genres as well.

Equally important in the equation for the future of the German movie industry are the attempts to establish a European framework for the production, distribution, and exhibition of audiovisual material. European integration has made great strides forward on the practical, political, and economic levels in the past ten years, and despite the ongoing frictions between the various members of the European Union it is evident that they consider the general direction to be positive.[7] These developments have implications for the European cultural agenda as well. In the last ten years the legal infrastructure and economic support mechanisms for the European movie industry have been established, but the actual product—the European film—has not yet made its appearance, unless we are speaking of the "Euro-puddings," those multinational coproductions financed by the combined resources of several European state agencies and television networks and usually filmed in English in the hope that they will travel beyond the borders of European distribution. Such films are more properly referred to as international productions and have little or nothing to do with a European cultural identity, while the obstinately local productions, those small films that emerge precisely from the specificity of a community, seem to continue to define the very essence of European identity—its diversity and difference.[8]

Given this state of affairs, it comes as no surprise that the discussion about moving images and culture became one of the major stumbling blocks for the renegotiation of the General Agreement on Tariffs and Trade (GATT) during the last months of 1993. The first GATT agreement in 1947 had included provisions for regular adjustments, and the eighth renegotiation (the so-called Uruguay Round), which began in 1986, provoked the crisis of 1993 when the United States argued that it was time finally to open the audiovisual market—as had already been agreed for other markets—to the unrestricted circulation of goods.[9] If the European partners saw the American initiative as a thinly veiled economic ploy to dominate the media and communications market, their grandstanding in defense of national cultures was no less a disguise on the part of politicians, businesspeople, and intellectuals for their own commercial interests. Europe's protection of its movie industry has historically been economic, relying on quota, contingency, or levy systems to shelter investment and employment. The cultural value of the industry's products has been secondary and derivative of the commercial value. In other words, film content and aesthetics have rarely been proposed as a reason for protecting a national movie industry anywhere in Europe. Thus, although the rhetoric of "invasion" by (American-produced) mass culture commodities and the defense of a more authentic national culture echoes earlier controversies of the

1920s and 1930s, the impassioned argument that film and television are both crucial for cultural identity is a new one, and in this sense the GATT talks might be more properly regarded as a marker for the way cultural space will be negotiated in the global future, joining other controversial issues such as culinary traditions, linguistic autonomy, and intellectual property rights.

The discussion about cultural particularity in Europe is advancing, but the particularity is defended by policymakers and bureaucrats almost exclusively within the context of global economic players, that is, as a contest between Europe and America. For these purposes the polemical rhetoric simply assumes the existence of a unified cultural space called "Europe." Rather than considering the marginalization of European tradition within a global context and the competing local and regional interests within Europe, such a position makes claims to cultural legitimacy and hegemony based on a European collective identity to be defended against an external threat. Germany, for instance, seen from Spain or Portugal, is a major exporter of television series and entertainment that competes to the detriment of domestic fare. Similarly, a global media giant like Bertelsmann, a holding company located in Germany, competes with other transnational concerns for market shares and market domination.

The putative opponent in this David and Goliath contest is Hollywood, seen as the industrial producer of profit-oriented mass culture commodities based on the lowest common denominator of audience appeal. The reality of the American movie industry with its differentiated products that include blockbusters, low-budget and independent features, and popular and art cinema in fact does not differ systemically from the European industry but rather differs in economies of scale. That American movies dominate European screens, on the other hand, is unarguable. In 1991, for example, a typical year for the entire decade, U.S. productions accounted for 81 percent of the screenings in European Union cinemas, 70 percent of the European box-office take, and 54 percent of all dramas and comedies broadcast on European television.[10] But American filmmakers, many of them immigrants themselves, have perfected a cinematic imaginary with tropes, styles, genres, and characters that are familiar in many different cultures and can be translated into local contexts. This has fed the previously mentioned myth of a universalized Hollywood enemy and has led to the defense of European cinema with recourse to an aggregate idea of Europe made up of discrete national cultures.

Yet the very notion of national cinema is itself a precarious one, and the developments in Germany during the 1990s reveal other, more fruitful ways of understanding how a variety of local cultures compete with a single transnational source of readily adaptable cultural tropes. First of all, it is questionable whether cinema is even the appropriate or logical ground on which to defend European cultural identity against Americanization. Today television is a more relevant site for visual culture, especially in view of the opportunities opened up by digitalization. Some 600 movies are produced each year in Europe, but fewer than 250 actually find their way through distribution and exhibition channels to the cinema screen.[11] The remainder usually ends up on television. Meanwhile, technological advance and the convergence of broadcasting, computing, and telecommunications that occurred in the second half of the 1990s are transforming the entire media environment. With the decline of analogue communication the national systems of media regulation that seek to control content by means of quotas are rendered obsolete. In this highly technological, commodified culture industry that allows access on many different levels, competition is leading inexorably to consolidation and more conformity. The issue, however, as I already stated, is how cultural space will be negotiated. As a result of the controversy surrounding the latest round of GATT talks, it becomes clear that the very character of the public sphere is being contested: what does and does not deserve subsidy or legal protection? In other words, it may be more fruitful to compare apples with apples rather than apples with oranges. Thus, when a citizen in Germany chooses to watch on television a German-produced soap like *Gute Zeiten, schlechte Zeiten* or a detective series like *Polizeiruf 110, Tatort,* or *Derrick* over an American product of similar nature, it is a decision to engage with a specifically German social context whose referent and style obliterate identification to a "relatively" lesser degree.

Second, beyond the discourse of European culture and identity occasioned by the recent GATT controversy, there have been more practical efforts undertaken by the European Union, whose goals have been characterized in an official document as "to strengthen our companies' competitiveness in order to use our cultural diversity and transform growth into jobs."[12] My hunch is that the latter, the employment goal, is the priority, if not from the perspective of the filmmakers and audiences then at least from that of the European bureaucrats and movie industry investors. Two main agencies were created, Eurimages and Media. Eurimages, established in 1989 by the Council of Europe, is the pan-European fund for multilateral coproductions. It funds primarily full-length feature films but also documentaries, the exhibition sector, and marketing initiatives among the member states. Funding is dispersed to projects involving at least three producers from member states in the form of interest-free production loans, repayable from producers' net receipts.[13] The second complementary agency, Media, also established in 1989, is an umbrella program responsible for pre- and postproduction support of the European audiovisual industry.[14] Its activities are divided into three areas: professional training, film development, and promotion and marketing, including support of local film festivals and prizes. The largest portion of Media's annual budget (about two-thirds) goes to the activities in the third category, in particular to help "national" fiction from the five largest member states (Germany, Italy, Spain, France, and the United Kingdom) penetrate the regional television market.[15] Both of these European agencies have developed programs oriented toward the audiovisual industry as a volatile international meeting place of art and commerce. Culture is regarded as a high-technology, high-investment marketplace with new employment opportunities for skilled labor.

Germany has conformed to the trends of the past decade in European funding and development. Both the film subsidy board (Film-förderungsanstalt)—created in the early 1970s in the Federal Republic to support the production of quality films in conjunction with public television cofinancing—and the various regional funding boards have been expanded and restructured since 1990. Especially the competitive bidding wars that arose between regional film funds, which were trying to attract national and European productions to their respective facilities, and the resulting fragmentation in production led in 1994 to the pooling of some subsidy programs and better coordination of regional resources. What becomes apparent here is the shift from criteria of quality to market-driven considerations of local and regional investment. The major impetus was the revision of the federal film subsidy law (Filmförderungsgesetz) in December 1992 that placed more emphasis on commercially promising (i.e., box office oriented) scripts but then made subsidy payouts dependent on a filmmaker's willingness to use regional shooting locations and technical services.

A 1999 informational brochure of the Berlin-Brandenburg Film Board (established in 1994) touts, for example, its subsidy program for "sophisticated, artistic films as well as popular entertainment" and goes on to assure potential applicants that the board does more than support entertainment and culture: it is "also an important economic factor." A similar brochure of the Filmstiftung Nordrhein-Westfalen (established in 1991) stresses that it promotes economic and cultural objectives (in that order!) with the goal of creating jobs through great filmmaking. The new Filmakademie Baden-Württemberg, which opened in Ludwigsburg in 1991, conceives its program explicitly against the myth of the *Autorenfilm* director, training instead specialists for the modern entertainment industry who can be integrated "into the rationalized labor of media business."[16] In general, the discussions about film production and subsidy occur now within the framework of market returns, investment opportunities, and creating or maintaining employment, while the films or television productions themselves are commodities that enter the larger context of capital circulation. Thus, at the same time that the cinema is becoming more and more contextualized within a global media network that includes technological innovations, telecommunications, and tourist-oriented event culture, the regionalization of funding policies and actual filmmaking are becoming more and more important. This plays itself out with cities like Cologne, Stuttgart, and Karlsruhe now competing with traditional film studios in Munich, Berlin, or Hamburg, offering training facilities, audiovisual service industries, media and informational know-how, and so forth.

This leads back to the question of finance and economies of scale mentioned earlier. In the 1990s the average entertainment film in Germany cost 3–5 million deutsche mark (DM) to produce. A big film, such as Dietl's box-office success *Schtonk,* cost about 16 million DM in 1992, and Volker Schlöndorff's sleeper *Der Unhold* was budgeted at an unheard of 27 million DM in 1996. Yet such films could expect to earn only about 4 million DM from the combined cinema exhibition, sale of television broadcasting rights, and video sales in Germany. Since comedy, in particular German humor, is basically nonexportable, that meant anything budgeted over 4 million DM had to be earned at the domestic box office.[17] Both on the federal and European level, recommendations have been made to limit the number of productions and thereby to subsidize fewer large-scale productions that can really compete on an international scale to amortize production costs. Yet this overlooks, of course, the traditional diversity of functioning cinema markets, first and foremost in the United States but also in commercially competitive markets like those of Japan, India, and Hong Kong. These latter cases have demonstrated that it is possible to build an audience with both domestic and international appeal that can compete with Hollywood products. Moreover, the many small and marginally distributed films in all of these countries function as a form of fertilizer for the major box-office successes, as well as for the wider media infrastructure.

There are two developments that can round out this overview. First, the growth of television programming in Germany during the decade of the 1990s represents possibly the single most important factor in the audiovisual market. Polls have indicated that at the end of the century German television audiences increasingly preferred domestic products to imports—either American or European. Hence, it is no surprise when statistics show that, on the one hand, the number of German films shown on television diminished by about half since 1992 (in particular, the number of reruns of older German films) but that, on the other hand, the number of new, made-for-television films increased, to the point where about two hundred are being produced per year in Germany and shown primarily during prime time.[18] Even a cursory glance at the weekly television guides indicates an incredible number of program hours filled by movies, series, comedies, and thrillers. Like never before both the German audience and the television broadcasters are seeking young directors and screenplay writers and even older New German Cinema directors to fill this programming space. In fact, Germany leads Europe in the production and screening of domestic television productions, and many of these are regionally inflected, set in particular cities or geographical locales that reflect the regional broadcasting company of the federal broadcasting system.[19]

Meanwhile, Europe counted over 250 television broadcasters in 1996, of which two-thirds are privately owned, at least double the number in 1990. Here is probably where the future of any new German wave will have to gather its forces. Yet, as in the past, the greatest barrier will be the distribution system. Just as the New German Cinema was blocked from the domestic exhibition market of the 1970s because the distribution and cinema circuits in Germany were to a large extent in the hands of American corporations, today the box-office successes of the German cinema are backed and distributed by Buena Vista (Disney's German affiliate), Warner, Columbia, United International, and Fox and are booked into cinema chains and multiplexes owned by multinationals. More importantly, private television broadcasters increasingly purchase packages of television programming from large transnational producers and distributors (e.g., Bertelsmann and Kirch Media) rather than individual products from independents or even small companies.

Second, a vital group of multicultural directors and actors emerged in the last decade as another facet of regionalization in Germany, enriching and contributing to a local-bound sense of cultural distinctiveness and difference that stands in contrast to the more conventional comedies that otherwise dominated the German cinema.[20] These vernacular filmmakers stake their claims on the search for a new identity, on the pleasure of cultural exchange that results from making films in Europe but not necessarily from Europe. Of course, identity cannot be constructed in a vacuum but rather is forged through the active demarcation of a self in relation to some Other. Arguably, this comparative and competitive spirit still valorizes German or European culture as the reference point in relation to which particularity is claimed, and similarly even the most local of these films enters a transnational space through the international festival circuits and publics they seek to address. Since reunification, the discussion of nation and national identity in Germany has revived in all areas of cultural and intellectual discourse. The challenge coming from the periphery in the cinema, from the multiethnic filmmakers, is new because it aims neither at the American competition—the main "enemy" of European cinema—nor at the mainstream national cinemas—the object of traditional national new waves. The extent to which audiovisual culture and policies can accommodate such resistances on the path to political and economic unity will reveal how serious Germany and Europe actually are about linking pluralism, diversity, and democracy.

NOTES

An earlier version of this essay was researched and presented in 1999 in Australia at the Sydney German Studies Symposium and appears under the title "European Cinema in the 90s: Whither Germany?" in *Schreiben nach der Wende: Ein Jahrzehnt deutscher Literatur, 1989–1999,* ed. Gerhard Fischer and David Roberts (Tübingen: Stauffenburg Verlag, 2001), 317–30. The version in this volume has been substantially revised and updated based on research conducted in January 2001.

    1. Statistics for both Europe and Germany show a gradual increase in the number of films produced annually, in the number of admissions sold, and in the number of new cinemas (especially multiplex construction). The explanation can be found, however, in the dominance of American productions: Germany is the second largest export market for American box-office hits after Japan, and, from the American perspective, a healthy German movie industry is an asset, especially when the distribution channels are owned by the American majors. Although the traditional cinema venues maintain their vigor, their fare is an increasingly inter-

national commodity defined by American production values and professionalism and marketed by means of American distribution strategies, with the result that more and more spectators are seeing fewer and fewer movies.

2. These and the following figures have been gleaned from the yearly statistics reported in Carsten Pfaff, ed., *Filmstatistisches Taschenbuch* (Wiesbaden: Spitzenorganisation der Filmwirtschaft [SPIO], 1990–98), 1990ff.

3. It should be noted that in 1996–97 the Hollywood studios entered a phase of troubled commercial returns when the spiral of ever fewer but more expensive films began, a development that had some impact on the distribution of American block bookings in Germany and thus indirectly facilitated the temporary success of German releases.

4. Some of these record-breaking comedies include *Werner Beinhart* (1990, Gerhard Hahn, Michael Schaak, and Niki List); *Pappa ante portas* (1991, Vicco von Bülow alias Loriot); *Allein unter Frauen* (1991, Sönke Wortmann); *Go, Trabi, Go* (1991, Peter Timm); *Manta—Der Film* (1992, Uwe Timm); *Otto—Der Liebesfilm* (1992, Otto Waalkes); *Schtonk* (1992, Helmut Dietl); *Abgeschminkt!* (1993, Katja von Garnier); *Manta Manta* (1993, Wolfgang Büld); *Wir können auch anders* (1993, Detlev Buck); *Stadtgespräch* (1995, Rainer Kaufmann); *Keiner liebt mich* (1995, Doris Dörrie); *Irren ist männlich* (1996, Sherry Hormann); *Echte Kerle* (1996, Rolf Silber); *Ballermann 6* (1997, Gernot Roll); *Widows* (1997, Sherry Hormann); *Die Apothekerin* (1998, Rainer Kaufmann); *Late Show* (1999, Helmut Dietl); and *Otto—Der Katastrofenfilm* (2000, Otto Waalkes).

5. These statistics reflect the numbers in 1999 as reported in *Kinobesucher in der MA [Medienanalyse]* (Düsseldorf: PR und Forschungsgesellschaft Werbung im Kino, 2000), 11. For a more general discussion of the cinema audience in the 1990s, see Caroline Beer, *Die Kinogeher: Eine Untersuchung des Kinopublikums in Deutschland* (Berlin: Vistas, 2000), esp. chap. 3.

6. On the miserable export history of European comedy genres and especially German comedies of the 1990s, see Thomas Elsaesser, "Introduction: German Cinema in the 1990s," in *The BFI Companion to German Cinema,* ed. Thomas Elsaesser with Michael Wedel (London: BFI, 1999), 5.

7. For an overview of media policy discussions in the European Union and the European Parliament, see Philip R. Schlesinger, "From Cultural Protection to Political Culture? Media Policy and the European Union," in *Constructing Europe's Identity: The External Dimension,* ed. Lars-Erik Cederman (Boulder: Lynne Reiner, 2001), 91–114; and Tobias Theiler, "Why the European Union Failed to Europeanize Its Audiovisual Policy," in *Constructing Europe's Identity,* 115–37.

8. One could point to European-funded small films such as *Der achte Tag* (1990, Reinhard Münster); *La haine* (1995, Mathieu Kassovitz); *The English Patient* (1996, Anthony Minghella); *Trainspotting* (1996, Danny Boyle); and *Breaking the Waves* (1996, Lars von Trier).

9. Ian Jarvie, "Free Trade as Cultural Threat: American Film and TV Exports in the Post-war Period," in *Hollywood and Europe: Economics, Culture, National Identity: 1945–95,* ed. Geoffrey Nowell-Smith and Steven Ricci (London: BFI, 1998), 40.

10. David Ellwood, "Introduction: Historical Methods and Approaches," in *Hollywood in Europe: Experiences of a Cultural Hegemony,* ed. David W. Ellwood and Rob Kroes (Amsterdam: VU University Press, 1994), 8.

11. Angus Finney, *The State of European Cinema: A New Dose of Reality* (London: Cassell, 1996), 114.

12. "die Verstärkung der Wettbewerbsfähigkeit unserer Unternehmen, um unsere kulturelle Vielfalt zu nutzen und das Wachstum in Arbeitsplätze umzusetzen." Jean-Michel Baer, ed., *Politik im audiovisuellen Bereich der europäischen Union 1998* (Brussels: Amt für amtliche Veröffentlichungen der Europäischen Gemeinschaften, 1997), 4.

13. Finney, *State of European Cinema,* 108–13. Eurimages's official literature and reports scrupulously avoid the word "subsidy," emphasizing their funding program as "repayable loans." Some of the successful features supported with Eurimages funds have included *Breaking the Waves* (Lars von Trier); *Smilla's Sense of Snow* (Bille August); *Antonia's Line* (Marleen Gorris); *Mutters Courage* (Michael Verhoeven); and *Beyond the Clouds* (Michelangelo Antonioni and Wim Wenders). In 1996 more than $500 million of national and European Union public money was spent to support the production of European films (Finney, *State of European Cinema,* 114), but Eurimages's own budget is so modest that its impact on the audiovisual sector can be judged as negligible (Theiler, "Why the European Union Failed," n 37).

14. Media is an acronym for "mesures pour encourager le développement de l'industrie audiovisuelle" (measures to encourage the development of the audiovisual industry).

15. Nikolaus Mirza, ed., *Media Info.* Newsletter des Informationsbüros des Media-Programms der Europäischen Union in der Bundesrepublik Deutschland, February 1999, 1. Statistics from 1996–97 indicate that only about 8.5 percent of the total number of hours of fiction broadcast on European television consisted of "Euro-fiction" (Jacques Delmoly, ed., *Media 17.* Media Programme Newsletter, European Commission, October 1998, 6).

16. The sources here are informational brochures distributed at the Berlinale Film Festival in February 1999. The original German for the quotes are, respectively, "anspruchsvolle, künstlerische Filme genauso wie populäre Unterhaltung"; "auch ein bedeutender Wirtschaftsfaktor"; and "in den arbeitsteiligen Medienalltag." It should be noted that most of this promotional material is printed in English as well as German; the regional film boards are increasingly seen as launch pads for marketing regional business facilities on an international level.

17. Dieter Menz, "Von Sissi bis zum Bewegten Mann: Vertrieb deutscher Filme ins Ausland," in *Der Bewegte Film: Aufbruch zu neuen deutschen Erfolgen,* ed. Heike Amend and Michael Bütow (Berlin: Vistas, 1997), 123.

18. Amend, "Deutsche Filme im Fernsehen," in *Der Bewegte Film,* ed. Amend and Bütow, 58, table 1. American television productions provide on the average about 25 percent of series and entertainment on German television but almost exclusively outside of prime-time slots (Johannes Kreile, "Stellung der Produzenten in Deutschland," in *Der Bewegte Film,* ed. Amend and Bütow, 190).

19. One article cites an unnamed study that reports in 1997 Germany pro-

grammed 1,815 hours of made-in-Germany soaps, television dramas, and television movies, while the comparable numbers for England were 1,225 hours and for France 576 hours (Nikolaus von Festenberg, "Viele Jäger, arme Hasen," *Der Spiegel* 48 [1998]: 244–46.)

20. The largest group of multicultural filmmakers are of ethnic Turkish background, for example, Fatih Akin (born in 1973 of Turkish parents in Hamburg, where he studied film): *Kurz und schmerzlos* (1998) and *Im Juli* (2000); Thomas Arslan (born in 1962 in Braunschweig of Turkish parents, lived in Ankara from 1967 to 1971, studied film in Berlin): *Mach die Musik leiser* (1994), *Geschwister—Kardesler* (1996), *Dealer* (1998), and *Der schöne Tag* (2000); Yilmaz Arslan (born in 1968 in Turkey, moved to Germany in 1975): *Langer Gang* (1992) and *Yara* (1998); Kutlug Ataman (born in Istanbul, studied in Paris and Los Angeles, lives in Istanbul and Berlin): *Lola + Bilidikid* (1998); Tefvik Baser (born in 1951 in Turkey, settled in Hamburg in 1980): *40 m² Deutschland* (1986), *Abschied vom falschen Paradies* (1989), and *Lebewohl Fremde* (1991); Merlyn Solakhan (born in Istanbul in 1955, moved to Germany in 1979, studied film in Berlin from 1980 to 1985): *Tekerleme* (1986) and *Hayal* (1990); Yüksel Yavuz (born in 1964 in Turkey, emigrated to Germany in 1980, studied film in Hamburg): *Mein Vater, Der Gastarbeiter* (documentary, 1995) and *Aprilkinder* (1998).

Tom Tykwer's *Run Lola Run* and the Usual Suspects: The Avant-Garde, Popular Culture, and History

Barbara Kosta

Tom Tykwer's 1998 film *Run Lola Run* has surprised even the most hardened critics of German cinema. As many have noted with uninhibited astonishment, it is rare that a German film is so clever while being an absolute pleasure to watch. The film has swept box offices and, with a budget of 3 million marks, has managed to run in over forty countries as well as win numerous film prizes.[1] The film has launched its director into the international limelight and has fulfilled most every contemporary German filmmaker's dream.

Why has *Lola* been such a box-office success? An important factor, no doubt, is Franka Potente's performance as the flaming red–headed Lola, who participates in an all-out race against time to save her boyfriend, Manni. She is a hipster, "a young tearaway Lola," as Robert Falcon writes.[2] In a film review in the fashion magazine *Bazaar,* Richard Rayner describes Potente as "a performer of potentially mythic charisma." In addition to her magnetic quality, he attributes the film's success to its accomplished deployment of the finest of European avant-garde traditions combined with Hollywood's pacing; to use his words, the film "brings Hollywood pizzazz to the European art movie."[3] Other critics, equally enthusiastic, zoom in on the film's "Germanness" and applaud its profound philosophical musings on chance and time (Tykwer studied philosophy) and its hermeneutic and cinematographic depth. Tom Whalen is fascinated by the film's "ludic spirit willing to see life and art as a game. It's as tightly wound and playful as a Tinguely machine and constructed with care." He is quick to note that the film "leaps lightly over the typical Teutonic metaphysical mountains."[4] There seems to be something in this film for everyone—romantics, rave enthusiasts, chaos theorists, adrenaline freaks, film critics, and scholars—everyone except filmmaker/actor Detlev Buck, a one-time hopeful for a new German cinema. In his estimation, the film leaps far beyond the national boundaries of German issues: "*Run Lola Run* doesn't have anything [shit] to say about Germany. It is pure entertainment."[5] In other words, to cite Niklas Luhmann's understanding of entertainment, which seems to complement Buck's, it is "one component of modern leisure culture, charged with the function of destroying superfluous time."[6]

Luhmann's and Buck's statements reveal a deeply ingrained belief in an unbridgeable divide between entertainment and having something to say about Germany. Their statements echo a modernist distrust of mass culture, a fear of selling out, and express a troubled relationship between German national identity and "Americanization" or commercialization that seems to be a German issue. When Buck uses the term *einen Dreck* (smut/shit), he seems to be referring to mass culture as the abject, as kitsch, and to be seeing the film as a version of an old-fashioned love song disguised in techno beats. Is Buck lamenting the end of the New German Cinema and/or of a cinema invested in producing an oppositional public sphere and a general turn to Hollywood? For critics who still work within the mass culture paradigm, popular culture, as opposed to "high" art, still has the reputation of being formulaic, as lacking critical insight and complexity. It is made in the United States and produced solely for mass consumption, that is, profit. As John Storey notes: "The claim that popular culture is mass American culture has a long history within the theoretical mapping of popular culture."[7]

Tykwer belongs to a generation of Germans that embraces popular culture rather than criticizes it as a colonization of the mind and a form of cultural imperialism, as Wenders and his generation of filmmakers maintained during the 1970s and 1980s. Yet Tykwer's postmodern merging of diverse art forms and genres and his incorporation of U.S. popular culture (comics, Westerns, slapstick, editing techniques) function as boundary breaking and liberating in their potential to launch viewers into the realm of fantasy. Tykwer traverses national boundaries in his choice of aesthetic practices and seems to relish his role as a *bricoleur* of the cultural offerings that this German-American merger affords. Thus, while *Run Lola Run* is entertaining, it does say quite a bit about the new Germany, about its cinematic aspirations and the turn it has taken, and about the image that the new nation wants to project for its own consumption as well as for its international audiences. In addition, the fast-paced editing that defies memory and that locks the spectator into the present may be saying even more about contemporary Germany than Buck is loath to admit. It reflects on contemporary Germany's relationship to history, which I will discuss later. Rather than just killing superfluous time, it seems that time as well as place—in its specificity as well as its indistinctness—are of the essence in *Run Lola Run*. First, Lola only has twenty minutes to come up with one hundred thousand marks in order to save her petty-criminal boyfriend, Manni (Moritz Bleibtreu), from the hands of the racketeer Ronnie, whose money Manni accidentally left in the subway train when he tried to escape a policeman checking tickets. A street person (Joachim Król) consequently becomes the lucky recipient of the bag.

The story that ensues gets replayed three times with slight variations that affect different outcomes. Besides the obsessive attention to time—clocks are everywhere—the film itself is largely a product of its own time. Instead of shying away from popular culture, it subscribes to a pop culture wave that has come to define the literary scene in contemporary Germany. "Pop" is the "key to the present," as Thomas Assheuer woefully notes.[8] The indulgent meshing of art and commercialism, sensation and surfaces, music and images belongs to pop culture's allure and success. The film incorporates the elements of popular culture that are nonconformist, rebellious (Lola's scream), and subversive and that test mainstream forms of representation. And, as far as place is concerned, Tykwer insists that the film is a Berlin film—a city that is as much in progress as it is a product of the new millennium and globalization. The fast-paced editing that lends vitality to the urban setting and its resilient and determined protagonist Lola suggest a new cultural identity in a postwall era that is local as much as it is global in its multicultural setting. Tykwer develops a new formal language to represent the New Berlin and a new direction in German filmmaking that goes with it. Out of the union of "Hollywood pizzazz" and the European art film emerges a complex visual commentary on fantasy, narrative, and history.

Run Lola Run represents a new Germany unhinged from its all too familiar narratives. It is a highly self-conscious collage of filmic styles and genres that are brought into tension with one another, exploited, reinforced, undercut, and challenged simultaneously. Ironically, the explosion that is said to signal Lola's and Manni's love for each other, which Thomas D sings about in "Komm zu mir" (Come to me), expressed as "we shattered every framework [*Rahmen*] when we came together; it was like an explosion. I still feel the jolt," reveals a seismic disintegration of classical narrative forms.[9] Tykwer brazenly dips into the grab bag of cinematic genres and trends and samples and exploits their potential while breaking with them. The film's visual playfulness and its copious allusions to game (roulette and video games) and risk taking emphasize a wild and reckless pleasure in experimenting with cinema's recently discovered possibilities. *Lola*'s hybridity is reflected in the run-together title of an interview with Tykwer by Michael Töteberg that accompanies the film script. Töteberg calls it "A romantic-philosophical actionloveexperimentalthriller."[10] Tykwer merges genres and styles only to dismiss their limitations. The emerging visual/narrative arrangement reveals a fundamental suspicion of narrative that allies his aesthetic project with early avant-garde cinema. He reveals: "I did not want one moment in the film that was motivated by dramaturgy, but rather directness and spontaneity" (130). The plot that serves as a mere skeleton is condensed into the first few minutes of the film. It offers just enough glue to hold together the visual kaleidoscope—while it unglues its protagonists, Lola and Manni, from the realm of realism.

Tykwer resorts to a variety of avant-garde aesthetic practices and in doing so acknowledges contemporary cinema's debt to its cinematic/phantasmatic precursors. Particularly, the suggestive salute to repetition through the film's thrice-told structure alludes to a return to the forms of visual experimentation associated with the invention of cinema. The possibilities inherent in a liberal exploration of a panoply of styles, and use of intertextuality in order to produce new experiences and perspectives are anticipated in the quote taken from the modernist icon T. S. Eliot's "Little Gidding" that introduces the film: "We shall not cease from exploration and the end of all our exploring will be to arrive where we started and know the place for the first time." The use of the spirals (movement) throughout the film, for example, is a visual reference to Fritz Lang's *M;* the painting of the woman's head from behind in the casino is a tribute to Hitchcock's *Vertigo,* which Tykwer includes among his favorite films. The film also returns to the various avant-garde styles in its use of montage, split screen, and slanted angles. Let us for a moment consider the suggestive detail of the avant-garde's influence beginning with the Man Ray photograph entitled "Glass Tears" in Lola's apartment or the glorification of speed and momentum that could be ascribed to the futurists. Tykwer actually claims that if the title had not been *Run Lola Run* it may have been *Speed.*[11] The fascination with movement and time at the end of the twentieth century resonates with the futurist manifesto that Filippo

Marinetti, founder of the futurist movement in 1909, expressed as "Speed is our God, the new canon of beauty; a roaring motorcar, which runs like a machine gun."[12]

The fast-paced editing, the innovative thrice-told story, the transnational techno beat that energizes the visuals, and the variety of media—animation, video, and 35 mm stock, as well as time-lapse effects, flashforwards and various editing techniques, and photography (stop-motion photography pioneered by Méliès, chief in the development of trick effects in the emergent cinema)—is the arsenal needed to produce the fantasy that is bound by the convention of ninety minutes. *Run Lola Run* cashes in on the postmodern mantra of "everything goes" and entertains the multiple options implicit in constructing a story, a notion that a number of filmmakers have tested (Ramis's *Groundhog Day* [1993], Tarantino's *Pulp Fiction* [1994], and Howitt's *Sliding Doors* [1998]). Most importantly, it builds on cinema's essential premise of fantasy or make-believe that is the juice of popular culture. Cinema is the site of desire—a dream machine.

Tykwer's description of the image that inspired the film is one that conflates movement, emotion, and the female body:

> There was the image of a woman running, who for me represented the primal image [*Urbild*] of cinema because it connects dynamism and emotion. You conceptualize a dynamic series of events that may be viewed as only mechanical and that you simultaneously infuse with emotion. I imagined a woman with red hair and her hair had to blow and she had to project desperation and passion.[13]

The film thus explores the cinematic medium and uses Lola as its vehicle. She literally embodies the animated image and the essence of cinema. Intrinsic to Tykwer's understanding of cinema is the idea that the moving image is magical, which means that it is not bound to a time-space continuum. Lola is the fantasy, the specularized body that arouses pleasure; she is the source of visual pleasure that is erotic in its potential to seduce. At the same time, Lola is the new woman: athletic, determined, and powerful.

The film begins with a cartoon of a female figure who enters a time tunnel and smashes all of the obstacles in her path—demons, spider webs, and clocks—until she is swept into the spiraling time tunnel. As a cartoon figure, Lola is aggressive and tenacious, a new tough girl and a national hero. Her metamorphosis into a "real" image emphasizes the invention of the character, and her transformation from cartoon to "real" image places her firmly in the realm of the imaginary. Her red hair and the other vibrant high-gloss colors of the mise-en-scène (the yellow subway, the phone booth) resemble the primary colors used in comics. They stand in contrast to the muted colors in the video footage used to set Lola off from other minor characters who are locked in conventional narratives. Interestingly, Lola bears a striking resemblance to Leeloo, the female character in French filmmaker Luc Besson's 1997 film *The Fifth Element.* The renowned comic book artists Moebius and Jean-Claude Mezieres provided his visual designs. Like most cartoon characters, Lola overcomes obstacles; her greatest power is her determination, her ability to change the course of the narrative and to resist death. When she is shot in the first round, or when Manni gets run over by an ambulance in the second round, Lola wills away their death and begins her quest anew. She also can mend a broken heart or, rather, rescue the guard who has suffered a heart attack by the touch of her hand. More importantly, she does get the money to save Manni within the allotted twenty minutes—a preposterous and insurmountable task that she is able to fulfill. And she certainly can run.

Besides endowing Lola with supernatural powers, the cartoon self-consciously represents the animated image (Lola running) and places the film at the juncture between avant-garde and popular culture. By setting up the film as a cartoon, Tykwer plays with the unlimited potential of animated films, which, as Roger Cordinal suggests, "suppress the categories of normal perception; indeed its logic might even be to suppress all differential categories, and annihilate the very conditions of rationality."[14] The cartoon launches the viewer into a fantasy world in which anything is possible, any game can be won, any obstacles overcome, any evil destroyed. As William Marston, the creator of Wonder Woman, wrote in 1943, "comics defy the limits of accepted fact and convention, thus amortizing to apoplexy the ossified arteries of routine thought."[15] The cartoon enables Lola; it lends her the power to perform the impossible, anchors her in the world of fantasy, leads her audience into a collective dream world.

To be sure, the cartoon also anticipates Lola's boundary-breaking movement through the metropolis that captivates her audience. In *Run Lola Run,* the female body commands the urban space and breaks with the spatial confines that define traditional femininity. Lola's image is sharply juxtaposed with that of her mother, who is dressed in a pink negligee and who functions as an ornament in the private sphere. Lola's stride carries her through the eastern and western parts of Berlin. She thus defies spatial logic in terms of the ground she covers in

Berlin, as Margit Sinka precisely observes: "Tykwer forcibly merges areas scattered throughout Berlin, thereby artificially creating spatial unity where none exists."[16] But Lola also defies spatial logic in terms of the clearly gendered messages that spaces transmit. Lola takes over the space of the metropolis and appropriates it in a way that her more sedentary namesake, Lola Lola in von Sternberg's 1930 film *The Blue Angel,* could never dream of, even though they both seem to be made for love/consumption. In sharp contrast to Lola, Manni is stationary, limited to the phone booth where he must remain while Lola attempts to restore equilibrium. He is trapped and infantilized through his dependence on Lola (the phone cord is like an umbilical cord) and the blind woman (played by Moritz Bleibtreu's mother, Monica Bleibtreu). The space that encloses him is claustrophobic and undermines his manliness (Manniness). And, more unusually, he must wait for Lola and consequently must subscribe to a trope that traditionally is reserved for the female character. He challenges her to perform her gendered role so that Lola must prove her love and return events to their status quo. "You see," he charges,

> I knew that you wouldn't have any bright ideas either. I told you that something'll happen one day and that you won't know how to get out of it either. Not if you die sooner! So much for love being able to do everything, except for conjuring up 100,000 marks in 20 minutes.[17]

Manni invokes the "love conquers all" myth, which gets played out time and again in popular renditions of romance. It is one that *Run Lola Run* falls back on because, as Tykwer admits, he needed to fuel the image with emotion. The question is whether the film features love as its primary interest or exhausts the conventional narrative of love.

Do visual innovation and eclectic structure and, more importantly, animation, which should complicate the issue of realism, only deceive the viewer into believing/fantasizing that something new is taking place and that traditional sensibilities are being tested and its narratives undone? Do the fast-paced editing and the film's pseudo-philosophical bent actually mask the emotional economy that sparks the narrative and that sets Lola running, or does that economy get left in the wake of the run? What is at the heart of the very sparse narrative? Is it the romance between Lola and Manni? Or does the film exploit the power of cartoons, which Sherrie Inness places "at the cutting edge of exploring new definitions of gender because of their marginalization."[18] The juxtaposition of genre, avant-garde aesthetics, and the spectacle of the female body racing through the metropolis, energized by techno music, guarantees for the film's rapture. But what are the fantasies that the film produces, and do they allow for a new image of gender? Do gender coordinates get recoded?

Romance

The film flirts with the compulsions of the past, as in the narrative of romantic love. Manni and Lola's relationship is visually underscored by the shot of Mattel's Barbie and Ken dolls that the camera sights in Lola's room after Manni's phone call. The brief shot of the dolls (a creation of the 1950s) ironically comments on the repertoire of love fantasies that girls rehearse and perform and establishes these cultural icons as fixtures of the popular imagination. It also launches the representation of Lola and Manni's relationship into the realm of play and fantasy, where gender gets negotiated. The film constantly employs, undercuts, and edges along the narrative conventions of romance without getting itself caught in its clichés. It can hardly be disputed that Lola runs to save Manni, but it is significant that the primacy of Lola's image racing through Berlin, her hyper-presence, eclipses the actual reason for her running and undermines the film's interest in romance. The crosscuts of Lola and Manni and the split-screen image function to remind the viewer, who is engrossed in her exuberant sprint through the metropolis, of Lola's goal. The techno music functions similarly.[19] In fact, when Lola dashes into her father's office to ask him for the money, the father's befuddled response—"Who is Manni?"—chips away at Manni's significance.

The film features assorted genres that stage romantic love—fairy tale, melodrama, and soap opera. They appear as signposts along Lola's route, which the film encounters and undoes. When Lola bursts in on her father, she finds him entangled in a bourgeois melodrama. Shot in close-ups to lend the scenes an atmosphere of intimacy, and in extreme close-ups that create a sense of claustrophobia, the tempestuous drama between her father (Herbert Knaup) and his lover unfolds with each episode. The viewer learns that the overworked breadwinner is estranged from his home. His lover and colleague, Jutta Hansen (Nina Petri), needs to know whether he is prepared to leave his wife for her. The plot thickens as we learn that she is pregnant, but it is not his biological child. Ironically, his story gets repeated because, as Lola finds out, she is *"ein Kuckucksei"* (not his biological child). The repetition reflects the inherent circular thematic structure of melodrama or soap operas. The subplot of the father's adulterous liaison is shot with a more coarsely grained film stock than the shots of Lola's run. The muted colors in these scenes lend a television-like quality to the image. Significantly, the melodramatic romance retards the ecstatic pace that Lola's goal demands. In effect, it presents an obstacle to Lola's running and delays the visual pleasure it provides. The same holds true for the shots of Lola and Manni in bed, which are staged twice between runs. Tykwer refers to these scenes as the film's heart. With Manni and Lola lying on spiral-print pillows, the intimate close-ups, shot with red gel on the lamps, show them talking about love and death. The "he says–she says" dialogue after the first run reveals the intangibility of love and Lola's uncertainty; after the second run Manni asks Lola what she would do if he died (producing a hypothetical script) and concludes that life goes on. The scenes are static and tedious relative to the exciting kaleidoscope of images that display Lola's dart through Berlin.

The tale of romantic love gets spun differently in relation to the guard, Schuster (Armin Rohde), who literally kicks off the game, the film, and the odyssey with the soccer ball. Tykwer threads a fairy tale–like relationship to Lola into each encounter with him. Each time Lola arrives at the bank, the guard promotes her. At first he sarcastically calls her the princess of the house (Holla, holla, Lolalola, die Hausprinzessin, welch seltenes Glück); the second time around he lectures her on the virtues of a queen; the third time around he proclaims, "you're finally here darling." Lola runs on. Schuster stands still, and the soundtrack is mixed with the loud pounding of his heart. When Lola revives him in the ambulance, which she hops into when it crosses her path, she assures the paramedic: "I belong to him."

Is three times a charm, as we learn from fairy tales? Will love conquer all? The mistrust of narrative convention peaks in the third and final performance of Lola's run. At first she seems to negotiate better the obstacles she encounters and to gain strength. At the outset of the third run, she leaps over the dog and growls back, yet when she finds that she has missed her father at the bank her powers wane. As a last resort, Lola surrenders agency and appeals to a higher being: "Come on. Help me. Please. Just this one time. I'm just going to continue running, OK. I'm waiting." She closes her eyes and runs into the street. Traffic screeches to a halt, and a truck driver who has just missed her yells: "What's wrong, are you sick of life?" But Lola trusts in fantasy. She has put her life on the line in order to save Manni. Her reward is the discovery of a casino, where, despite all odds, Lola wins one hundred thousand marks. The camera that anticipated the roulette game at the beginning of the film with the image of Lola turning has come full circle. The black ball falls twice on the number 20. Twenty has now become her lucky number instead of leading to Manni's demise. Yet, when Lola arrives with the cash, she sees Manni exiting Ronnie's car in good spirits. With the help of the blind woman—a reference to the blind man in Lang's *M* who leads the police to the serial killer—Manni discovers the street person bicycling past the phone booth and recovers the bag of money. His brief sprint, much shorter than Lola's, ends up being as fruitful.

Noticing Lola's fatigue, he asks whether she ran. Lola's race against time turns out to be superfluous. In other words, the convention of the happy ending necessitates a restoration of equilibrium and of a traditional gender arrangement and, last but not least, a casino. It is happy, at least, within the logic of the overarching narrative but is ultimately disappointing because it undermines Lola's success. Manni has regained his mobility, restored his masculinity, and taken control of his circumstance. Yet this perfunctory ending falls short of the complex visual spectacle that has dominated the film. The ending, spurious at best, is a self-conscious reenactment of a Hollywood convention. What is more, the happy ending is unsettled by the final image of Lola, who remains detached and reserved and does not arouse confidence in this "union of the heart" as suggested in the song "Komm zu mir." Lola does not respond to Manni's question concerning the contents of her bag. She has a mysterious and mischievous Mona Lisa–like smile that remains open-ended and uncompromised by the convention of the happy ending. The spectator and Lola share the knowledge of her abilities, while Manni remains clueless. After approximately eighty-one minutes, the film is over. Lola has one hundred thousand marks in the bag and has won the game on her own terms. She remains an image of fantasy that is not reabsorbed into the convention of the happy heterosexual couple. Lola retains a transcendent quality that is captured in the non-diegetic lyrics sung by Franka Potente at various times throughout the film in which she enumerates all of the things she wishes she were. She shouts: "I wish I were." Her wish list includes wanting to be a hunter, a starship, a princess, a ruler, a writer, a prayer—all powerful images that energize the visual representation of Lola. She has broken boundaries just like the film. The excitement ceases but identities have been transformed, and another female image can be added to the repertoire of representations that feeds popular culture.

History

For all of Tykwer's technical innovation, his recourse to avant-garde traditions and to popular culture, and his challenge to conventional narrative forms, the question that remains is whether this game allows for a transition into another way of living. In other words, to return to Detlev Buck's assertion, what else does the film have to say about Germany other than to call for a new type of German cinema (that dismisses history)? The relationship of the film to Germany's history is ambivalent indeed. With the exception of the traditional narratives (melodrama, romance, and so forth) that she encounters, Lola is barely impeded. Unlike the New German Cinema or the German heritage films, which Lutz Koepnick discusses in the present volume, it is significant that *Run Lola Run* hardly concerns itself with history, except when it trips Lola up. She is late in meeting Manni not only because her moped was stolen but also because a taxi driver mistakenly took her to the Grunewald Street in the eastern part of Berlin rather than the one in the western part. The mix-up reflects a postunification confusion owing to the divide that still exists between the eastern and western parts of Berlin. Besides this one explicit reference to history, history, for the most part, is only visually insinuated. For instance, Lola sails past the Garnison Cemetery (in the east) at the beginning of each segment. At the end of the third segment, she barrels across the Gendarmenmarkt (in the east). Her race against time (and thus history) then takes her over the Oberbaumbrücke—a border crossing for Germans during the time of the wall—and past the Friederichsstrasse and Kochstrasse (in the west) that bordered Checkpoint Charlie—the crossing points between East and West Berlin before the fall of the wall for citizens of allied nations. These sites and spaces are traversed, and it may be argued that the past and present are visually connected. Yet while Lola's twenty-minute sprint (a tribute to the end of the twentieth century) takes her past these sites, she never takes them in or reflects on them. Unlike Walter Benjamin's angel of history, who looks back in shock at the pile of debris that history has left and desires to return to fix it but cannot, Lola is oriented toward the future.[20] Her stride is resolute and unwavering; she never gazes back. The piles of bricks and open ditches, the construction sites that she passes, represent renewal. Berlin, Germany's new capital, stands for the future of a new Germany. Berlin is a city under construction that must reinvent itself, and Lola becomes its agent—a superhero of the contemporary German cultural scene.

The first cut on the CD soundtrack, which is not included in the film but accompanies it, is entitled "Believe." It begins with an inventory of the things in which the female protagonist does not believe. She does not believe in trouble, silence, panic, fear, history, truth, chance, prophecy, or destiny. She does, however, believe in fantasy, the stuff of popular culture. It is a type of fantasy that has the power to overcome the spatial divide of a newly unified Berlin, which Lola navigates with exceptional skill. Indeed, *Run Lola Run* is, as Sinka argues, the feature film that best portrays "the spirit of a New Berlin generation." This generation, she writes, does not "shun confrontations with Germany's fractured tortured past, this past no longer has a hold on them."[21] Perhaps it is not only the New Berlin generation that is celebrated but also more significantly a new Germany that is less invested in remembering and more invested in looking ahead. Is it by chance that Lola emerges at a time when Germany is struggling to redefine itself as a nation and that the film has become synonymous with the new direction that Germany is taking?

Run Lola Run does not reflect the Germany that the New German filmmaker Fassbinder envisioned. After all, Fassbinder fatalistically returned to the past to identify the moment in postwar Germany history in which the game was won and thus lost simultaneously. I am referring here to Fassbinder's 1979 film *The Marriage of Maria Braun,* which ends with Germany's victory in the soccer match against Hungary in 1954. For Fassbinder, this victory marks a turning point in the direction the Federal Republic took in establishing its democracy and a failed opportunity to reflect on Germany's fascist past. In the last scene Maria's house explodes and with it her dreams of love and a new beginning. Tykwer's open admiration for the New German Cinema may have influenced his first feature, *Die tödliche Maria* (The Deadly Maria, 1994), but with *Lola* Tykwer steps outside of the politically motivated framework of the New German Cinema and its compulsive preoccupation with national identity and the past. The question of "who we are" at the beginning of the film is posed tellingly by the well-known voice of Hans Paetsch, a storyteller of fairy tales, that is, popular culture. Ironically, Tykwer picks up where Fassbinder left off but changes the course. In the last scene of *Maria Braun,* the radio broadcaster exclaims that Germany has won the soccer match against Hungary. At the beginning of *Run Lola Run,* the questions of "who we are" and "why we believe" are answered in a quotation by Sepp Herberger, the same legendary soccer coach who took Germany to victory in the 1954 World Cup: "The ball is round, the game lasts 90 minutes. Everything else is theory." Yet the film only lasts eighty-one minutes, which means that Tykwer again did not stick to the rules. With *Run Lola Run,* he let his imagination run, placed his bets ("Rien ne va plus"), and became "the king" of a new wave in German cinema.

A subjective engagement in the film's fantasy may open up a space for a new type of German cinema and lend a new cultural identity to Germany that is focused more on the future. The premise on which the film operates, as Tykwer admits, is that "you have no chance, therefore, use it."[22] And he did. The film is celebrated as signaling a new beginning for German cinema that is bold, dynamic, and indulgent and that overcomes self-doubt and "artistic cowardliness," according to Helmut Krausser, who compares the film to opera and applauds Tykwer's courage to produce visual pathos.[23] Considering its international success and Hollywood's interest in engaging *Lola*'s filmmaker for its own productions, it comes as no surprise that the German Film Prize that is awarded annually now fondly is called *Lola.*[24] With *Lola* Tykwer has struck a new chord that serves Germany well.

NOTES

I would like to thank my colleagues Irene d'Almeida, Mary Beth Haralovich, Susan White, and Linda Zwinger for our lively discussions of the film that helped to shape this essay.

1. Michael Töteberg, "Über die Karriere eines Films," in *Szenenwechsel: Momentaufnahmen des jungen deutschen Films,* ed. Michael Töteberg (Reinbeck and Hamburg: Rowohlt, 1999), 45–49.

2. Robert Falcon, "Run Lola Run/Lola rennt," *Sight and Sound* 9, no. 11 (1999): 52.

3. Richard Rayner, "Franka Potente: This German Actress Makes Her U.S. Film Debut in Run Lola Run," *Harper's Bazaar* 3451 (June 1999): 85.

4. Tom Whalen, "Run Lola Run," *Film Quarterly* 53, no. 3 (2000): 22.

5. Cited in Margit Sinka, "Tom Tykwer's *Lola rennt:* A Blueprint of Millennial Berlin," *Glossen* 11 (2000): n 14: "*Lola rennt* erzählt von Deutschland einen Dreck. Das ist reines Entertainment." All translations in this essay are my own.

6. Niklas Luhmann, *The Reality of the Mass Media* (Palo Alto: Stanford University Press, 2000), 51.

7. John Storey, *An Introduction to Cultural Theory and Popular Culture* (Athens: University of Georgia Press, 1998), 11.

8. Thomas Assheuer, "Im Reich des Scheins," *Die Zeit,* April 11, 2001, 16.

9. The original reads: "wir sprengten jeden Rahmen, als wir zusammenkamen. Es war wie eine Explosion. Ich spür die Erschütterung immer noch" (my translation). It is interesting to note the tension in the blending of the songs "Wish"

(a female vocalist) and "Komm zu mir" (a male vocalist). While the female vocalist fantasizes about all of the things that she wishes to become, the male vocalist is intent on drawing her back to him.

10. Michael Töteberg, "Ein romantisch-philosophischer ActionLiebesExperimentalThriller" (interview with Tom Tykwer), in *Lola rennt* (Reinbeck and Hamburg: Rowohlt, 1998), 129–42.

11. Töteberg, "Ein romantisch-philosophischer ActionLiebesExperimentalThriller," 129.

12. Cited in Giovanni Lista, *Futurism,* trans. Charles Lynn Clark (New York: Universe Books, 1986), 5. There is a resonance with futurism also in the fragmented representation of Lola in some advertisements for the film. Also, the *New Yorker* film advertisement includes a quote from Peter Rainer, of the *New York Magazine.* He writes: "Lola's like a human stun gun."

13. Tom Tykwer, "Generalschlüssel furs Kino," in *Szenenwechsel: Momentaufnahmen des jungen deutschen Films,* ed. Michael Töteberg (Reinbeck and Hamburg: Rowohlt, 1999), 32: "Bei *Lola rennt* war es das Bild dieser rennenden Frau, für mich so ein Urbild von Kino, weil es Dynamik und Emotion verbindet. In der Wahrnehmung fasst du einen dynamischen Ablauf zusammen, der einfach mechanisch sein könnte, den du aber gleichzeitig emotional auflädst. Ich hatte vor Augen eine Frau mit roten Haaren, und die Haare mußten auch so wehen, und sie mußte Verzweiflung und Leidenschaft ausdrücken. Das ist ein Bild, das hab ich immermal wieder gehabt."

14. Cited in Paul Wells, *Understanding Animation* (London and New York: Routledge, 1988), 26.

15. Cited in Les Daniels, *Wonder Woman: The Complete History. The Life and Times of the Amazon Princess* (San Francisco: Chronicle Books, 2000), 11.

16. Sinka, "Tom Tykwer's *Lola rennt.*"

17. "Siehste, ich wusste, dass dir da auch nix mehr einfällt, ich hab's dir ja gesagt, eines Tages passiert was, da weisst auch du keinen Ausweg mehr, und nicht erst, wen du stirbst, das kommt viel früher. Du wolltest mir ja nicht glauben, und jetzt stehste da. Von wegen die Liebe kann alles, aber nicht in zwanzig Minuten hunderttausend Mark herzaubern."

18. Sherrie A. Inness, *Tough Girls: Women Warriors and Wonder Women in Popular Culture* (Philadelphia: University of Pennsylvania Press, 1999), 141.

19. My special thanks to Caryl Flynn, who gave me her unpublished paper on the music in *Run Lola Run* entitled "That Music That Lola Ran To."

20. Flash-forwards of the nameless passersby that Lola encounters in each run, the guy on the bike or the woman pushing a baby carriage, suggest that she changes the course of their personal histories. Some critics have pursued a chaos theory reading of Lola and talked about the ripple effect that the smallest alteration to the narrative produces. I think that Tykwer plays with the endless possibilities and combinations that storytelling provides and, much like a constructivist, believes in the alterability of reality.

21. Sinka, "Tom Tykwer's *Lola rennt.*" Sinka offers an incisive analysis of the impact of the film on the political landscape in Berlin. Both the conservative and social democratic parties appropriated the image of Lola's vitality and determina-

tion to inject their campaigns with a message for the future. Each candidate (Diepgen and Naumann) donned the Lola look.

22. Cited in Sinka, "Tom Tykwer's *Lola rennt.*"

23. Helmut Krausser, "Lola: Ein Nachwort, viel zu früh," in *Szenenwechsel: Momentaufnahmen des jungen deutschen Films,* ed. Michael Töteberg (Reinbek bei Hamburg: Rowohlt, 1999), 35.

24. "Der Kanzler und die Kaiserin: In Berlin wird der Deutsche Filmpreis 2001 zelebriert," SZdigital- Süddeutsche Zeitung (June 22, 2001) <www.diz-muenchen.de> A012.502.877.

Hollywood in Altona: Minority Cinema and the Transnational Imagination

Gerd Gemünden

> The image, the imagined, the imaginary—these are all terms which direct us to something critical and new in global cultural processes: *the imagination as social practice.* . . . The imagination is now central to all forms of agency, is itself a social fact, and is the key component of the new global order.
>
> —Arjun Appadurai

At the press screening of his second feature, *Im Juli* (In July) (2000), at the 2001 Berlin Film Festival, director Fatih Akin introduced the film with the following words (in English): "*Im Juli* is a German film. It was made in Germany. [Pause] It was shown here in German theaters." Vaguely familiar with the film through some reviews, I found Akin's words puzzling. Why this emphasis on Germany as the film's country of origin and exhibition? Couldn't this be assumed since the film was showing in the so-called Neue deutsche Reihe, a sampling of German films from the last year for international journalists who have limited opportunities to see them? And why such an emphatic self-positioning within the national German cinema? To disavow being typecast as a hyphenated filmmaker? To assert a position within a German national cinema that encompasses, rather than marginalizes, Turkish-German directors? Or, more simply, to deflect expectations that *Im Juli* be a follow-up to the portrayal of minority culture of his first feature, *Kurz und schmerzlos* (A short sharp shock), and to assert, instead, the right to make different kinds of films, with different target audiences, in different genres, and with different social concerns?

Akin's remarks are straightforward and unambiguous, yet they are also puzzling and full of irony. I quote them here because they point toward the difficulty of articulating what German national cinema has come to mean in the new millennium. Over the last ten years, minority filmmakers have emerged as a significant creative force, contributing to what Hamid Naficy calls "the genre of independent transnational cinema" or what Ella Shoat and Robert Stam label "postcolonial hybrid films," a development that challenges us to rethink the meaning of "German" in German popular culture.[1] In the first part of this essay, I want to review the function of cinema within the construction of the nation as an imagined community, showing how global and local concerns have overtaken national ones. In the second part, a reading of two films attempts to demonstrate that one very significant agent in this development has been a changed stance toward discourses and representations of Americanization. Fatih Akin's *Kurz und schmerzlos* (1998) as well as Angelina Maccarone and Fatima El-Tayeb's *Alles wird gut* (Everything will be fine) (1998) register a disavowal of the rhetoric of cultural imperialism and Coca-colonization that was dominant during the 1970s and 1980s, instead presenting U.S. popular culture as liberating and empowering; for the diverse protagonists of these films, it provides a most viable alternative to a German culture that is perceived to be too limiting and exclusive in its insistence on homogeneity, purity, and authenticity. On a deeper political level, the United States is sought out as a model for social and ethnic integration, cultural hybridity, and progressive notions of immigration and citizenship.

In his influential study *Imagined Communities,* Benedict Anderson has linked the emergence of the modern nation-state as a sovereign and limited entity since the eighteenth century to the epistemological, political, and technological changes that have allowed the nation to *imagine* itself possessing these attributes. A fundamental role in producing such an imaginary has been played by the novel and the newspaper, "creating that remarkable confidence of community in anonymity which is the hallmark of modern nations."[2] Following Anderson's concept that the nation is to be understood as a construct that needs to be envisioned and sustained primarily by mass media, recent film theory has addressed the question of how particularly *cinema,* as the most important mass medium of the twentieth century, participates—in both enabling and critical modes—in representations and discourses of community building.[3] In his recent essay "The Limiting Imagination of National Cinema," Andrew Higson raises the question of the degree to which Anderson's concept of the nation—imagined as a limited, finite, and sovereign community—provides an appropriate framework for conceptualizing the specificity of national cinema.[4] Higson suggests that an account of national cinema must acknowledge not only the nationalizing effect of certain discourses and state politics but also the increasingly *trans*national dimensions of cinematic production, distribution, and reception. The boundaries defining cinema culture, claims Higson, do not coincide with Anderson's limits of the nation-state. On the contrary, the communities imagined by cinematic means tend to be local or transnational rather than national. In the words of Rob Wilson and Wimal Dissanayake: "[As] the crucial genre of transnational production and global circulation for refigured narratives, [film] offers speculative ground for the transnational imaginary and its contention within national and local communities."[5]

The emergence of a German-Turkish cinema in Germany during the last ten years needs to be situated within the developments just outlined. Films such as *Sommer in Mezra* (Summer in Mezra) (Hussi Kutlucan, 1991); *Schattenboxer* (Shadow boxer) (Lars Becker, 1992); *Nach dem Spiel* (After the match) (Aysun Bademsoy, 1997); *Yara* (Yilmaz Arslan, 1998); *Aprilkinder* (April children) (Yüksel Yavuz, 1998); *Ich Chef, du Turnschuh* (Me boss, you sneaker) (Hussi Kutlucan, 1998); *Dealer* (Thomas Arslan, 1999); *Lola und Bilidikid* (Kutlug Ataman, 1999); *Kanak Attack* (Lars Becker, 2000); and *Im Juli* (Akin, 2000) call into question existing definitions of national German cinema. Made by directors born in both Germany and Turkey, the transnational dimension of these films is not anchored in the biography of the filmmakers, nor is it informed by any claim to record authentic or personal experiences. These films form part of a wider European and non-European cinema that is "driven by its sensitivity to the production and consumption of films in conditions of transnationality, liminality, multiculturality, multifocality, and syncretism."[6]

These films from the last decade introduce us to German-Turkish relationships that differ significantly from those represented in the New German Cinema of the 1970s and early 1980s, taking leave of the stereotype of portraying immigrant communities in Germany as lost between two cultures and insisting instead on fluid notions of *both* German and Turkish identity. They thus confirm Deniz Göktürk's observations regarding "the development from a [1970s] 'cinema of duty' to 'the pleasures of hybridity'," which she sees exemplified in Sinan Cetin's *Berlin in Berlin* (1993).[7] Yet the films cited previously are even more playful and ironic in their reversal of cultural stereotypes than the example she chooses to discuss, showing many incidents of humorous enactments of ethnicity; ridiculing essentialized notions of racial or ethnic identity; and relying on performance and masquerade, comedy, irony, and pastiche to portray the complex lives of minorities in Germany. They also attest to a change in German popular culture, allowing the vernacular a flexibility to reflect these changes that high culture apparently still lacks (see also Sabine von Dirke, "Hip Hop Made in Germany," this vol.).

As Göktürk shows, representation of so-called guest workers and other minorities in films such as *Katzelmacher* (Fassbinder, 1969); *Angst essen Seele auf* (Ali: Fear Eats the Soul) (Fassbinder, 1973); *Shirins Hochzeit* (Shirin's wedding) (Helma Sanders, 1975); and *Yasemin* (Hark Bohm, 1988) emphasized the status of the victim, the oppressed, the silenced, and the abject. Made by German leftist filmmakers, these films aim to raise the consciousness of viewers about social and gender injustice and racial prejudice, as do the films of Turkish filmmaker Tevfik Baser, *40 m² Deutschland* (1986) and *Abschied vom falschen Paradies* (Farewell to a false paradise) (1988). Yet by insisting on the fundamentally different experiences of Germans and non-Germans, they invariably cement the popular narrative of "lost between two cultures." These films, claims Göktürk, "are informed by a social worker's perspective and haunted by residual notions of cultural purity, community and authenticity," often relying on reified notions of exile and diaspora that have little to do with the filmmakers' own biography—as in the case of Baser—and that comply with the label "ethnic" or "third world" cinema in order to profit from funding policies and to target specific audiences.[8]

There is yet no overview of German-Turkish or minority cinema of the last decade.[9] My following remarks about the role of U.S. popular culture in this development and its effects on understanding the national remain therefore somewhat speculative. As I want to argue, one very significant aspect of German-Turkish cinema, and German minority cinema in general, is a relationship to Hollywood filmmaking and U.S. popular culture that is very different from the New German Cinema. As I have shown elsewhere, the famed auteurs of the 1970s entertained a highly ambivalent relationship to the United States, exposing in their respective films the ways in which Hollywood has shaped the social, psychological, and political dimension of the postwar generation.[10] U.S. popular culture functioned in this scenario as catalyst *and* antagonist, providing both foil and engine to articulate the paradoxical predicament of those born around the end of World War

II. Filmmakers such as Akin and Maccarone and El-Tayeb, in contrast, belong to a generation of Germans who have learned from Hollywood in a way that Wenders and Fassbinder never wanted to. Like other successful filmmakers of the 1990s, they put emphasis on fast editing, stylized interiors, witty dialogues, and well-paced plot development—as well as a strong emphasis on entertainment rather than consciousness raising—aiming for professional standards and a visual style that their Hollywood-reared audience expects. Yet, unlike Doris Dörrie, Sönke Wortmann, Joseph Vilsmaier, or Tom Tykwer, they do understand themselves as part of an alternative cinema that gives voice to minorities and indeed shows the centrality of the margins. Thus despite their aspirations to be commercially viable and entertaining, one must see *Kurz und schmerzlos* and *Alles wird gut* as films that are "minor" in Deleuze and Guattari's sense—by definition these films are always political; they mark the "double movement of deterritorialization and reterritorialization of the image"; and they insist on the minor as a "collective assemblages of enunciation."[11] It is this tension between the major and the minor that makes the two films I now turn to a significant new development within the tradition of cultural productions that address Americanization in Germany.

Called by critics a mixture of gangster film and multicultural *Milieustudie, Kurz und schmerzlos* revolves around the friendship of Gabriel (a Turk), Costa (a Greek), and Bobby (a Serb), in the hoods of Hamburg-Altona. Released from prison, Gabriel rejoins the lives of his would-be gangster and small-time mafiosi buddies, despite resolutions to stay legit. When conflicting love interests intersect with a deal to purchase illegal weapons, the inevitable happens, leaving Bobby and Costa dead and Gabriel heading for Turkey. With an international soundtrack including U.S. and Hamburg hip-hop, Turkish and Greek traditional music, and the Spanish-language punk band Niños Con Bombas, the film tries to re-create the dense atmosphere of 1980s U.S. crime films as well as that of more contemporary films revolving around life in the hood. As multilayered subjects, the three protagonists show themselves to be well versed in a variety of idioms and languages that they can mimic, parody, or employ as their own most authentic means of exchange. They ridicule the infantile language that Germans adopt when they speak to foreigners, as well as German efforts to create a multicultural society: "Ich steig bei den Albanern ein—das nennt man heute Multi-Kulti," says Bobby before joining the Mafia.[12] While the three remain outsiders to German culture, they do participate in the prevalent everyday racism, belittling Asians and uttering remarks like: "Silvio hat mich zum Neger gemacht. Er hat mir nicht vertraut."[13]

The youths can speak the respective languages of their parents, yet their true moment of bonding occurs through the lingo of U.S. gangsters. All three show themselves to be well versed in the language and gestures of Al Pacino and Robert de Niro. Particularly Bobby loves Americanisms, calling Gabriel "my baddest mother-fucker," while constantly donning the swagger and demeanor of the two American stars in the hope of commanding some respect in the mean streets of Altona. In a particularly memorable scene, we witness the three young men watching an Asian karate film, the hero of which is derided for his failure to live up to the toughness and masculinity of Al Pacino. Sitting next to each other on a sofa, Costa, Gabriel, and Bobby communicate with each other without making eye contact, merely looking at the screen in front of them—their relationship is structured around projections and perceptions of which they are not the authors. Yet such other-directedness is not criticized as a colonization of the subconscious—as one protagonist famously quipped in Wim Wenders's *Im Lauf der Zeit* (1976)—but celebrated as a moment of true experience. As in Pacino's struggle to fit into U.S. society as a Cuban (in *Mean Streets*), they recognize their own problems of assimilating to German society. Yet *Kurz und schmerzlos* is not entirely complicit with its protagonists' emulation of things American, for the viewers realize that the incongruity between the three youths' lives and the fictions they want to live is what costs Bobby and Costa their lives.

By resorting to the Hollywood gangster film as its generic model, *Kurz und schmerzlos* situates itself in a long line of German postwar films. Yet Akin's film is quite different from famous precursors such as Klaus Lemke's *48 Stunden bis Acapulco* (1967), Rainer Werner Fassbinder's *Liebe ist kälter als der Tod* (1969) and *Der amerikanische Soldat* (1971), Rudolf Thome's *Rote Sonne* (1970), or Wenders's *Der amerikanische Freund* (1977). Whereas these earlier films are examples of modernist and experimental filmmaking that present Hollywood cinema as an aesthetic and political model of fascination and rejection, Akin's film seems far less paradoxical. Aesthetically, it marks its relation to features of Scorsese, de Palma, or Coppola as one of unadulterated fascination and emulation, employing a camera and editing style that invokes the American precursors without irony. Yet in terms of gender politics, Akin remains much closer to the German auteurs cited previously. As with many films by Thome and Wenders, *Kurz und schmerzlos* also presents an unquestioned embrace of codified gender roles by its male protagonists. The homosocial bond between the three men comes at the expense of stable and equal heterosexual relationships. Indeed, it is not the gap between foreigners and Germans that cannot be closed but the one between men and women. The three men are victims not of German oppression but rather of their own misunderstood masculinity, shown here to be a mixture of native tradition and Hollywood deception. For the modern Turkish and German women in the film, this machismo may at first be attractive and titillating, yet ultimately it is not tolerable.

If the Hollywood to be emulated in *Kurz und schmerzlos* is that of 1970s and 1980s crime films and more recent films set in the hood, it is 1930s screwball comedy that defines the trajectory of *Alles wird gut.* Also set in Hamburg, the film follows its gender-bending Afro-German heroines' pursuit of love and fulfillment in the face of everyday racism. A "mainstream black lesbian comedy,"[14] as screenwriter Fatima El-Tayeb describes it, the made-for-television film tackles sensitive issues of race and sexuality while trustfully relying on the upbeat nature of a Hollywood-style narrative that delivers what its title promises—in the end, everything will be fine.

Even more so than in *Kurz und schmerzlos,* in *Alles wird gut* American popular culture provides the means through which the characters define themselves and relate to each other. Nabou, a dropout with dreams of winning the lottery, is a fan of Skunk Anansie and Tina Turner and styles herself like urban young blacks in the United States; Kim, a workaholic designer in an advertising company, was once inspired by Angela Davis to leave behind her white rural home (and her real name, Erika) and to seek self-fulfillment in the city. She is clearly representative of many radical intellectuals her age who have been absorbed by the culture industry they once decried. Kim's dormant disavowal of German *Spiessertum* is reawakened when she meets Nabou, for whom she will, in the end, forego a bourgeois marriage and career. For Giuseppa, Kofi, and his son Kwame—the respective friends surrounding the two protagonists—the heroes and heroines of contemporary popular culture likewise supply points of commonality and give meaning to their lives, be they Greta Garbo, Michael Jackson, or the Ninja Turtles, respectively.

Yet the film clearly divides between appropriate and inappropriate modes of reception of U.S. culture—between cultural poaching and mere consumption. In a particularly humorous scene, Kim and Dieter, her boyfriend and boss, emerge from the movie theater to discuss the performance of Julia Roberts and Kevin Costner.

DIETER: "Endlich mal wieder 'n guter Film, nicht so platt, von wegen aus Hollywood kommt keine sozialkritische Message . . ."

KIM: "Sozial*kitschig* wolltest du wohl sagen . . ."

DIETER: "Sei doch nicht immer so. Wie die Julia Roberts, da am Schluss im Elendsviertel, da musst ich fast heulen."

KIM: [ironically] "Ja, ich auch. Julia Roberts als Mutter Teresa und Kevin Costner ihr indischer Liebhaber!"

DIETER: "Also manchmal verstehe ich dich nicht. Diesen französischen Frauenfilm fandste eurozentrisch und der hat dir jetzt auch nicht gefallen . . . ausserdem war Costner ja'n *Halb*inder."[15]

While Kim derides the manipulative tearjerker, Dieter defends the performance of the two stars because they disappear into their roles; he does not see through the ethnic drag of Kostner as Halbinder (reminiscent of his performance in *Dances with Wolves*). Whereas Dieter lauds the culture industry's ability both to entertain and to provide social critique, Kim—like Adorno—only sees mass deception. Dieter's shallowness is also visible in the many Americanisms with which he peppers his language: "der Deal, das Brainstorming, sorry, Mäuschen, ich bin total busy." The dichotomy between the two is obvious and, following genre conventions, intentionally overdrawn—white boys don't dig popular culture. Dieter, of course, represents not only the yuppie-esque German manager in Armani suit and sneakers but the mainstream of German men (and women). For Nabou, Guiseppa, and Kim, in contrast, *certain aspects* of American popular culture provide a means to articulate their racial and sexual difference in playful and yet politically relevant ways. As savvy recipients, they appropriate and reinterpret popular culture. While Dieter raves about Julia Roberts's phony humanism, Kim lights two cigarettes at once, imitating Paul Henreid's chivalry toward Bette Davis in *Now, Voyager*—a gesture of emancipation and role reversal that shows her creative use of pop culture, the meaning of which will certainly escape Dieter. Interestingly, German popular culture, represented in the film only in the form of techno music favored by Katja, Nabou's "ex," provides Afro-Germans with no resources for cultural poaching. German culture, whether high brow or commercial, offers these minorities no source for appropriation or even subversion.

In *Kurz und schmerzlos* the biggest gap opens not between non-Germans and Germans (there are hardly any in the film) but between men and women. The biggest divide in *Alles wird gut,* in contrast, is not class or gender but race. Both Nabou and Kim abandon their white German love interest. While one film ends in tragedy and the other in bliss, both advocate a retreat—Gabriel will return to the country of his parents and Kim and Nabou will cultivate an island existence within a society that clearly has difficulties accepting difference, as symbolized by their holding on to the buoy amidst the Hamburg harbor in the final frame.

The two films' portrayal of how German minorities use U.S. popular culture raises, of course, questions about the political implications of such a reception. As stated earlier, these films take leave from discourses of cultural imperialism of the 1970s and early 1980s, from the fierce anti-Americanism of Edgar Reitz or Hans Jürgen Syberberg, and from the paradoxical, highly ambivalent stance of Wim Wenders or Rainer Werner Fassbinder. Yet one should be careful not to misread this as a naive co-optation by the U.S. culture industry. Rather, what is at stake is a different understanding of the national and of what it means to be German. For the New German auteurs, the national itself was a minor that needed to be upheld against the dominance of the U.S. film industry. Self-marginalization became an attitude with which the auteurs defined themselves as minor vis-à-vis the dominance of Hollywood—always eager to identify with the other (as in the films depicting foreigners cited earlier) yet never questioning how the government's funding of their films served the legitimization of Germany's larger postwar political strategy to reintegrate itself into the West.[16] Born to parents who immigrated to the Federal Republic, directors such as Akin and Maccarone have a very different relationship to the "German question" than the postwar New German directors. Gone are the brooding meditations on one's parents' alleged complicity in the Third Reich; gone are the attempts to claim victim status, the self-hatred, and the triangulation of U.S. popular culture with German fascism. The minorities in these films are not voiceless and disempowered outsiders as the "Griech aus Griechenland" from Fassbinder's *Katzelmacher* but rather the articulate representatives of a new generation of Germans who fight xenophobia through creativity and parody.

For German minority cinema, Americanization is that part of globalization that is willfully accepted and incorporated. The protagonists of *Kurz und schmerzlos* and *Alles wird gut* do not experience U.S. culture as something that is imposed from above or merely happens—rather, these young Germans Americanize themselves because U.S. popular culture offers opportunities to articulate ethnic and racial differences that do not (yet) exist in Germany. To that extent—and to that extent only—Hollywood is not an other but is part of almost every national cinema. The positive effects of its global, and indeed universal, aspirations are the fostering of supranational imagined communities that displace those of the nation-state. For minorities living in a nation such as Germany, which refuses to see itself as *Einwandererland,* this is an attractive position.

But, of course, "globalization" remains a far more ambiguous and problematic term. For those who believe in it, it promises openness—the free flow of people, goods, and information; political liberalization; and transparent, more democratic societies. Others fear its effects, which range from homogenization and exploitation to the erosion of individual cultures and the consolidating of power in the hands of big, unaccountable corporations. U.S. film production is still hegemonic and fiercely capitalist, even if now more subtle and dispersed, and it affects transnational cinema not only in productive ways, as Maccarone and El-Tayeb experienced themselves: the original title of their film, *Hakuna Matata,* had to be dropped because it was preempted by the release of Disney's *The Lion King*—perhaps in the end not everything will be fine.

NOTES

1. Hamid Naficy, "Phobic Spaces and Liminal Panics: Independent Transnational Film Genre," in *Global/Local: Cultural Production and the Transnational Imaginary,* ed. Rob Wilson and Wimal Dissanayake (Durham and London: Duke University Press, 1996), 119; and Ella Shoat and Robert Stam, *Unthinking Eurocentrism: Multiculturalism and the Media* (London and New York: Routledge, 1994), 42.

2. Benedict Anderson, *Imagined Communities: Reflections on the Origin and Spread of Nationalism* (New York and London: Verso, 1983), 40.

3. See Robert Burgoyne, *Film Nation: Hollywood Looks at U.S. History* (Minneapolis: University of Minnesota Press, 1997); Susan Hayward, *French National Cinema* (London and New York: Routledge, 1993); Andrew Higson, "The Concept of National Cinema," *Screen* 30, no. 4 (1989): 36–46; Mette Hjort and Scott Mackenzie, eds., *Cinema and Nation* (London and New York: Routledge, 2000); Marc Silberman, "What Is German in the German Cinema?" *Film History* 8 (1996): 297–315.

4. Andrew Higson, "The Limiting Imagination of National Cinema," in *Cinema and Nation,* 63–74.

5. Wilson and Dissanayake, *Global/Local,* 11.

6. Naficy, "Phobic Spaces," 121.

7. Deniz Göktürk, "Turkish Delight—German Fright: Migrant Identities in Transnational Cinema," *Transnational Communities—Working Paper Series,* An Economic and Social Council Research Programme, University of Oxford, January 1999, 1.

8. Göktürk, "Turkish Delight—German Fright." Fatih Akin's remarks quoted earlier have to be seen as an attempt to escape being labeled a German-Turkish, or ethnic, director. Yet the struggle against such labeling is a difficult task. In conversation, Kutlug Ataman told me how relatively easy it was for him, a Turkish-born, U.S.-trained film director currently residing in London, to receive funding for *Lola and Bilidikid,* a drama set in the Turkish transvestite community of Berlin-Kreuzberg. Yet his plans to make a film about Sigmund Freud have not yet found support from German or Austrian sources because officials, Ataman suspects, do not trust an "ethnic" filmmaker with this material. Ataman's model for filmmaking is Ang Lee, who can make films about Hong Kong with equal credibility as adapting a Jane Austen novel (*Sense and Sensibility*) or depicting a family crisis in small-town America (*The Icestorm*).

9. The best surview of the German cinema of the last decade is provided by Eric Rentschler, "From New German Cinema to the Post-Wall Cinema of Consensus," in *Cinema and Nation,* 260–77. In order to underscore the political shortcomings of what he calls "a cinema of consensus," he intentionally excludes more "offbeat voices and less reconciled visions" (of whose existence he is well aware), because "this cinema remains for the most a minority opinion and a marginal perspective" (275). Rentschler thus forgoes any discussion of the place of that more marginal cinema within German national cinema and, in particular, any speculation to what extent films by Turkish-German filmmakers question the very notion of the national as he employs it.

10. Gerd Gemünden, *Framed Visions: Popular Culture, Americanization, and the Contemporary German and Austrian Imagination* (Ann Arbor: University of Michigan Press, 1998).

11. Gilles Deleuze and Felix Guattari, *Kafka: Toward a Minor Literature,* trans. Dana Polan (Minneapolis: University of Minnesota Press, 1985), 16 ff.

12. "I'll join the Albanians. That's what they call multiculturalism these days."

13. "Silvio turned me into a negro. He didn't trust me."

14. Conversation with author, Hanover, NH, May 2000.

15. Fatima El-Tayeb and Angelina Maccarone, *Alles wird gut: Das Filmbuch* (Berlin: Orlanda Frauenverlag, 1999), 31. (*Dieter:* Finally, a good film, not so predictable. And people say, Hollywood films have no social critique. / *Kim:* You probably mean social kitsch. / *Dieter:* Don't give me that. At the end, with Julia Roberts in the slums—I was close to crying / *Kim* [ironically]: Yeah, right. Julia Roberts as Mother Teresa, and Kevin Costner as her half-Indian lover. / *Dieter:* Sometimes I just don't understand you. The French woman's film you found too eurocentric, and this one you didn't like either . . . even though Kevin Costner was only *half*-Indian.)"

16. See John E. Davidson, *Deterritorializing the New German Cinema* (Minneapolis: University of Minnesota Press, 1999).

"Amerika gibt's überhaupt nicht": Notes on the German Heritage Film

Lutz Koepnick

The mid-1980s saw the emergence of what Andrew Higson has called the British heritage film, a cycle of period pieces whose central pleasures lay in "the artful and spectacular projection of an elite, conservative vision of the national past."[1] As defined by Higson, the heritage film avoided the stylistic signatures of the European art film yet often explored literary sources and domestic cultural traditions as marks of authenticity. Heritage films privileged mise-en-scène over narrative development, fluid camera moves over fast cutting, self-conscious panorama shots over close-ups. Concerned with character, place, and atmospheric detail rather than goal-oriented action, the British heritage films of the 1980s reproduced English history as a museal object of identification, consumption, and exportability. In the United States, these films—e.g., *Another Country* (1984), *A Room with a View* (1985), *A Passage to India* (1985), and *Little Dorrit* (1987)—were shown primarily in art house theaters. In their European context, however, they represented a new cinema of high production values and popular appeal that aspired to supplement, rather than challenge, the dominant role of Hollywood on the global market.

However conservative in outlook, the British heritage film evidenced a dialectic of reification and utopia that Fredric Jameson locates in all works of modern mass culture, namely, the fact that even when their function lies in the legitimation of the present order these works "cannot do their job without deflecting in the latter's service the deepest and most fundamental hopes and fantasies of the collectivity, to which they can therefore, no matter in how distorted a fashion, be found to have given voice."[2] British heritage films of the 1980s served as both a complement and a corrective to Margaret Thatcher's neoliberal call for universal entrepreneurship. In converting national history into a viable commodity, heritage films on the one hand echoed and capitalized on Thatcher's celebratory view of the marketplace. Carefully crafted, their mise-en-scène reconstructed the past as a profitable showcase of sights and sounds. On the other hand, however, at the level of narrative development, the heritage cycle often confronted Thatcher's economic policies with memories of a past in which liberal-humanist values triumphed over the logic of the market. Though rigorously commodifying the past, the emplotment of national history in these films could only succeed because it, in so many ways, defied Thatcher's credo of competitive individualism and instrumental reason. The national thus emerged as a site of striking ambivalence, becoming an imaginary in which different modes of identification and consumption competed with each other.

Shell-shocked by the demise of New German Cinema, a climate of cultural stagnation, and a radical transformation of the domestic media landscape, the German cinema of the 1980s offered little that matched the historicist fantasies of British cinema. A few exceptions proving the rule, it was in fact not until the second half of the 1990s that German cinema set out to develop its own version of the heritage genre. The last years of the old and the first year of the new millennium saw the sudden rise of sweeping historical melodramas that reproduced the national past, including that of the Nazi period, as a source of nostalgic pleasures and positive identifications. Similar to what a number of British directors produced in the mid-1980s, German feature productions such as *Comedian Harmonists* (1997, Joseph Vilsmaier); *Aimée & Jaguar* (1999, Max Färberböck); *Viehjud Levi* (1999, Didi Danquart); *Ein Lied von Liebe und Tod—Gloomy Sunday* (1999, Rolf Schübel); *Marlene* (2000, Joseph Vilsmaier); and *Gripsholm* (2000, Xavier Koller) turned the nation's past into a space for the spectacular display of heritage properties, whether material or symbolic in nature. And yet, due to a fundamentally different political, social, economic, and cultural context, German cinema's turn to the past diverged from its British forerunner in both aesthetic and ideological terms. First, whereas the British heritage film displaced the experience of a multicultural present with pastoral images of upper-class imperial grandeur, most of the new German melodramas aspire nothing less than to reclaim sites of social consensus against the grain of historical trauma. Unlike the British heritage film, which reconstructed national history through the eyes of the past's social elite, the German model by and large pictures political elites (i.e., the Nazis) as the true nemesis of the nation's (multicultural) story. Second, in contrast to the prominent role of highbrow literary material in the British heritage film, recent German melodramas are eager to parade the textures and traditions of the popular. They index German mass culture as a site of authenticity that once provided powerful alternatives to Hollywood. In some cases, these films even reinscribe the popular as the nation's most viable common ground—one that dissolved under the historical pressure of Nazi politics but that German filmmakers ought to recuperate for the present. Third, and finally, whereas the British heritage cycle relied on a visual style reminiscent of early cinema's aesthetics of attraction, German historical melodramas spend considerable time staging the past as a sonic spectacle of first rank. Recalling the extent to which German cinema since the early 1930s was bound up with sound and film music, German heritage films around 2000 produce the acoustical domain as the primary site at which national identity comes into being and can be consumed most pleasurably.

As seen from the vantage point of ideology criticism, the new German heritage film no doubt serves urgent political needs and functions. The cycle's retrospective images of Jewish-German reconciliation, as well as its juxtaposition of pleasurable privacy and violent publicness, feed directly into formative discourses of the self-proclaimed Berlin Republic. Many of these films glorify successful moments of German-Jewish cooperation prior to or even during the Nazi period in order to reconstruct the nation's narrative and reintegrate German Jews into hegemonic definitions of German cultural identity. As they frequently play out the seemingly authentic textures of the popular against the disintegrating force of the political, these films clear historical debts so as to open a path for a normal German future. But to understand the rise of the German-Jewish heritage film merely in terms of ideological opportunism misses the point. For the heritage film's self-confident reinscription of the historical and the national, at the same time, reflects a radical transformation of German film production and consumption caused by new government subsidy policies on both the federal and the regional level; by greater influence of television officials on film boards and funding decisions; by new arrangements between film academies, television stations, and commercial producers; by technological revolutions in the exhibition sector; and last, but not least, by significant investments of prominent American distributors in a select number of German film productions.[3] Unlike the German auteurs of the 1970s and early 1980s, this new cinema of heritage properties is clearly guided by Hollywood standards of industrial filmmaking and

box-office success. It embraces the national not in defiance of Hollywood but in a conscious effort to inhabit certain niches left uninhab-
ited by Hollywood's transnational drive. The rediscovery of national
history thus emerges as an integral moment of globalization itself, not
as its other. It illustrates the fact that globalization, far from leveling
local differences, has produced new desires for localization, that is, a
global resurgence of demarcated group identities predicated on often
narrowly defined markers of ethnic, regional, or religious belonging.

Breaking with the dissident designs of New German Cinema, German heritage films circa 2000—unwittingly—exhibit the national as a
thoroughly globalized category. They crisscross former territorializations of culture, yet at the same time they re-vision the nation as
bounded and distinctive. In doing so, these films not only challenge the
ways in which previous generations of German filmmakers sought to
define German national cinema in critical opposition to and conversation with American filmmaking. They also urge us (1) to question
whether, in face of today's global flows of sounds, images, technologies, moneys, and meanings, concepts such as Americanism and Hollywoodization are still persuasive; and (2) to rethink whether we still can
or should uphold one of the principal tropes of modernist film discourse, namely, the grounding of cultural diversity and critical film
practice in the normative concept of national cinema. It is to these two
questions that I shall turn in the following pages, reading the rise of the
German heritage film during the late 1990s not as a return of nine-
teenth-century inventions of national identity but, on the contrary, as
a symptomatic and theoretically challenging expression of postmodern
globalization.

THE NARRATIVE OF German-American film relations between the mid-
1960s and the early 1980s has often been told. Curiously combining
Americanist and anti-Americanist stances, the auteurs of New German
Cinema viewed Hollywood cinema simultaneously as a legitimate
alternative to German popular filmmaking and as a harbinger of cultural imperialism. In most cases, they embraced America not as a tan-
gible space but as a playground for the imagination, an imaginary
where tormented German subjects could realize identity by experienc-
ing themselves as others.[4] Thomas Elsaesser has separated New German Cinema's projective fantasies about America into three different
scenarios.[5] In the perspective of one group of filmmakers, postwar
American cultural imperialism simply continued the Nazi destruction
of authentic German culture. In a gesture of Oedipal revolt, German

cinema's task was to contest Germany's colonization and, by exploring the darkest chapters of German history, find new forms of national authenticity (Syberberg, Herzog). Represented by directors such as Wenders or Fassbinder, the second strategy was that of a discriminating exploration of Hollywood cinema as a source of possible identifications. It entailed the orphan's search for alternative father figures (Ford, Ray, Sirk) who would not trigger neurotic dependencies. The third prototype, finally, focused on the painful formation of German subjectivity, though with the conspicuous omission of any reference to American popular culture or Hollywood at all. Mother-daughter bonds in this paradigm became the primary trope of recalling the ruptures of twentieth-century German history and of recapturing a lost sense of expressive authenticity (Sanders-Brahms, Brückner).

However projective it may have been, the image of America and Hollywood allowed German filmmakers of the 1970s to reject certain institutional practices at home and to build a critical cinema of formal experimentation and social commentary. A reverse image that German auteurs loved to hate, Hollywood demonstrated the need for a German cinema in which government subsidies could allow for the possibility of cultural diversity, political awareness, and modernist innovation. New German Cinema's struggle against Hollywood thus clearly affirmed Paul Willemen's argument that we should not equate discourses about cinema's national specificity with nationalist ideology, that is, with the invention of national identity as homogenous, unified, and primordial.[6] Defining their own aesthetic practices against the backdrop of both Hollywood filmmaking and Nazi coordination, the filmmakers of the 1970s considered the nation not only as something that could be reinvented and reappropriated by historically situated actors but also as a space of internal diversification and contestation, a space of fractured identifications, heterogeneous traditions, and embattled hegemonies. Shaped by the experience of the 1960s revolutions, filmmakers such as Wenders and Fassbinder were far from envisaging the national as a site of unproblematic consensus and archaic belonging, a site free of dispute, difference, or pluralistic possibility.

And yet, the point I would like to make here is that this reinvention of the nation as a space of difference and multiplicity in large measures rested on a binary and often essentializing reading of Hollywood filmmaking and its relation to the category of national cinema. Eager to establish frameworks for critical authorship, the auteurs of New German Cinema understood the concept of national cinema mostly in terms of a cinema's geographical base of production. National cinemas, according to this view, entailed distinct sets of artistic signatures, production strategies, and state policies territorializing cultural expressions within the demarcated space of the nation-state. In their thinking about national cinema, the filmmakers of the 1970s were, on the other hand, much less concerned about the viewer's productivity of consumption and how German audiences might produce differential articulations of non-German films within local contexts. This production-oriented reading of national cinema was then projected back onto Hollywood; it instigated a reifying definition of Hollywood filmmaking as American national cinema. Time after time, the auteurs of the 1970s reduced Hollywood to a mere tool implanting American values, meanings, and styles of expression in the world's subconscious. They did not see Hollywood as a, however ideological, lingua franca of international film production and consumption, nor did they recognize Hollywood's constitutive ability to negotiate between different cultural and ethnic constituencies; to open its doors to foreign talent, themes, and styles; and to cater to worldwide markets with products that may yield many, locally specific appropriations. Determined to reconstruct "a legitimate film culture in Germany again,"[7] New German Cinema often denied possible tensions in Hollywood's simultaneous role as a capitalist industry and as a fantastic country of the mind.[8] It obscured Hollywood's own narrative of cross-cultural barter and imaginary dislocation and, thereby, obscured the fundamental ambiguity of Hollywood filmmaking regarding the issue of national identity.

Any critical account of film history, writes Douglas Gomery, must begin with Hollywood, "not because the cinema industry based in the United States has produced the best films (by some criteria) but because it has forced all other national cinemas to begin by dealing with the power of Hollywood as an industry."[9] Whether we like it or not, Hollywood always precedes any thinking about cinema in national terms, for any labeling of cinemas as national today reacts to the already established rule of Hollywood transnationalism. Itself unthinkable without a long history of migration, exile, and cultural give-and-take, Hollywood is best understood as a supraterritorial language in which—or at the margins of which—other cinemas set up the national as a minor language. Though we may laud their vision of German cinema as a critical space of identity *and* difference, of questioning hegemonic ideology and the marketplace, German filmmakers of the 1970s often failed to recognize the curious belatedness and relational nature of national cinemas. Instead of understanding Hollywood as a global industry forcing different film industries to define themselves as national in the first place, New German Cinema secretly hoped for nothing less than the impossible: to restore German national cinema as an originary presence, a self-regulatory space of authentic expressiveness independent from anything beyond its institutional demarcations.

At first sight one might easily assume that German heritage films around 2000 directly continue the anti-American strands of postwar German culture, including the anti-American tirades of such filmmakers as Werner Herzog and Hans Jürgen Syberberg. German heritage films abound with stereotypes about American culture as inauthentic. The stereotype, which—according to Homi Bhabha—is a discursive strategy that "vacillates between what is always 'in place,' already known, and something that must be anxiously repeated,"[10] here serves the ideological construction and demarcation of a negative other. In Joseph Vilsmaier's *Comedian Harmonists,* the act of translating American musical models—The Revelers—into German expression is shown as an act of setting the foreign straight and replacing it with homemade objects of greater cultural depth.[11] When the Dietrich character in Vilsmaier's *Marlene* returns to Germany after shooting *Morocco,* she laments: "The Americans are meshuga. No culture. Goethe, Schiller—they're unheard of. Mozart, Brahms, Schubert—what's that? And the food—ugh." Vilsmaier's America is a full-fledged society of the spectacle. Anxiously repeating what German discourses on modern America seem to have known all along, Vilsmaier's stereotypical America privileges superficial distraction over interpretation, appearance over essence. Accordingly, American culture overwhelms individual minds and generates artificial emotions. Sensory bombardments produce either narcotic intoxication or endless stupor, while mass cultural technologies displace the real and leave no space for lived experience.

Nothing would be more wrong, however, than to think that in its effort to capitalize on the national the heritage film would simply reiterate New German Cinema's dream of cinematic nation building. Supplying postwall Germany with a chimera of national normalcy, the German heritage film in fact reveals a thinking about nation, national cinema, and Hollywood filmmaking that differs greatly from the films of the 1970s. Unlike New German Cinema, heritage films want to be user-friendly and easy to digest. Their visual surfaces look like designer products, their narrative shapes are powered by melodramatic formulae. Mellifluous editing replaces the elongated, pensive takes of New German Cinema. Self-contained stories and special effects gloss over what looked fractured and artisinal more than twenty years earlier. The German heritage film's foregrounding of national themes thus no longer results in a formal challenge of Hollywood cinema, but it instead relies on a straightforward adoption of Hollywood modes of production and storytelling. It is not the audience's but rather the critic's toes on which this newest German cinema seeks to step. Whatever we may consider national about it, this cinema achieves its status because it understands how to gratify audiences for whom Hollywood filmmaking represents a native idiom, a major language. Whatever this cinema may do in order to reorder the paths of German national history, it does so by abandoning the oppositional stance of New German Cinema. That in spite of such fundamental differences the heritage film, at the level of textual enunciation, repeats some of the anti-American stereotypes of New German Cinema might be puzzling at first. As I will argue in a moment, however, the anti-Americanist tropes of the heritage film serve dramatically different functions from those during the 1970s. Whereas the figure of anti-Americanism, for the auteurs of the 1970s, was meant to produce national identity through demarcating external difference and emphasizing internal diversification, the postwall heritage film enlists anti-Americanism in order to mask what it knows all too well, namely, the fact that in a world of global flows national belonging is an effect of the transnational rather than a primordial essence.

German heritage films circa 2000 document the extent to which in today's world touristic self-representations have become one of the dominant ways of articulating collective belonging. They actively produce nationality and locality on the basis of what David Harvey has called the postmodern rule of flexible accumulation: a regime of capitalist reproduction that places dissimilar meanings, traditions, images, sounds, and experiences on a single plane of instant availability.[12] Heritage identity emerges as a property, as something one can stick in one's pocket and take along. It withstands geographical border crossings, cultural crossovers, and "the inevitability of fantasy."[13] While for the authors of New German Cinema identity resulted from encountering and leaving behind the American other, the heritage film pictures the self as originary and authentic. Heritage identity can do without passing through states of otherness. Rather than emulating, mimicking, or inverting the other, the German self is shown as a given. It is firmly anchored in the semantic inventories of banal nationalism—the circulation of national symbols in everyday life, the seemingly trivial evocation of the nation in sporting events, news broadcasts, or musical performances.[14] Heritage films reinvent the national past with the help of an excessive accumulation of visual and sonic signifiers. Their image of Germany provides what foreign tourists expect to see when traveling to exotic locales: the pleasures of uncontaminated and perennial locality. Heritage films nourish fantasies of contiguity powerful enough to mend the decentering of home, identity, and body in modern history; but they do so by placing the nation's subjects outside of their own culture, asking them to look at their own lives like tourists who typify different cultures as sites of radical—and, hence, pleasurable—alterity.

Nowhere perhaps does the German heritage film's reconstruction of the national as a global tourist attraction become clearer than in Joseph Vilsmaier's two-hour opus *Marlene* (2000). Ever since his first successful feature film, *Herbstmilch* (1988), Vilsmaier (born in 1939) has occupied the role of a German Merchant-Ivory: a producer, director, screenwriter, and cinematographer of historical melodramas transforming the national past into a decorative figure that is designed to fascinate. However, unlike his Indian-American counterparts, whose most well-known films have reviewed British history through the eyes of high-literary sources, Vilsmaier has dedicated his films to recuperating the popular as a site of national coherence and self-representation. The popular, in Vilsmaier's films, opposes the disruptive violence of public history and enables liminal spaces of authenticity and self-expression. It bridges local particularity and sutures what is different into a unified whole, including the dissimilar fates of Jews and Germans as suggested in the 1997 *Comedian Harmonists.*

Vilsmaier's *Marlene* attempts to reclaim Marlene Dietrich as a national icon whose popular appeal preceded Hollywood, undermined Nazi power, and therefore can retrospectively heal the open wounds of German history. A stylish 18 million deutsche mark production, *Marlene* presents the heroine's sights and sounds as a national heritage: a source of nostalgic identification and present-day regeneration. It is therefore no coincidence that it takes Vilsmaier almost an hour to have the protagonist arrive in southern California and start shooting on Paramount's sets. For Vilsmaier's project is not to explore the trade of European images and imaginaries as a constitutive element of Hollywood filmmaking during the 1930s and 1940s. Rather, what Vilsmaier's film wants to show is that Weimar Germany entertained a Hollywood of its own and that—in contrast to Hollywood—Weimar culture, by integrating industrial mass culture (the film industry) with preindustrial forms of entertainment (cabaret, theater, popular song and dance), provided meanings and pleasures far superior to the Fordist products of American cinema. *Marlene* introduces Dietrich as a sensual, carefree pleasure seeker who prior to going to Hollywood galvanized the popular and the national, the industrial and the preindustrial, into timeless expressions. Josef von Sternberg may have recast her physical appearance in Hollywood, but Dietrich's success in America was made entirely in Germany. It was predicated on her Germanness, her intuitive grounding of modern mass culture in premodern legacies of the popular. Vilsmaier's Dietrich is an exemplary German, not because she revoked her German citizenship during the 1930s and worked for the United Service Organization (USO) and against the Nazis but because she offered something that bonds past and present and can unify Germans across divisions of ideology, generation, gender, and class.

The success of German émigré and exile actors in Hollywood during the Nazi era often relied on an excessive performance of ethnic clichés. In order to feed the New World's hunger for profitable images of the Old World, émigré actors had to turn their heritage into a brand name, a hyperreal signifier of exotic otherness. Vilsmaier's Dietrich, by way of contrast, is far from masquerading as a German. She temporarily camouflages herself as an American, but her heart continues to beat in Germany. Identity, for Vilsmaier, is that which exceeds the mandates of representation; it is incommensurable with any willful act of self-performance or masquerade. While Dietrich's American life is one of alienating make-believe, Dietrich's return to Europe during the last months of the war allows the diva to shed the spectacle and rediscover her inalienable German self. When Dietrich travels to the European battlefields, Vilsmaier offers the viewer a captivating open-air song number—"See What the Boys in the Backroom Will Have"—staged in front of a crowd of frenzied GIs. Yet it is not Marlene's performance for her American friends that interests Vilsmaier most but rather her encounter with a young German soldier who recognizes the diva as she visits a POW camp. "You know me?" she asks the dying soldier with melancholic surprise. While nondiegetic piano music produces a sonic image of simultaneous mourning and recovery, the camera cuts to a series of meditative close-ups of singer and soldier that convert a chance encounter into a national communion. Too young to have witnessed Dietrich during the Weimar era, the soldier testifies to the timeless power of Dietrich's stardom, an appeal untainted by Nazi cultural politics. Dietrich, in turn, recovers her Berlin accent, strips off her American facade, and bridges the gulf between enemies: "So, let's be friends again, alright?" we hear her say right before the soldier dies. Finally returning to Europe, the legend consumes the real and opens the path for German reconciliation.

Vilsmaier's heritage films picture popular culture—not public history—as the primary scene at which national affiliation comes into being. In *Marlene* the popular heals the political rift between soldier and singer, the Nazi war machinery and the German emigrant. A product and producer of Weimar Germany, Vilsmaier's Dietrich returns to Europe in order to reexperience the national as a site of original plentitude. Minimizing the role of Hollywood in the making of the Dietrich persona, *Marlene* thus recalls the diva's biography as if ethnic identity was a nonrelational category preceding discourse and resilient to cultural transfer or dislocation. Accordingly, the film defines the specificity of German cultural expressions—contrary to the Americanist fantasies of New German Cinema—no longer in an ongoing conversation and confrontation with other cultures but rather as if this specificity existed independent of any other as a self-contained presence. In a sense, Vilsmaier recalls modern German culture as if a Germanified Hollywood had always been in existence—just better, more authentic, more modern, and more emancipated than in the United States. Unlike Los Angeles, Weimar Germany provides the Dietrich character with a perfect site to practice her mobile sexuality. In the opening minutes, the film makes a great effort to picture Dietrich as a bisexual libertine who consumes her life to the fullest. Whether involved in hetero- or homosexual relations, Dietrich appears as modernity incarnate: a woman easily transgressing the former threshold between public and private while playfully mocking the norms, values, and identity constructions of the past. Once in America, however, Dietrich is forced to leave her German liberties behind, even though the Hollywood film industry—hypocritically, as it were—capitalizes on her image as a vamp. Dietrich challenges conventional morality on screen, but the studio's public relation managers demand that she appear as ordinary mother and wife in front of press reporters. Whereas Vilsmaier reconstructs Weimar mass culture as a playground of spontaneity and unadulterated difference, he decries modern America as a fortress of conventional morality and normative heterosexuality. Unlike Weimar, where the popular withstands the homogenizing logic of the culture industry, America commodifies the female body and sacrifices (German) sensuality on the altar of the Protestant work ethic and its modern heir, the ruthless rule of capital.

Vilsmaier's heritage films, including *Marlene,* rest on the twofold proposition that (1) popular culture is the primary site at which national identity is constituted and maintained and that (2) Nazi Germany, by instrumentalizing cultural material for political purposes, not only drained the cohesive power of the popular but in doing so also betrayed the idea of the nation. National socialism, rather than embodying nationalism at its peak, undercut German nation building, and according to Vilsmaier it is the task of the filmmaker today to redeem the unpolitical heritage of domestic popular traditions and thereby recuperate what may allow Germans proudly to say "we" to each other again. Contrary to both New German Cinema and the British forerunner of the 1980s, the new German heritage film does not view the popular as a bad object, as a source of anxiety, contamination, or perverse pleasure. Neither the modernist dialectic of high and low nor the critical catchword of "Americanism" as cultural imperialism has any true bearing on this cinema. Whereas New German Cinema refuted the world of the fathers and worried about its American friends, Vilsmaier's cinema showcases the heritage value of domestic legends and markets it to national and international audiences. It screens the legends of the past so as to transform myth into fact. Reviewed through the lenses of Hollywood-like filmmaking, domestic history here becomes German cinema's international marketing label—a souvenir bartered on the stands of global cinematic tourism.

That German heritage films, in spite of their Hollywood-like design, nevertheless often recycle the rhetoric of anti-Americanism symptomatically expresses what I consider an act of double repression. On the one hand, the anti-American stereotype (badly) conceals the extent to which the heritage film's reinvention of the national relies on the very process of globalization it seems to defy. The heritage film's critique of America as inauthentic posits the idea of the German nation as mythic and primordial, while at the same time obscuring the fact that today's interest in cultural specificity, diversity, and marginality is a result of, rather than an antidote to, processes of globalization. On the other hand, the heritage film's anti-American stereotype simultaneously shows and conceals the degree to which this cinema is actively involved in reordering German national history. Unlike New German Cinema, whose anti-American anxieties expressed an often overdetermined battle against the burdens of German history, the heritage film enlists anti-American sentiments so as to reinscribe historical self-confidence and redefine the national consensus. New German Cinema's anti-Americanism attempted to challenge the viewer's perception and unsettle political hegemonies; it spoke for the nation by speaking against postwar silence and consensus. Rhetorical anti-Americanism in the heritage film, by way of contrast, conveys the fact that the true other of postwall film culture is not Hollywood at all but rather the oppositional politics and disruptive designs of critical filmmaking, that is to say, the legacy of the 1968 generation and its hope to couple aesthetic innovation to political reform.

IN 1913 THE Austrian novelist and critic Robert Müller suggested that the notion of Americanism, far from describing any concrete process of development, should be seen as a figment of the imagination, a fiction rather than a reality. Unlike many of his contemporaries, Müller understood Americanism not as a logic of cultural homogenization or social modernization. Instead, he identified it as a way of seeing the world, an imaginary, a noncontiguous fantasy deeply affecting how people maneuvered their paths through the modern world. The real America, according to Müller, either was on the moon or—as he claimed polemically in one of his essays—didn't even exist.[15] Whatever one might see of it was mediated by modern machines of image production: a copy without original. America, for Müller, was a media construct, a wish fantasy, and projection screen, not an experiential reality.

Almost ninety years later, Müller's untimely insights have become part of the heritage film's political unconscious. Films such as *Marlene* and *Comedian Harmonists* might have their protagonists journey to America, but these films' images of the New World are nothing but projections, reverse images, virtual realities. They lack any sense of reference, context, and material texture. America, in the German heritage film, emerges as a specter—a site of seductive, albeit empty, forms and images. It initially teases the German visitor's senses, but due to its heavy reliance on visual representation America denies the possibility of sensual engagement and authentic experience. An intoxicating culture of display and mediation, America turns out to be anaesthetic. It numbs the traveler's sense perception and impedes his or her pleasure. Seemingly true to Müller's 1913 claim, the heritage film's America doesn't really exist.

As I argued earlier, however, it would be utterly misleading to describe the heritage film's American imaginary as a direct continuation of modernist discourses on American mass culture. The modernist optic of Americanism—whether negative or affirmative—was based on the perception of American culture as something initially foreign and particular. It understood difference and alterity as the precondition of social critique and transformation, alternatively arguing either for more or for less American culture in order to rebuild modern Germany. Modernist discourses on America by and large relied on universalist pleas for cultural relativism and specificity. Far from homogenizing difference, universalism here implied the recognition of diversity and otherness—whether at home or abroad—as sources of cultural transfer, critical engagement, and self-transformation, of reframing the self in light of the other. The heritage film, by contrast, departs from the idea of cultural transmission as an unsettling process of reframing self and other, of critical introspection, experience, and emancipation. In spite of all its German "aboutness" at the level of narrative and mise-en-scène, the heritage cycle rests firmly on postindustrial modes of production, distribution, and exhibition not much different from Hollywood. Similar to mainstream Hollywood cinema, the heritage film is a product of the accelerated vertical and horizontal integration of media and entertainment industries during the last decade at the global level. Designed for the diverse channels of postindustrial consumption, the heritage film catalyzes fantasies of cultural particularity by putting an accent on the aesthetic surfaces and narrative arrangements of Hollywood cinema. However, instead of explicitly exploring the extent to which the national today has become an effect of or a supplement to the transnational, the German heritage film reintroduces essentializing images of the local through the global backdoor. That America, in *Marlene* and *Comedian Harmonists,* looks as spectral as it does is a symptom of these films' paradoxical (and, ultimately, regressive) ambitions. Vilsmaier pictures America as anaesthetic because his films—in contrast to the modernist engagement with America—are eager to reconstruct cultural boundaries in such a way that symbolic transfers between here and there, or past and present, do not unsettle the reinscription of nationality as primordial. In the final analysis, the ghostly image of Vilsmaier's America shows what the heritage narrative does not dare to say, namely, that in our present world of transnational flows Hollywood—in however indigenized form—has always already inhabited the home and structures our views of past, present, and future. Vilsmaier's heritage optic is so steeped in Hollywood transnationalism that it lacks the means to picture Hollywood itself.

In closing, I would like to draw two conclusions from the millennial emergence of the German heritage film. First, contrary to its own rhetoric, the heritage film reveals the degree to which, under the sign of global media conglomerates and marketing strategies, critical concepts such as "Americanism" and "Hollywoodization" have lost their grasp.

To be sure, it would be cynical to deny the kind of asymmetries that structure the transnational transfer of images, technologies, meanings, and capital today. To speak of globalization cannot mean to ignore that "certain nationalisms, cultures, ideas and interpretations are more transnationally powerful, assertive, and successful than others."[16] However, by articulating and territorializing Germanness *within* the global language and economy of Hollywood cinema itself, the heritage film at least urges us to understand that bipolar models of influence, causation, and colonization are no longer adequate to map the sites of contemporary cinema. Although the heritage film often reverts to anti-American stereotypes, it documents the fact that "Hollywood" can mean very different things to global viewers, producers, and filmmakers. Unlike New German Cinema, for which Hollywood was mostly identical with American culture and for which both embodied cultural imperialism, the heritage film sees Hollywood as a global lingua franca that German cinema can put to local use. The heritage film thus indicates that, even under conditions of asymmetrical globalization, Hollywood can have local or minor accents—accents that stamp particular meanings and visions on the cinematic product and hence do not allow us to think of Hollywood as a unified and overpowering institution of cultural homogenization. Although it often toys with the image of a much simpler past, the heritage film demonstrates that modernist notions of Americanism have been consumed by the historical process, that these notions have become too simple to conceptualize the present moment. What we can learn from the heritage film is that Americanism no longer exists.

Second, the rise of the postwall heritage film asks us to revise the normative concept of national cinema as it informed film scholarship in particular prior to the 1980s. In this writing, the idea of national cinema was directly tied to the promotion of critical, non-Hollywood filmmaking. "Along with the name of the director-auteur, [the concept of national cinema] has served as a means by which non-Hollywood films—most commonly art films—have been labelled, distributed, and reviewed. As a marketing strategy, these national labels have promised varieties of 'otherness'—of what is culturally different from both Hollywood and the films of other importing countries."[17] To speak of national cinemas meant to support semi- or noncommercial film practice, to commend the critique or subversion of mainstream conventions, to privilege experimental, fragmented, or highly self-reflexive designs over narrative totalization and spectatorial identification. German cinema played a prominent role in this kind of writing. Primarily focusing on the 1920s and 1970s, critics celebrated expressionist filmmaking and New German Cinema as heralds of oppositional meaning and cultural experimentation, as a national cinema whose insistence on product differentiation warranted cultural diversity and self-critique. In postwall Germany, by way of contrast, the idea of national cinema has ceased to catalyze counter-hegemonic film art. Although the national defines their topic, recent German heritage films illustrate Higson's claim that the limits of the national today are no longer "the most productive way of framing arguments about cultural diversity and cultural specificity."[18] There is surely no need to discard the category of national cinema as a heuristic device and epistemological tool, nor to disband the national out of some strange postcolonial embarrassment about cultural particularity. However, what the postwall heritage film exemplifies is that national terms per se do little today to articulate a meaningful critical distance to Hollywood. Though obsessed with transforming national legends into contemporary cinema's selling point, the heritage film reveals that to argue for national cinemas in today's world does by no means mean to promote a more diverse and culturally specific film culture.

Does this imply, then, that we must bury any hope for a future German cinema that could shatter dominant hegemonies and fracture cultural identities? Is there any space left for experimental, critical, and unpopular filmmaking, for cinematic diversity, in a world of transnational media conglomerates? This is clearly not the place to speculate about the prospects of oppositional film production and consumption in Germany. Let it be said, though, that critical filmmaking today has to develop a cinematic style capable of working through the often paradoxical disaggregation of space and time in our globalized world. Rather than fleeing from or fleeing into the transnational, this cinema would—as Naficy has suggested—"operate both within and astride the cracks and fissures of the system, benefiting from its contradictions, anomalies, and heterogeneity."[19] Critical filmmaking today is located at the intersection of the global and the local, and—unlike the heritage film—it actively explores the extent to which the most relevant questions of identity and belonging today are articulated either at the subnational or the transnational level. Projecting itself beyond and across national territorializations of culture, critical film practice is well aware of its own limitations, its temporariness, its imperfection, its deterritorialized outlook, its lack of shine. Rather than offering reified visions of self and other, it stresses the fundamental contingency, openness, and malleability of inside/outside distinctions.

Rather than recuperating the national as a self-referential space of authenticity, it elaborates on the fact that our notions of home, community, and identity are necessary fictions—transitory imaginaries that effectively allow us to negotiate the increasing disarticulation of space and time in global cyber culture. Paradoxical though it may seem, then, oppositional cinemas today on the one hand enable the viewer to recognize that things such as "Germany" and "America" do not really exist. On the other hand, however, they also emphasize that experiences of cultural difference remain essential to any attempt at challenging dominant templates of power and splintering the user-friendly consensuses of the day.

NOTES

This essay continues a set of arguments raised in particular at the end of my *The Dark Mirror: German Cinema between Hitler and Hollywood* (Berkeley: University of California Press, 2002), as well as in my essay "Reforming the Past: Heritage Cinema and Holocaust in the 1990s," *New German Critique* 87 (fall 2002): 47–82. I am grateful to both publishers for allowing me to make use here of a very few previously published paragraphs.

1. Andrew Higson, "The Heritage Film and British Cinema," in *Dissolving Views: Key Writings on British Cinema,* ed. Andrew Higson (London: Cassell, 1996), 233. See also Andrew Higson, "Re-presenting the National Past: Nostalgia and Pastiche in the Heritage Film," in *Fires Were Started: British Cinema and Thatcherism,* ed. Lester Friedman (Minneapolis: University of Minnesota Press, 1993), 109–29; and Ginette Vincendeau, "Issues in European Cinema," in *The Oxford Guide to Film Studies,* ed. John Hill and Pamela Church Gibson (Oxford: Oxford University Press, 1998), 440–48.

2. Fredric Jameson, "Reification and Utopia in Mass Culture," *Signatures of the Visible* (New York: Routledge, 1992), 30.

3. Eric Rentschler, "From New German Cinema to the Post-Wall Cinema of Consensus," in *Cinema and Nation,* ed. Mette Hjort and Scott MacKenzie (Routledge: London, 2000), 260–77.

4. Eric Rentschler, "How American Is It? The U.S. as Image and Imaginary in German Film," *Persistence of Vision* 2 (1985): 5–18.

5. Thomas Elsaesser, "German Postwar Cinema and Hollywood," in *Hollywood in Europe: Experiences of a Cultural Hegemony,* ed. David W. Ellwood and Rob Kroes (Amsterdam: VU University Press, 1994), 283–302; see also Thomas Elsaesser, *New German Cinema: A History* (New Brunswick: Rutgers University Press, 1989).

6. Paul Willemen, "The National," *Looks and Frictions: Essays in Cultural Studies and Film Theory* (Bloomington: Indiana University Press, 1994), 210.

7. Werner Herzog, "Tribute to Lotte Eisner (1982)," in *West German Film-*

makers on Film: Visions and Voices, ed. Eric Rentschler (New York: Holmes and Meier, 1988), 117.

8. Thomas Elsaesser, "To Be or Not to Be: Extra-territorial in Vienna Berlin—Hollywood," *Weimar Cinema and After: Germany's Historical Imaginary* (London: Routledge, 2000), 381.

9. Douglas Gomery, "Hollywood as Industry," in *Oxford Guide to Film Studies,* ed. John Hill and Pamela Church Gibson (Oxford: Oxford University Press, 1998), 245.

10. Homi K. Bhabha, "The Other Question: Stereotype, Discrimination, and the Discourse of Colonialism," *The Location of Culture* (London: Routledge, 1994), 66.

11. For an expanded version of this argument, see Lutz Koepnick, "'Honor Your German Masters': History, Memory, and National Identity in Joseph Vilsmaier's *Comedian Harmonists* (1997)," in *Light Motives: Perspectives on Popular German Cinema,* ed. Margaret McCarthy and Randall Halle (Detroit: Wayne State University Press, 2003), 349–75.

12. David Harvey, *The Condition of Postmodernity: An Enquiry into the Origins of Cultural Change* (Oxford: Basil Blackwell, 1989).

13. John Durham Peters, "Exile, Nomadism, and Diaspora: The Stakes of Mobility in the Western Canon," in *Home, Exile, Homeland: Film, Media, and the Politics of Place,* ed. Hamid Naficy (New York: Routledge, 1999), 36.

14. Michael Billig, *Banal Nationalism* (London: Sage, 1995).

15. Robert Müller, "Der Roman des Amerikanismus," *Saturn* 9 (September 1913): 253–58, quoted in Deniz Göktürk, *Künstler, Cowboys, Ingenieure: Kultur- und mediengeschichtliche Studien zu deutschen Amerika-Texten* (Munich: Fink, 1998), 211.

16. Ulf Hedetorf, "Contemporary Cinema: Between Globalisation and National Interpretation," in *Cinema and Nation,* 280.

17. Stephen Crofts, "Concepts of National Cinema," *Oxford Guide to Film Studies,* 385.

18. Andrew Higson, "The Limiting Imagination of National Cinema," in *Cinema and Nation,* 73.

19. Hamid Naficy, "Between Rocks and Hard Places: The Interstitial Mode of Production in Exilic Cinema," in *Home, Exile, Homeland,* 134.

Bibliography

Adelson, Leslie. "Touching Tales of Turks, Germans, and Jews: Cultural Alterity, Historical Narrative, and Literary Riddles for the 1990s." *New German Critique* 80 (2000): 93–124.

Adorno, Theodor W. "Perennial Fashion-Jazz." In *Prisms*, 119–32. London: Spearman, 1967.

Amend, Heike. "Deutsche Filme im Fernsehen." In *Der Bewegte Film: Aufbruch zu neuen deutschen Erfolgen*, ed. Heike Amend and Michael Bütow, 57–63. Berlin: Vistas, 1997.

Amend, Heike, and Michael Bütow, eds. *Der Bewegte Film: Aufbruch zu neuen deutschen Erfolgen*. Berlin: Vistas, 1997.

Anderson, Benedict. *Imagined Communities: Reflections on the Origin and Spread of Nationalism*. New York and London: Verso, 1983.

Ang, Ien. *Watching Dallas*. London: Methuen, 1985.

Appadurai, Arjun. "Disjuncture and Difference in the Global and Cultural Economy." *Public Culture* 2, no. 2 (1990): 1–24.

Appadurai, Arjun. *Modernity at Large: Cultural Dimensions of Globalization*. Minneapolis: University of Minnesota Press, 1996.

Assheuer, Thomas. "Im Reich des Scheins." *Die Zeit* (April 11, 2001): 16–17.

Baer, Jean-Michel, ed. *Politik im audiovisuellen Bereich der Europäischen Union 1998*. Brussels: Amt für amtliche Veröffentlichungen der Europäischen Gemeinschaften, 1997.

Barber, Benjamin R. *Jihad vs. McWorld: How Globalism and Tribalism Are Reshaping the World*. New York: Ballantine, 1995.

Barthes, Roland. "The Death of the Author." In *Image, Music, Text*, trans. Stephen Heath, 142–48. New York: Hill and Wang, 1977.

Bathrick, David. "Max Schmeling on the Canvas: Boxing as an Icon of Weimar Culture." *New German Critique* 51 (fall 1990): 113–36.

Becker, Frank. *Amerikanismus in Weimar: Sportsymbole und politische Kultur 1918–1933*. Wiesbaden: Deutscher Universitäts-Verlag, 1993.

Becker, Hinrich. *Das Beste aus* Reader's Digest: *Ideologische Grundzüge in der Zeitschrift* Das Beste aus Reader's Digest: *Untersucht an den Jahrgängen 1949/50, 1973, 1979/80*. Kiel: n.p., 1984.

Becker, Jörg, et al., eds. *Informationstechnologie und internationale Politik*. Bonn: Friedrich-Ebert-Stiftung, 1983.

Beer, Caroline. *Die Kinogeher: Eine Untersuchung des Kinopublikums in Deutschland*. Berlin: Vistas, 2000.

Berendt, Joachim-Ernst. *Der Jazz: Eine zeitknitische Studie.* Stuttgart: DVA, 1950.

Berendt, Joachim-Ernst. "Zum Thema Jazz." In *Frankfurter* Hefte 7 (October 1952): 768–79.

Berendt, Joachim-Ernst. "Americana: Erlebnisse und Gedanken von einer US-Reise." *Melos* 18 (March 1951): 78–82.

Berendt, Joachim-Ernst. "Für und wider den Jazz." *Merkur* 7 (1953): 887–90.

Berendt, Joachim-Ernst. *Das Jazzbuch: Entwicklung und Bedeutung der Jazzmusik.* Frankfurt a.M.: Fischer, 1953.

Berghahn, Volker. *America and the Intellectual Cold Wars in Europe: Shepard Stone between Philanthropy, Academy, and Diplomacy.* Princeton: Princeton University Press, 2001.

Berghahn, Volker. "Philanthropy and Diplomacy in the 'American Century'." In *The Ambiguous Legacy: U.S. Foreign Relations in the 'American Century,'* ed. Michael Hogan. New York: Cambridge University Press, 1999.

Berman, Marshall. *All That Is Solid Melts into Air: The Experience of Modernism.* London: Verso, 1983.

Bhabha, Homi K. *The Location of Culture.* London: Routledge, 1994.

Billig, Michael. *Banal Nationalism.* London: Sage, 1995.

Bliersbach, Gerhard. *So Grün War die Heide: Der Deutsche Nachkriegsfilm in neuer Sicht.* Weinheim: Beltz, 1985.

Blumler, Jay G. "Political Communication Systems All Change: A Response to Kees Brants." *European Journal of Communication* 14 (1999): 245–46.

Bohrer, Karl Heinz. "Was alles fraglich ist: Rolf Dieter Brinkmanns erster Gedichtband." *Frankfurter Allgemeine Zeitung,* November 11, 1967.

Borchers, Hans, Gabriele Kreutzner, and Eva-Maria Warth, eds. *Never-Ending Stories: American Soap Operas and the Cultural Production of Meaning.* Trier: Wissenschaftlicher Verlag, 1994.

Breidenbach, Joana, and Ina Zukrigl. *Tanz der Kulturen. Kulturelle Identität in einer globalisierten Welt.* Hamburg: Rowohlt, 2000.

Brinkmann, Rolf Dieter. "Angriff aufs Monopol: Ich hasse alte Dichter." In *Roman oder Leben: Postmoderne in der deutschen Literatur.* ed. Uwe Wittstock, 65–77. Leipzig: Kiepenheuer, 1994.

Brinkmann, Rolf Dieter. "Anmerkungen zu meinem Gedicht 'Vanille'." In *Mammut: März Texte 1 & 2, 1969–1984,* ed. Jörg Schröder. Herbstein: März, 1984.

Brinkmann, Rolf Dieter. *Briefe an Hartmut, 1974–1975.* Reinbek: Rowohlt, 1999.

Brinkmann, Rolf Dieter. "Der Film in Worten." In *Der Film in Worten,* 223–47. Reinbek: Rowohlt, 1982.

Brinkmann, Rolf Dieter. "Die Lyrik Frank O'Haras." In *Der Film in Worten,* 207–22. Reinbek: Rowohlt, 1982.

Brinkmann, Rolf Dieter. "Ein unkontrolliertes Nachwort zu meinen Gedichten." *Literaturmagazin* 5 (1976): 228–48.

Brinkmann, Rolf Dieter. "Fragment zu einigen populären Songs." *Literaturmagazin* 2 (1975): 105–22.

Brinkmann, Rolf Dieter. "Notizen 1969 zu amerikanischen Gedichten und zu der

Anthologie 'Silverscreen'." In *Der Film in Worten,* 248–69. Reinbek: Rowohlt, 1982.

Brinkmann, Rolf Dieter. *Rom, Blicke.* Reinbek: Rowohlt, 1979.

Brinkmann, Rolf Dieter. *Standphotos: Gedichte, 1962–1970.* Reinbek: Rowohlt, 1980.

Brinkmann, Rolf Dieter. *Westwärts 1 & 2: Gedichte.* Reinbek: Rowohlt, 1974.

Brinkmann, Rolf Dieter, ed. *Silver Screen: Neue amerikanische Lyrik.* Cologne: Kiepenheuer und Witsch, 1969.

Brinkmann, Rolf Dieter, and Ralf-Rainer Rygulla, eds. *ACID: Neue amerikanische Szene.* Frankfurt am Main: März, 1969.

Brzezinski, Zbigniew. *Between Two Ages: America's Role in the Technetronic Era.* New York: Penguin, 1976.

Burgoyne, Robert. *Film Nation: Hollywood Looks at U.S. History.* Minneapolis: University of Minnesota Press, 1997.

Buscombe, Edward. "Film History and the Idea of a National Cinema." *Australian Journal of Screen Theory* 9–10 (1981): 141–53.

Butler, Judith. *Gender Trouble: Feminism and the Subversion of Identity.* New York and London: Routledge, 1990.

Carter, Erica. *How German Is She? Postwar West German Reconstruction and the Consuming Woman.* Ann Arbor: University of Michigan Press, 1997.

Cederman, Lars-Erik, ed. *Constructing Europe's Identity: The External Dimension.* Boulder: Lynne Reiner, 2001.

Chambers, Iain. *Migrancy, Culture, Identity.* London and New York: Routledge, 1994.

Charney, Leo, and Vanessa R. Schwartz, eds. *Cinema and the Invention of Modern Life.* Berkeley: University of California Press, 1995.

Chiellino, Carmine, ed. *Interkulturelle Literatur in Deutschland: Ein Handbuch.* Stuttgart and Weimar: Metzler, 2000.

Cinquin, Chantal. "President Mitterand Also Watches Dallas: American Mass Media and French National Policy." In *The Americanization of the Global Village,* ed. Roger Rollin. Bowling Green: Bowling Green State University Popular Press, 1989.

Clarke, John, et al. "Subcultures, Cultures, and Class: A Theoretical Overview." In *Resistance through Rituals: Youth Subcultures in Post-War Britain,* ed. Stuart Hall and Tony Jefferson, 9–74. London: Hutchinson, 1976.

Collins, Robert M. *More: The Politics of Economic Growth in Postwar America.* New York: Oxford, 2000.

Cooper, Frederick, and Ann Laura Stoler. "Between Metropole and Colony: Rethinking a Research Agenda." In *Tensions of Empire: Colonial Cultures in a Bourgeois World,* ed. Cooper and Stoler, 1–56. Berkeley: University of California Press, 1997.

Corten, H. W. "Kann der Jazz unserer Jugend schaden?" *Die Welt,* July 21, 1957.

Cowen, Tyler. *In Praise of Commercial Culture.* Cambridge: Harvard University Press, 1998.

Crofts, Stephen. "Concepts of National Cinema." In *The Oxford Guide to Film*

Studies, ed. John Hill and Pamela Church Gibson. Oxford: Oxford University Press, 1998.

Cross, Gary S. *An All-Consuming Century: Why Commercialism Won in Modern America*. New York: Columbia University Press, 2000.

Cuomo, Glenn, ed. *National Socialist Cultural Policy*. New York: St. Martin's, 1995.

Daniels, Les. *Wonder Woman: The Complete History. The Life and Times of the Amazon Princess*. San Francisco: Chronicle Books, 2000.

Davidson, John E. *Deterritorializing the New German Cinema*. Minneapolis: University of Minnesota Press, 1999.

de Grazia, Victoria. "Nationalising Women: The Competition between Fascist and Commercial Cultural Models in Mussolini's Italy." In *Cultural Transmissions and Receptions: American Mass Culture in Europe*, ed. R. Kroes, R. W. Rydell, and D. F. J. Bosscher, 84–99. Amsterdam: VU University Press, 1993.

Deleuze, Gilles, and Felix Guattari. *Kafka: Toward a Minor Literature*. Trans. Dana Polan. Minneapolis: University of Minnesota Press, 1985.

Delmoly, Jacques, ed. *Media* 17, Media Programme Newsletter, European Commission, October 1998.

Denham, Scott, Irene Kacandes, and Jonathan Petropoulos, eds. *A User's Guide to German Cultural Studies*. Ann Arbor: University of Michigan Press, 1997.

DeVeaux, Scott. "Constructing the Jazz Tradition: Jazz Historiography." *Black American Literature Forum* 25.3 (fall 1991): 525–60.

Die Fantastischen Vier. *Die letzte Besatzermusik: Die Autobiographie*. Ed. Ralf Niemczyk. Cologne: Kiepenheuer und Witsch, 1999.

Diederichsen, Diedrich. *Freiheit macht arm: Das Leben nach Rock'n'Roll. 1990–93*. Cologne: Kiepenheuer und Witsch, 1993.

Diederichsen, Diedrich. "Wort Auf!" *Spex* 9 (1988): 34–35.

"'Dieser Song gehört uns!' Interview mit Imran Ayata, Laura Mestre Vives und Vanessa Barth von Kanak Attak." *diskus: Frankfurter StudentInnen Zeitschrift* 1 (May 1999), http://www.passagiere.de/ka/ presse/ diskus5_99.htm.

Doering-Manteuffel, Anselm. "Dimensionen von Amerikanisierung in der deutschen Gesellschaft." *Archiv für Sozialgeschichte* 35 (1995): 1–34.

Dorfman, Ariel, and Armand Mattelart. *How to Read Donald Duck: Imperialist Ideology in the Disney Comic*. New York: International General, 1996.

Duberman, Martin B. *Paul Robeson*. New York: Knopf, 1988.

Elflein, Dietmar. "From Krauts with Attitudes to Turks with Attitudes: Some Aspects of Hip-hop History in Germany." *Popular Music* 17.3 (October 1998): 255–265.

Ellwood, David W. "Anti-Americanism in Western Europe: A Comparative Perspective." *Occasional Paper No. 3, European Studies Seminar Series*, 25–33. Bologna: Johns Hopkins University Bologna Center, 1999.

Ellwood, David W. "Introduction: Historical Methods and Approaches." In *Hollywood in Europe: Experiences of a Cultural Hegemony*, ed. David W. Ellwood and Rob Kroes, 2–18. Amsterdam: VU University Press, 1994.

Ellwood, David W. *Rebuilding Europe: Western Europe, America, and Postwar Reconstruction*. London: Longman, 1992.

Elsaesser, Thomas. "German Postwar Cinema and Hollywood." In *Hollywood in Europe: Experiences of a Cultural Hegemony,* ed. David W. Ellwood and Rob Kroes, 283–302. Amsterdam: VU University Press, 1994.

Elsaesser, Thomas. "Introduction: German Cinema in the 1990s." In *The BFI Companion to German Cinema,* ed. Thomas Elsaesser with Michael Wedel, 3–16. London: BFI, 1999.

Elsaesser, Thomas. *New German Cinema: A History.* New Brunswick: Rutgers University Press, 1989.

Elsaesser, Thomas. "To Be or Not to Be: Extra-territorial in Vienna—Berlin—Hollywood." In *Weimar Cinema and After: Germany's Historical Imaginary.* London: Routledge, 2000.

El-Tayeb, Fatima, and Angelina Maccarone. *Alles wird gut: Das Filmbuch.* Berlin: Orlanda Frauenverlag, 1999.

Enzensberger, Hans Magnus. "Gemeinplätze, die neueste Literater betreffend." *Kursbuch* 15 (November 1968): 187–97.

Erbe, Günter. *Die verfemte Moderne: Die Auseinandersetzung mit dem "Modernismus" in Kulturpolitik, Literaturwissenschaft und Literatur der DDR.* Opladen: Westdeutscher Verlag, 1993.

Erenberg, Lewis A. *Steppin' Out: New York Nightlife and the Transformation of American Culture, 1890–1930.* Chicago: University of Chicago Press, 1981.

Fachinger, Petra. "Writing Back to Liberal Discourse: Feridun Zaimoglu's Grotesque Realism." In *Rewriting Germany from the Margins: Other German Literature of the 1980s and 1990s,* ed. Petra Fachinger, 98–111. Montreal and London: McGill-Queens University Press, 2001.

Falcon, Robert. "Run Lola Run/Lola rennt." *Sight and Sound* 9, no. 11 (1999): 52.

Fehrenbach, Heide. *Cinema in Democratizing Germany: Reconstructing National Identity after Hitler.* Chapel Hill: University of North Carolina Press, 1995.

Fehrenbach, Heide, and Uta G. Poiger, eds. *Transactions, Transgressions, Transformations: American Culture in Western Europe and Japan.* New York: Berghahn Books, 2000.

Festenberg, Nikolaus von. "Viele Jäger, arme Hasen." *Der Spiegel* 48 (1998): 244–46.

Finney, Angus. *The State of European Cinema: A New Dose of Reality.* London: Cassell, 1996.

Fiske, John. "Moments of Television: Neither the Text nor the Audience." In *Remote Control: Television, Audiences, and Cultural Power,* ed. Ellen Seiter, Hans Borchers, Gabriele Kreutzner, and Eva-Maria Warth, 56–78. London: Routledge, 1989.

Fiske, John. "Popular Culture." In *Critical Terms for Literary Study,* ed. Frank Lentricchia and Thomas McLaughlin, 321–35. 2d ed. Chicago: University of Chicago Press, 1995.

Fiske, John. *Power Plays, Power Works.* London: Verso, 1993.

Fiske, John. *Understanding Popular Culture.* Boston: Hyman, 1989.

Fluck, Winfried. "Aesthetic Experience of the Image." In *Iconographies of Power: The Politics and Poetics of Visual Representation,* ed. Ulla Haselstein, Berndt Ostendorf, and Hans Peter Schneck, 11–41. Heidelberg: Carl Winter, 2003.

Fluck, Winfried. "The 'Americanization' of History in New Historicism." *Monatshefte* 84, no. 2 (1994): 220–28.

Fluck, Winfried. "'Amerikanisierung' der Kultur: Zur Geschichte der amerikanischen Populärkultur." In *Die Amerikanisierung des Medienalltags*, ed. Harald Wenzel, 13–52. Frankfurt am Main: Campus, 1998.

Fluck, Winfried. "Amerikanisierung und Modernisierung." *Transit* 17 (1999): 55–71.

Fluck, Winfried. "*Close Encounters of the Third Kind:* American Popular Culture and European Intellectuals." *Annals of Scholarship* 12 (1998): 235–51.

Fluck, Winfried. "Emergence or Collapse of Cultural Hierarchy? American Popular Culture Seen from Abroad." In *Popular Culture in the United States*, ed. Peter Freese and Michael Porsche, 49–74. Essen: Die blaue Eule, 1994.

Foucault, Michel. "What Is an Author?" In *Textual Strategies: Perspectives in Poststructuralist Criticism*, ed. Josué Harari, 141–60. Ithaca: Cornell University Press, 1979.

Friedan, Betty. *The Feminine Mystique*. New York: Dell, 1970.

Führer, Karl Christian. "A Medium of Modernity? Broadcasting in Weimar Germany, 1923–33." *Journal of Modern History* 69 (1997): 722–53.

Garncarz, Joseph. "Hollywood in Germany: The Role of American Films in Germany." In *Hollywood in Europe: Experiences of a Cultural Hegemony*, ed. David Ellwood and Rob Kroes, 94–135. Amsterdam: VU University Press, 1994.

Gassert, Phillip. *Amerika im dritten Reich: Ideologie, Propaganda und Volksmeinung, 1933–1945*. Stuttgart: Franz Steiner, 1997.

Gates, Henry Louis, Jr. *The Signifying Monkey: A Theory of African-American Literary Criticism*. New York and Oxford: Oxford University Press, 1988.

Geduldig, Gunter, and Marco Sagurna. "'Es genügten ihm seine Empfindungen der Welt gegenüber': Ein Gespräch mit Ralf-Rainer Rygulla." In *too much: Das lange Leben des Rolf Dieter Brinkmann*, ed. Gunter Geduldig and Marco Sagurna, 95–108. Aachen: Alano, 1994.

Gemünden, Gerd. "The Depth of the Surface, or, What Rolf Dieter Brinkmann Learned from Andy Warhol." *German Quarterly* 68 (1995): 235–50.

Gemünden, Gerd. *Framed Visions: Popular Culture, Americanization, and the Contemporary German and Austrian Imagination*. Ann Arbor: University of Michigan Press, 1998.

Giese, Fritz. *Girlkultur: Vergleiche zwischen amerikanischem und europäischen Rhythmus und Lebensgefühl*. Munich: Delphin-Verlag, 1925.

Glickman, Lawrence B. "The 'Ism' That Won the Century." *Nation*, December 4, 2000, 33–38.

Göktürk, Deniz. *Künstler, Cowboys, Ingenieure: Kultur- und mediengeschichtliche Studien zu deutschen Amerika-Texten*. Munich: Fink, 1998.

Göktürk, Deniz. "Turkish Delight—German Fright: Migrant Identities in Transnational Cinema." *Transnational Communities—Working Paper Series*. An Economic and Social Council Research Programme, University of Oxford, January 1999.

Gomery, Douglas. "Hollywood as Industry." In *The Oxford Guide to Film Studies*, ed. John Hill and Pamela Church Gibson. Oxford: Oxford University Press, 1998.

Graf, Herbert, et al., eds., *Black American English: A Glossary.* Straelen: Straelener Manuskripte, 1994.

Gramsci, Antonio. *Selections from the Prison Notebooks.* Ed. and trans. Quintin Hoare and Geoffrey Nowell Smith. New York: International, 1971.

Gumbrecht, Hans Ulrich. *In 1926.* Cambridge: Harvard University Press, 1997.

Gunning, Tom. "The Cinema of Attractions: Early Film, Its Spectator, and the Avant-Garde." In *Early Cinema: Space-Frame-Narrative,* ed. Thomas Elsaesser, 56–62. London: BFI, 1990.

Hake, Sabine. "In the Mirror of Fashion." In *Women in the Metropolis: Gender and Modernity in Weimar Culture,* ed. Katharina von Ankum, 185–201. Berkeley: University of California Press, 1997.

Hannerz, Ulf. *Cultural Complexity.* New York: Columbia University Press, 1992.

Hannerz, Ulf. "Networks of Americanization." In *Networks of Americanization: Aspects of the American Influence in Sweden,* ed. Rolf Lunden. Uppsala: Almquist and Wiksell, 1992.

Hansen, Miriam. *Babel and Babylon: Spectatorship in American Silent Film.* Cambridge: Harvard University Press, 1991.

Hardkor Kingxz. "Sprengt die Brücken."<http://www.epoxweb.de/lyrics/hiphplyricsesk.htm>.

Hartmann, Susan. *The Home Front and Beyond: American Women in the 1940s.* Boston: Twayne, 1982.

Harvey, David. *The Condition of Postmodernity: An Enquiry into the Origins of Cultural Change.* Oxford: Basil Blackwell, 1989.

Hauch-Fleck, Marie-Luise. "Die Rollen werden neu verteilt: Europäische Produzenten wehren sich gegen die Vormachtstellung der Amerikaner." *Die Zeit,* overseas ed., May 25, 1990, 10.

Hayward, Susan. *French National Cinema.* London and New York: Routledge, 1993.

Hebdige, Dick. *Subculture: The Meaning of Style.* London: Methuen, 1979.

Hedetorf, Ulf. "Contemporary Cinema: Between Globalisation and National Interpretation." In *Cinema and Nation,* ed. Mette Hjort and Scott MacKenzie. Routledge: London, 2000.

Heineman, Elizabeth. "The Hour of the Women: Memories of Germany's 'Crisis Years' and West German National Identity." *American Historical Review* 101, no. 2 (April 1996): 354–95.

Heineman, Elizabeth. *What Difference Does a Husband Make? Women and Marital Status in Nazi and Postwar Germany.* Berkeley: University of California Press, 1999.

Herf, Jeffrey. *Reactionary Modernism.* Cambridge and New York: Cambridge University Press, 1984.

Herzog, Werner. "Tribute to Lotte Eisner (1982)." In *West German Filmmakers on Film: Visions and Voices,* ed. Eric Rentschler. New York: Holmes and Meier, 1988.

Higson, Andrew. "The Concept of National Cinema." *Screen* 30, no. 4 (1989): 36–46.

Higson, Andrew. "The Heritage Film and British Cinema." In *Dissolving Views: Key Writings on British Cinema*, ed. Andrew Higson. London: Cassell, 1996.

Higson, Andrew. "The Limiting Imagination of National Cinema." In *Cinema and Nation*, ed. Mette Hjort and Scott Mackenzie, 63–74. London and New York: Routledge, 2000.

Higson, Andrew. "Re-presenting the National Past: Nostalgia and Pastiche in the Heritage Film." In *Fires Were Started: British Cinema and Thatcherism*, ed. Lester Friedman, 109–29. Minneapolis: University of Minnesota Press, 1993.

Hjort, Mette, and Scott Mackenzie, eds. *Cinema and Nation.* London and New York: Routledge, 2000.

Hoenisch, Michael. "Film as an Instrument of the U.S. Reeducation Program in Germany after 1945 and the Example of 'Todesmühlen.'" *Englisch Amerikanische Studien* 4 (June 1982): 196–210.

Hoffman, Paul G. *Peace Can Be Won.* Garden City, NY: Doubleday, 1951.

Höhn, Maria. *GIs and Fräuleins: The German-American Encounter in 1950s West Germany.* Chapel Hill: University of North Carolina Press, 2002.

Hollinger, David A. *Postethnic America: Beyond Multiculturalism.* New York: Basic Books, 1995.

Horkheimer, Max, and Theodor W. Adorno. *Dialektik der Aufklärung.* Frankfurt am Main: Fischer, 1969.

Horkheimer, Max, and Theodor W. Adorno. *Dialectic of the Enlightenment.* Translated by John Cumming. New York: Herder and Herder, 1972.

"'Ich muß blöd gewesen sein': Rapper Hakan Durmus über seine Zeit in der Kreuzberger Türken-Gang 36 Boys." *Der Spiegel* 16 (1997): 79.

Imdahl, Max. "'Op,' 'Pop' oder die immer zu Ende gehende Geschichte der Kunst." In *Die nicht mehr schönen Künste: Grenzphänomene des Ästhetischen.* Ed. Hans Robert Jauß, 697. Munich: Fink, 1968.

Inglehart, Ronald, and Wayne E. Baker. "Modernization's Challenge to Traditional Values: Who's Afraid of Ronald McDonald." *Futurist* 35 (2001): 16–21.

Inness, Sherrie A. *Tough Girls: Women Warriors and Wonder Women in Popular Culture.* Philadelphia: University of Pennsylvania Press, 1999.

Iser, Wolfgang. *The Act of Reading: A Theory of Aesthetic Response.* Baltimore: Johns Hopkins University Press, 1978.

Jacob, Günther. *Agit-Pop: Schwarze Musik und weiße Hörer.* Berlin and Amsterdam: Edition ID-Archiv, 1993.

Jahn, Thomas. "Türksun = Du bist Türke. HipHop, House und Pop: In den türkischen Ghettos von München, Köln, Berlin pocht ein neues Wir-Gefühl." *Die Zeit* 3 (January 19, 1996): 21.

Jameson, Fredric. *Postmodernism, or the Cultural Logic of Late Capitalism.* Durham, NC: Duke University Press, 1991.

Jameson, Fredric. "Reification and Utopia in Mass Culture." In *Signatures of the Visible.* New York: Routledge, 1992.

Jarausch, Konrad, and Hannes Siegrist, eds. *Amerikanisierung und Sowjetisierung in Deutschland, 1945–70.* New York: Campus, 1997.

Jarvie, Ian. "Free Trade as Cultural Threat: American Film and TV Exports in the Post-war Period." In *Hollywood and Europe: Economics, Culture, National Identity: 1945–95,* ed. Geoffrey Nowell-Smith and Steven Ricci, 63–74. London: BFI, 1998.

Jessen, Jens. "Schicksal Denglisch: Gegen Hegemonie hilft kein Sprachgesetz." *Die Zeit,* August 3, 2001.

Johnson, Lesley. "'As Housewives we [*sic*] Are Worms': Women, Modernity, and the Home Question." In *Feminism and Cultural Studies,* ed. Morag Schiach, 475–91. New York: Oxford University Press, 1999.

Kaes, Anton. *From Hitler to Heimat.* Cambridge: Harvard University Press, 1989.

Kaes, Anton. *Weimar Republic Sourcebook.* Berkeley: University of California Press, 1994.

Kanak Attak. "Manifesto: Kanak Attak und Basta!" <http:www.passagiere.de /ka/manifest_dt.htm>

Kasson, John F. *Amusing the Million: Coney Island at the Turn of the Century.* New York: Hill and Wang, 1978.

Kater, Michael H. *Different Drummers: Jazz in the Culture of Nazi Germany.* New York: Oxford University Press, 1992.

Katz, Elihu, and Tamar Liebes. "Mutual Aid in the Decoding of *Dallas:* Preliminary Notes from a Cross-Cultural Study." In *Television in Transition,* ed. Philip Drummond and Richard Paterson, 187–98. London: BFI, 1986.

Kershaw, Ian. *The Nazi Dictatorship.* 4th ed. London: Arnold, 2000.

Kinobesucher in der MA [Medienanalyse]. Düsseldorf: PR und Forschungsgesellschaft Werbung im Kino, 2000.

Knauer, Wolfram, ed. *Jazz in Deutschland.* Hofheim: Wolke, 1996.

Knepler, Gorg. "Jazz und die Volksmusik." *Musik und Gesellschaft* 5 (June 1956): 181–83.

Korzybski, Alfred. *Science and Sanity: An Introduction to Non-Aristotelian Systems and General Semantics.* 4th ed., 1933. Reprint, Lakeville, CT: International Non-Aristotelian Library Publishing, 1958.

Koegler, Horst. "Jazz-theoretisch." *Der Monat* 12 (October 1959): 58–64.

Koepnick, Lutz. "Honor Your German Masters': History, Memory, and National Identity in Joseph Vilsmaier's *Comedian Harmonists* (1997)." In *Light Motives: Perspectives on Popular German Cinema,* ed. Margaret McCarthy and Randall Halle, 349–75. Detroit: Wayne State University Press, 2003.

Krausser, Helmut. "Lola. Ein Nachwort, viel zu früh." In *Szenenwechsel: Momentaufnahmen des jungen deutschen Films,* ed. Michael Töteberg, 35–39. Reinbek: Rowohlt, 1999.

Kreile, Johannes. "Stellung der Produzenten in Deutschland." In *Der Bewegte Film: Aufbruch zu neuen deutschen Erfolgen,* ed. Heike Amend and Michael Bütow, 189–201. Berlin: Vistas, 1997.

Krekow, Sebastian, and Jens Steiner. *Bei uns geht einiges: Die deutsche Hip Hop-Szene.* Berlin: Schwarzkopf und Schwarzkopf, 2000.

Kroes, Rob. "Americanisation: What Are We Talking About?" In *Cultural Transmissions and Receptions: American Mass Culture in Europe,* ed. R. Kroes,

R. W. Rydell, and D. F. J. Bosscher, 302–18. Amersterdam: VU University Press, 1993.

Kroes, Rob. *If You've Seen One, You've Seen the Mall: Europeans and American Mass Culture*. Urbana: University of Illinois Press, 1996.

Kroes, Rob, Robert W. Rydell, and Doeko F. J. Bosscher, eds. *Cultural Transmissions and Receptions: American Mass Culture in Europe*. Amsterdam: VU University Press, 1993.

Kruse, Holly. "Gender." In *Key Terms in Popular Music and Culture*, ed. Bruce Horner and Thomas Swiss, 85. Malden, MA, and Oxford: Blackwell, 1999.

Kühn, Heike. "'Mein Türke ist Gemüsehändler': Zur Einverleibung des Fremden in deutschsprachigen Filmen." In *"Getürkte Bilder": Zur Inszenierung von Fremden im Film*, ed. Ernst Karpf, Doron Kiesel, and Karsten Visarius, 41–62. Marburg: Schüren, 1995.

Kuisel, Richard. *Seducing the French: The Dilemma of Americanization*. Berkeley: University of California Press, 1993.

Lammersdorf, Raimund, ed. *GHI Conference Papers on the Web: The American Impact on Western Europe: Americanization and Westernization in Transatlantic Perspective*. <http://www.ghi-dc.org/conpotweb/westernpapers/index.html>.

Lange, Horst. *Jazz in Deutschland: Die deutsche Jazz-Chronik 1900–1960*. Berlin: Colloquium, 1966.

Langley, Stephen. "Multiculturalism versus Technoculturalism: Its Challenge to American Theatre and the Functions of Arts Management." In *The American Stage: Social and Economic Issues from the Colonial Period to the Present*, ed. Ron Engle and Tice L. Miller, 278–89. Cambridge: Cambridge University Press, 1993.

Leach, William. *Land of Desire: Merchants, Power, and the Rise of a New American Culture*. New York: Pantheon, 1993.

Lehmann, Hans-Thies. "SCHRIFT / BILD / SCHNITT: Graphismus und die Erkundung der Sprachgrenzen bei Rolf Dieter Brinkmann." In *Rolf Dieter Brinkmann: Literaturmagazin Sonderheft No 36*, ed. Maleen Brinkmann, 182–97. Reinbek: Rowohlt, 1995.

Levine, Lawrence W. *Highbrow/Lowbrow: The Emergence of Cultural Hierarchy in America*. Cambridge: Harvard University Press, 1988.

Light, Alan, ed. *The VIBE History of Hip Hop*. New York: Three River Press, 1999.

Link, Heiner, ed. *Trash-Piloten: Texte für die 90er*. Leipzig: Reclam, 1997.

Lista, Giovanni. *Futurism*. Trans. Charles Lynn Clark. New York: Universe Books, 1986.

Lottmann, Joachim. "Kanak Attak! Ein Wochenende in Kiel mit Feridun Zaimoglu dem Malcolm X der deutschen Türken." *Die Zeit* 47 (November 21, 1997): 24.

Lüdtke, Alf, Inge Maßolek, Adelheid von Saldern, eds. *Amerikanisierung: Traum und Alptraum im Deutschland des 20. Jahrhunderts*. Stuttgart: Franz Steiner, 1996.

Luhmann, Niklas. *The Reality of the Mass Media*. Palo Alto: Stanford University Press, 2000.

Lunden, Rolf, ed. *Networks of Americanization: Aspects of the American Influence in Sweden.* Uppsala: Almquist and Wiksell, 1992.

Lungstrum, Janet. "The Display Window: Designs and Desires of Weimar Consumerism." *New German Critique* 76 (winter 1999): 115–60.

Maase, Kaspar. *BRAVO Amerika: Erkundungen zur Jugendkultur der Bundesrepublik in den fünfziger Jahren.* Hamburg: Junius, 1992.

Maier, Charles S. "The Politics of Productivity: Foundations of American International Economic Policy After World War II." *International Organization* 31 (fall 1977): 607–33.

Mattelart, Armand. *Mapping World Communication: War, Progress, Culture.* Minneapolis and London: University of Minnesota Press, 1994.

May, Elaine Tyler. *Homeward Bound: American Families in the Cold War Era.* New York: Basic Books, 1988.

May, Lary. *The Big Tomorrow: Hollywood and the Politics of the American Way.* Chicago: University of Chicago Press, 2000.

Mayer, Ruth, and Mark Terkessidis, eds. *Globalkolorit: Multikulturalismus und Populärkultur.* St. Andrä-Wördern: Hannibal, 1998.

McChesney, Robert W. "The Internet and United States Communication Policy-Making in Historical and Critical Perspective." *Journal of Communication* 46 (1996): 98–124.

McKay, George, ed. *Yankee Go Home (& Take Me with You): Americanization and Popular Culture.* Sheffield: Academic, 1997.

Meinecke, Thomas. "Alles Mist." *Spiegel Spezial* 2 (1994): 83.

Menz, Dieter. "Von Sissi bis zum Bewegten Mann: Vertrieb deutscher Filme ins Ausland." In *Der Bewegte Film: Aufbruch zu neuen deutschen Erfolgen,* ed. Heike Amend and Michael Bütow, 117–23. Berlin: Vistas, 1997.

Meyer, Paul W. "Forschungsobjekt: Der Verbraucher." *Der Volkswirt* 42 (1954): 28–29.

Mirza, Nikola, ed. *Media Info.* Newsletter des Informationsbüros des Media-Programms der Europäischen Union in der Bundesrepublik Deutschland. February 1999.

Mitchell, Tony. *Popular Music and Local Identity: Rock, Pop, and Rap in Europe and Oceania.* London and New York: Leicester University Press, 1996.

Moeller, Felix. *Der Filmminister: Goebbels und der Film im Dritten Reich.* Berlin: Henschel, 1998.

Moeller, Robert G. *Protecting Motherhood: Women and the Family in the Politics of Postwar West Germany.* Berkeley: University of California Press, 1993.

Monson, Ingrid. "The Problem with White Hipness: Race, Gender, and Cultural Conceptions of Jazz Historical Discourse." *Journal of the American Musicological Society* 48 (fall 1995): 396–422.

Morley, David. "Television: Not So Much a Visual Medium, More a Visible Object." In *Visual Culture,* ed. Chris Jenks, 170–89. London: Routledge, 1995.

Mueller, Agnes C. *Lyrik "made in USA": Vermittlung und Rezeption in der Bundesrepublik.* Amsterdam and Atlanta: Rodopi, 1999.

Müller, Ludwig Richard. "Dekadenz und lebensfroher Neubeginn." *Musik und Gesellschaft* 5 (April 1955): 114–17.

Müller, Robert. "Der Roman des Amerikanismus." *Saturn* 9 (September 1913): 253–58.

Murray, Bruce A. "NBC's Docudrama, *Holocaust,* and Concepts of National Socialism in the United States and the Federal Republic of Germany." In *The Americanization of the Global Village: Essays in Comparative Popular Culture,* ed. Roger Rollin, 87–106. Bowling Green: Bowling Green State University Popular Press, 1989.

Naficy, Hamid. "Between Rocks and Hard Places: The Interstitial Mode of Production in Exilic Cinema." In *Home, Exile, Homeland: Film, Media, and the Politics of Place,* ed. Hamid Naficy. New York: Routledge, 1999.

Naficy, Hamid. "Phobic Spaces and Liminal Panics: Independent Transnational Film Genre." In *Global/Local: Cultural Production and the Transnational Imaginary,* ed. Rob Wilson and Wimal Dissanayake, 119–44. Durham, NC, and London: Duke University Press, 1996.

Naficy, Hamid, ed. *Home, Exile, Homeland: Film, Media, and the Politics of Place.* New York: Routledge, 1999.

Nasaw, David. *Going Out: The Rise and Fall of Public Amusements.* Cambridge: Harvard University Press, 1993.

Nenno, Nancy. "Femininity, the Primitive, and Modern Urban Space: Josephine Baker in Berlin." In *Women in the Metropolis: Gender and Modernity in Weimar Culture,* ed. Katharina von Ankum, 145–61. Berkeley: University of California Press, 1997.

Neumeister, Andreas. "Pop als Wille und Vorstellung." In *Sound Signatures: Pop-Splitter,* ed. Jochen Bonz, 19–26. Frankfurt am Main: Suhrkamp, 2001.

Nolan, Mary. "America in the German Imagination." In *Transactions, Transgressions, Transformations: American Culture in Western Europe and Japan,* ed. Heide Fehrenbach and Uta G. Poiger, 3–25. New York: Berghahn, 2000.

Nolan, Mary. *Visions of Modernity: American Business and the Modernization of Germany.* New York: Oxford University Press, 1994.

Noller, Ulrich. "'Man muss das Deutsche stark machen': Interview with Georg Klein." *die tageszeitung,* March 22, 2001.

O'Brien, Lucy. *She Bop: The Definitive History of Women in Rock, Pop, and Soul.* London: Penguin Books, 1995.

O'Hara, Frank. *Lunch Poems und andere Gedichte.* Ed. Rolf Dieter Brinkmann. Cologne: Kiepenheuer und Witsch, 1969.

Ostendorf, Berndt. "The Final Banal Idiocy of the Reversed Baseball Cap: Transatlantische Widersprüche in der Amerikanisierungsdebatte." *Amerikastudien/American Studies* 44, no. 1 (1999): 25–48.

Partsch, Cornelius. "Hannibal ante Portas: Jazz in Weimar." In *Dancing on the Volcano: Essays on the Culture of the Weimar Republic,* ed. Thomas Kniesche and Stephen Brockmann, 105–16. Columbia, SC: Camden House, 1994.

Peiss, Kathy. *Cheap Amusements: Working Women and Leisure in Turn-of-the-Century New York.* Philadelphia: Temple University Press, 1986.

Pells, Richard. *Not Like Us: How Europeans Have Loved, Hated, and Transformed American Culture since World War II.* New York: Basic Books, 1997.

Pennay, Mark. "Rap in Germany." In *Global Noise: Rap and Hip-Hop Outside of the USA,* ed. Tony Mitchell, 111–32. Middletown, CT: Weslyan University Press, 2001.

Peters, John Durham. "Exile, Nomadism, and Diaspora: The Stakes of Mobility in the Western Canon." In *Home, Exile, Homeland: Film, Media, and the Politics of Place,* ed. Hamid Naficy. New York: Routledge, 1999.

Peukert, Detlev. *Inside Nazi Germany.* Trans. R. Deveson. London: Penguin, 1987.

Peukert, Detlev. *The Weimar Republic.* Trans. R. Deveson. New York: Hill and Wang, 1992.

Pfaff, Carsten, ed. *Filmstatistisches Taschenbuch.* Wiesbaden: SPIO, 1990–98.

Poiger, Uta G. *Jazz, Rock, and Rebels: Cold War Politics and American Culture in a Divided Germany.* Berkeley: University of California Press, 2000.

Poiger, Uta G. "American Jazz in the Cold War." In *Music and German National Identity,* ed. Celia Applegate and Pamela Potter, 218–33. Chicago: University of Chicago Press, 2002.

Poschardt, Ulf. *DJ-Culture: Diskjockeys and Popkultur.* Reinbek: Rowohlt, 1997.

Potter, Russell A. *Spectacular Vernaculars: Hip-Hop and the Politics of Postmodernism.* Albany: SUNY Press, 1995.

Rabinowitz, Lauren. *For the Love of Pleasure: Women, Movies, and Culture in Turn-of-the-Century Chicago.* New Brunswick, NJ: Rutgers University Press, 1998.

Ramonet, Ignacio. "L'Ére du Soupçon." *Le Monde Diplomatique* (May 1991): 12.

Rauhut, Michael. *Beat in der Grauzone: DDR-Rock 1964 bis 1972—Politik und Alltag.* Berlin: Basisdruck, 1993.

Rayner, Richard. "Franka Potente: This German Actress Makes Her U.S. Film Debut in Run Lola Run." *Harper's Bazaar* 3451 (June 1999): 85.

Rentschler, Eric. "From New German Cinema to the Post-Wall Cinema of Consensus." In *Cinema and Nation,* ed. Mette Hjort and Scott Mackenzie, 260–77. London and New York: Routledge, 2000.

Rentschler, Eric. "How American Is It? The U.S. as Image and Imaginary in German Film." *Persistence of Vision* 2 (1985): 5–18.

Rentschler, Eric. *The Ministry of Illusion.* Cambridge: Harvard University Press, 1996.

Ribbat, Christoph. "'Ja, ja, deine Mudder!' American Studies und deutsche Populärkultur." In *Kulturwissenschaftliche Perspektiven in der Nordamerika-Forschung,* ed. Friedrich Jaege, 145–60. Tübingen: Stauffenburg, 2001.

Ritzer, George. *The McDonaldization of Society.* Rev. ed. Thousand Oaks: Pine Forge Press, 1996.

Robeson, Paul. "Pesni moega nevoda." In *Sovetskaia muzyka* (July 1949), quoted in Starr, *Red and Hot,* 221–22.

Robins, Kevin. "The Politics of Silence: The Meaning of Community and the Uses of Media in the New Europe." *New Formations* 21 (1994): 80–101.

Robinson, J. Bradford. "Jazz Reception in Weimar Germany: In Search of a Shimmy Figure." In *Music and Performance during the Weimar Republic,* ed. Bryan Gilliam, 107–34. Cambridge: Cambridge University Press, 1994.

Rollin, Roger, ed. *The Americanization of the Global Village: Essays in Compara-*

tive Popular Culture. Bowling Green: Bowling Green State University Popular Press, 1989.

Rose, Tricia. *Black Noise: Rap Music and Black Culture in Contemporary America.* Hanover: Wesleyan University Press, 1994.

Rosenberg, Emily S. "Cultural Interactions." In *Encyclopedia of the United States in the Twentieth Century,* ed. Stanley I. Kutler et al., 2:710. New York: Charles Scribner's Sons, 1996.

Rosenberg, Emily. *Spreading the American Dream: American Economic and Cultural Expansion, 1890–1945.* New York: Hill and Wang, 1982.

Rosenhaft, Eve. "Lesewut, Kinosucht, Radiotismus: Zur (geschlechter-) politischen Relevanz neuer Massenmedien in den 1920er Jahren." In *Amerikanisierung: Traum und Alptraum im Deutschland des 20. Jahrhunderts,* ed. Alf Lüdke et al., 119–43. Stuttgart: Steiner, 1997.

Rudorf, Reginald. *Jazz in der Zone.* Cologne: Kiepenheuer und Witsch, 1964.

Rudolf [sic], Reginald. "Für eine frohe, ausdrucksvolle Tanzmusik." In *Musik und Gesellschaft* 4, pt. 1 (February 1954): 51–56, pt. 2 (March 1954): 92–95.

Rudorf, Reginald. *Nie wieder links: Eine deutsche Reportage.* Frankfurt am Main: Ullstein, 1990.

Ryback, Timothy W. *Rock Around the Bloc: A History of Rock Music in Eastern Europe and the Soviet Union.* New York: Oxford University Press, 1990.

Rygulla, Ralf Rainer, and Rolf Dieter Brinkmann. "Der joviale Russe." In *Mammut: März Texte 1 & 2, 1969–1984,* ed. Jörg Schröder. Herbstein: März, 1984.

Said, Edward. *Culture and Imperialism.* New York: Knopf, 1993.

Said, Edward. *Orientalism.* New York: Random House, 1978.

Saunders, Thomas J. "A 'New Man': Fascism, Cinema, and Image Creation." *International Journal of Politics, Culture, and Society* 12 (1998): 227–46.

Saunders, Thomas J. *Hollywood in Berlin.* Berkeley: University of California Press, 1994.

Schäfer, Hans Dieter. *Das gespaltene Bewußtsein: Deutsche Kultur und Lebenswirklichkeit 1933–1945.* Munich: Carl Hanser, 1981.

Schiller, Herbert I. *Mass Communications and American Empire.* 2d ed. Boulder: Westview Press, 1992.

Schlesinger, Philip R. "From Cultural Protection to Political Culture? Media Policy and the European Union." In *Constructing Europe's Identity: The External Dimension,* ed. Lars-Erik Cederman, 91–114. Boulder: Lynne Reiner, 2001.

Schmidt, Alexander. *Reisen in die Moderne: Der Amerika-Diskurs des deutschen Bürgertums vor dem Ersten Weltkrieg im europäischen Vergleich.* Berlin: Akademie, 1997.

Schmidt-Wulffen, Stephan. "Die Kunst von heute braucht kein Haus: Warum das Museum seine gesellschaftliche Funktion verloren hat." *Die Zeit* 13 (March 25, 1999): 55.

Schneider, Peter. "Die falsche Gewissheit." *Der Spiegel* 35 (2002): 168–70.

Schoenbaum, David. *Hitler's Social Revolution.* Garden City, NY: Doubleday, 1966.

Schröder, Hans-Jürgen. "Marshall Plan Propaganda in Austria and Western Germany." In *The Marshall Plan in Austria,* ed. Günter Bischof, Anton Pelinka, and Dieter Steifel, 212–46. Contemporary Austrian Studies 8. New Brunswick: Transaction, 2000.

Schulte-Sasse, Linda. *Entertaining the Third Reich.* Durham, NC: Duke University Press, 1996.

Schumacher, Eckhard. "'Re-make/Re-model'—Zitat und Performativität im Pop-Diskurs." In *Zitier-Fähigkeit,* ed. Andrea Gutenberg and Ralph Poole. Berlin: Erich Schmidt, 2001.

Schumacher, Eckhard. *Die Ironie der Unverständlichkeit: Johann Georg Hamann, Friedrich Schlegel, Jacques Derrida, Paul de Man.* Frankfurt am Main: Suhrkamp, 2000.

Seiter, Ellen, Hans Borchers, Gabriele Kreutzner, and Eva-Maria Warth, eds. *Remote Control: Television, Audiences, and Cultural Power.* London: Routledge, 1989.

Sell Tower, Beeke. "'Ultramodern and Ultraprimitive': Shifting Meanings in the Imagery of Americanism in the Art of Weimar Germany." In *Dancing on the Volcano: Essays on the Culture of the Weimar Republic,* ed. Thomas Kniesche and Stephen Brockmann, 85–104. Columbia, SC: Camden House, 1994.

Shoat, Ella, and Robert Stam. *Unthinking Eurocentrism: Multiculturalism and the Media.* London and New York: Routledge, 1994.

Silberman, Marc. "What Is German in the German Cinema?" *Film History* 8 (1996): 297–315.

Sinka, Margit. "Tom Tykwer's Lola rennt: A Blueprint of Millennial Berlin." *Glossen* 11 (2000). <http://www.dickinson.edu/glossen/heft17/ navigation17 .html>.

Smelser, Ronald. *Robert Ley: Hitler's Labour Front Leader.* Oxford and New York: Berg, 1988.

Smith, Anthony. *The Geopolitics of Information: How Western Culture Dominates the World.* New York: Oxford University Press, 1980.

Snyder, Robert W. *The Voice of the City: Vaudeville and Popular Culture in New York.* New York: Oxford University Press, 1989.

Spigel, Lynn. *Make Room for TV.* Chicago: University of Chicago Press, 1992.

Spieker, Markus. *Hollywood unterm Hakenkreuz: Der amerikanische Spielfilm im Dritten Reich.* Trier: Wissenschaftlicher Verlag, 1999.

Starr, S. Frederick. *Red and Hot: The Fate of Jazz in the Soviet Union.* 2d ed. New York: Oxford University Press, 1983. Rpt., updated ed. New York: Limelight, 1994.

Storey, John. *An Introduction to Cultural Theory and Popular Culture.* Athens: University of Georgia Press, 1998.

Swann, Paul. "The Little State Department: Washington and Hollywood's Rhetoric of the Postwar Audience." In *Hollywood in Europe: Experiences of a Cultural Hegemony,* ed. David W. Ellwood and Rob Kroes, 176–95. Amsterdam: VU University Press, 1994.

Sznaider, Natan. "Amerika, Du hast es besser." *Süddeutsche Zeitung,* October 29, 1999.

Teraoka, Arlene Akiko. "Talking 'Turk': On Narrative Strategies and Cultural Stereotypes." *New German Critique* 46 (1989): 104–28.

Theiler, Tobias. "Why the European Union Failed to Europeanize Its Audiovisual Policy." In *Constructing Europe's Identity: The External Dimension,* ed. Lars-Erik Cederman, 115–37. Boulder: Lynne Reiner, 2001.

Thomson, Charles A., and Walter H. C. Leaves. *Cultural Relations and U.S. Foreign Policy.* Bloomington: Indiana University Press, 1963.

Thompson, John B. *The Media and Modernity: A Social Theory of the Media.* Palo Alto: Stanford University Press, 1995.

Thomson, Charles A., and Walter H. C. Leaves. *Cultural Relation and U.S. Foreign Policy.* Bloomington: Indiana University Press, 1963.

Tomlinson, John. *Cultural Imperialism: A Critical Introduction.* Baltimore: Johns Hopkins University Press, 1991.

Töteberg, Michael. Interview with Tom Tykwer. "Ein romantisch-philosophischer Action Liebes Experimental Thriller." In *lola rennt,* ed. Michael Töteberg, 129–42. Reinbek and Hamburg: Rowohlt, 1998.

Töteberg, Michael. "Über die Karriere eines Films." In *Szenenwechsel: Momentaufnahmen des jungen deutschen Films,* ed. Michael Töteberg, 45–49. Hamburg: Rowohlt, 1999.

Traufetter, Gerald. "Die Vermischung der Weltkulturen." *Der Spiegel* 44 (2000): 234–38.

Traufetter, Gerald. "'Ich bin die Mama, die Schwester mit dem Hammer': Der Musikkanal Viva bringt MTV in Zugzwang." *Die Welt,* February 10, 1996. On-line archive: <http://www.de/daten/1996/02/10/0210ku99270.htx>.

Trommler, Frank. "Neuer Start und alte Vorurteile. Die Kulturbeziehungen im Zeichen des kalen Krieges 1945–1968." In *Die USA und Deutschland im Zeitalter des Kalten Krieges: Ein Handbuch,* ed. Detlev Junker, 1:567–91. Stuttgart/Munich: Deutsche Verlags-Anstalt, 2001.

Trommler, Frank. "Kultur als transatlantisches Spannungsfeld 1968—1990." In *Die USA und Deutschland in Zeitalter,* 2:395–419.

Trommler, Frank, and Joseph McVeigh, eds. *America and the Germans: An Assessment of a Three-Hundred-Year History: I, Immigration, Language, Ethnicity; II, The Relationship in the Twentieth Century.* Philadelphia: University of Pennsylvania Press, 1985.

Tykwer, Tom. "Generalschlüssel fürs Kino." In *Szenenwechsel: Momentaufnahmen des jungen deutschen Films,* ed. Michael Töteberg. Hamburg: Rowohlt, 1999.

Ullmaier, Johannes. *Von Acid nach Adlon und zurück: Eine Reise durch die deutschsprachige Popliteratur.* Mainz: Ventil, 2001.

Verlan, Sascha, and Hannes Loh. *20 Jahre Hip Hop in Deutschland.* Höfen: Hannibal, 2000.

Vincendeau, Ginette. "Issues in European Cinema." In *The Oxford Guide to Film Studies,* ed. John Hill and Pamela Church Gibson, 440–48. Oxford: Oxford University Press, 1998.

von Bismarck, Klaus, et al. *Industrialisierung des Bewußtseins: Eine kritische Auseinandersetzung mit den 'neuen' Medien.* Munich and Zurich: Piper, 1985.

Von Eschen, Penny M. "'Satchmo Blows Up the World': Jazz, Race, and Empire during the Cold War." In *"Here, There, and Everywhere,"* ed. Wagnleitner and May, 163–78.

von Saldern, Adelheid. "Überfremdungsängste: Gegen die Amerikanisierung der deutschen Kultur in den zwanziger Jahren." In *Amerikanisierung: Traum und Alptraum im Deutschland des 20. Jahrhunderts,* ed. Alf Lüdke et al., 213–44. Stuttgart: Steiner, 1997.

Wagnleitner, Reinhold. "American Cultural Diplomacy, the Cinema, and the Cold War in Central Europe." In *Hollywood in Europe,* ed. David W. Ellwood and Rob Kroes, 197–210. Amsterdam: VU University Press, 1994.

Wagnleitner, Reinhold. *Coca-Colonisation und Kalter Krieg: Die Kulturmission der USA in Österreich nach dem Zweiten Weltkrieg.* Vienna: VG, 1991.

Wagnleitner, Reinhold. *Coca-Colonization and the Cold War: The Cultural Mission of the United States in Austria after the Second World War.* Trans. Diana M. Wolf. Chapel Hill: University of North Carolina Press, 1994.

Wagnleitner, Reinhold. "Propagating the American Dream: Cultural Policies as Means of Integration." In *Exporting America: Essays on American Studies Abroad,* ed. Richard P. Horwitz, 305–43. New York: Garland, 1993.

Wagnleitner, Reinhold. "The Empire of Fun, or Talkin' Soviet Union Blues: The Sound of Freedom and U.S. Cultural Hegemony in Europe." *Diplomatic History* 23 (summer 1999): 499–524.

Wagnleitner, Reinhold, and Elaine Tyler May, eds. *"Here, There, and Everywhere": The Foreign Politics of American Popular Culture.* Hanover and London: University Press of New England, 2000.

Wasser, Frederick. "Is Hollywood America? The Trans-Nationalization of the American Film Industry." *Critical Studies in Mass Communication* 12 (1995): 423–37.

Weber, Annette. "Du kannst es dir nicht aussuchen." *die tageszeitung,* June 27, 1995, 16.

Wells, Paul. *Understanding Animation.* London and New York: Routledge, 1988.

Werthebach, Eckart. "Die deutsche Sprache braucht gesetzlichen Schutz." *Berliner Morgenpost,* December 31, 2000.

Werthebach, Eckart. "Zeitbomben in den Vorstädten." *Der Spiegel* 16 (1997): 88.

Whalen, Tom. "Run Lola Run." *Film Quarterly* 53, no. 3 (2000): 22–40.

Whitfield, Stephen J. *The Culture of the Cold War.* Baltimore: Johns Hopkins University Press, 1991.

Wildt, Michael. *Am Beginn der "Konsumgesellschaft": Mangelerfahrung, Lebenshaltung, Wohlstandshoffnung in Westdeutschland in den fünziger Jahren.* Hamburg: Ergebnisse, 1994.

Wildt, Michael. "Changes in Consumption as Social Practice in West Germany during the 1950s." In *Getting and Spending: European and American Consumer Societies in the Twentieth Century,* ed. Susan Strasser, Charles McGovern, and Matthias Judt, 301–16. Washington, DC: German Historical Institute and Cambridge University Press, 1998.

Willemen, Paul. "The National." In *Looks and Frictions: Essays in Cultural Studies and Film Theory.* Bloomington: Indiana University Press, 1994.

Willett, Ralph. *The Americanization of Germany, 1945–1949.* London: Routledge, 1989.

Williams, Raymond. *The Sociology of Culture.* New York: Schocken, 1981.

Wolfsgrubern, Alex. "We want you, and you . . ." *Focus* 46 (November 2000): 50.

Zaimoglu, Feridun. *Kanak Sprak: 24 Mißtöne vom Rande der Gesellschaft.* Hamburg: Rotbuch, 1995.

Zaimoglu, Feridun. *Koppstoff: Kanaka Sprak vom Rande der Gesellschaft.* Hamburg: EVA/Rotbuch, 1998.

Zitelmann, Rainer. *Hitler: Selbstverständnis eines Revolutionärs.* Stuttgart: Klett-Cotta, 1987.

Žižek, Slavoj. "A Leftist's Plea for 'Eurocentrism.'" *Critical Inquiry* 24 (1998): 988–1009.

Contributors

Winfried Fluck's highly distinguished international career in American studies includes visiting professorships at Harvard, Yale, Princeton, and in Barcelona, as well as a Rockefeller Fellowship in Italy. He currently holds the chair of American culture at the Kennedy Institute for North American Studies at the Freie Universität Berlin. Some of his more recent publications are on the Americanization of German history.

Gerd Gemünden, professor of German and comparative literature at Dartmouth College, is the author of *Framed Visions: Popular Culture, Americanization, and the Contemporary German and Austrian Imagination* (1998). He coedited *The Cinema of Wim Wenders: Image, Narrative, and the Postmodern Condition* (1997) and *Germans and Indians: Fantasies, Encounters, Projections* (2002).

Lutz Koepnick is associate professor of German and film and media studies at Washington University, St. Louis. He is the author of *Nothungs Modernität: Wagners Ring und die Poesie der Macht im neunzehnten Jahrhundert* (1994), *Walter Benjamin and the Aesthetics of Power* (1999), and *The Dark Mirror: German Cinema between Hitler and Hollywood* (2002). His current book project is entitled "Framing Attention: Windows on Modern German Culture."

Barbara Kosta is associate professor of German studies at the University of Arizona. She is the author of *Recasting Autobiography: Women's Counterfictions in Contemporary German Literature and Film* (1994) and coeditor of *Writing against Boundaries: Ethnicity, Gender, and Nationality* (2003). Her publications include articles on twentieth-century German women writers, on German film, and on autobiography. She is currently working on a book-length study of Josef von Sternberg's *The Blue Angel.*

Sara Lennox is professor of German and director of the Social Thought and Political Economy Program at the University of Massachusetts at Amherst. During her distinguished career, she has published widely on Ingeborg Bachmann, feminism in German studies and in the academy, feminist approaches to literary and cultural theory, and issues of gender and race in German national identity. She also coedited *The Imperialist Imagination: German Colonialism and Its Legacy* (1999).

Thomas Meinecke lives and writes in Eurasburg (Bavaria) and has been touring Europe and the United States with his rock band FSK since 1980. He works for public radio stations in Germany and, in addition to *The Church of JFK* (1996), has published numerous essays on pop culture in music magazines. The prominent role of gender theory in his best-selling *Tomboy* (1998) stirred great interest in academia and beyond. In 2003, he received the Deutsche Literaturpreis after publication of his novel *Hellblau* (2001).

Agnes C. Mueller, assistant professor of German and comparative literature at the University of South Carolina, is the author of a monograph on the postwar German reception of U.S. poetry (*Lyrik "made in USA": Vermittlung und Rezeption in der Bundesrepublik,*1999). She has published essays on German-American relations and on Rolf Dieter Brinkmann. Her current research focuses on popular culture and literature after 9/11.

Uta G. Poiger is associate professor of German and European history at the University of Washington. She is the author of *Jazz, Rock, and Rebels: Cold War Politics and American Culture in a Divided Germany* (2000), and she is coeditor of *Transactions, Transgressions, Transformations: American Culture in Western Europe and Japan* (2000). Her current research interests include the intersections between commodity culture and changing German visions of empire.

Matthias Politycki holds a Ph.D. in German from Munich University and lives in Hamburg as a writer. His best-selling novel *Weiberroman* (1997) received wide critical acclaim well before the recent boom of pop literature was celebrated in the German media. His novel *Ein Mann von 40 Jahren* (2000) involved writing the first draft in an interactive forum on the Internet where readers could participate. Politycki's essays on the state of German literature appear regularly in periodicals such as *Neue Frankfurter Rundschau.*

Thomas J. Saunders is associate professor of history at the University of Victoria in British Columbia. His *Hollywood in Berlin: American Cinema and Weimar Germany* (1994) received significant attention in the fields of history, German studies, and film studies. He is currently writing a monograph on the intersection between cinema and other forms of public persuasion, exploring the ways in which scandal and sensation were exploited in Germany during the 1920s.

Eckhard Schumacher is assistant professor of German and media studies at the Kulturwissenschaftliches Forschungskolleg "Medien und kulturelle Kommunikation" at the University of Cologne. He is author of *Die Ironie der Unverständlichkeit: Hamann, Schlegel, Derrida, de Man* (2000) and *Gerade Eben Jetzt: Schreibweisen der Gegenwart* (2003) and coeditor of *Die Adresse des Mediums* (2001). He has also published articles on contemporary German literature and popular culture.

Marc Silberman is professor of German studies at the University of Wisconsin at Madison. His research and publications cover the history of German cinema, Bertolt Brecht and the tradition of political theater, and GDR literature and culture. He edited the *Brecht Yearbook* from 1990 to 1995 and is author of, among others, *German Cinema: Texts in Context* (1995).

Frank Trommler, professor of German and comparative literature and director of the Harry and Helen Gray Humanities Program at the University of Pennsylvania, has held visiting professorships at Princeton and Johns Hopkins Universities. He has authored and edited books on modern German literature as well as on issues of youth, socialism, Germanics, technology, and German-American cultural relations. His publications include *America and the Germans* (1985, also in German) and *The German-American Encounter: Conflict and Cooperation between Two Cultures, 1800–2000* (2001).

Sabine von Dirke is associate professor of German studies at the University of Pittsburgh. Her monograph *"All Power to the Imagination!" The West German Counterculture from the Student Movement to the Greens* (1997) has received significant attention in the fields of both German and history, and she is the author of numerous articles on multiculturalism in Germany, the West German Left, rock music, and questions of genre and gender.

Index